Comparing Political Journalism

Comparing Political Journalism is a systematic, in-depth study of the factors that shape and influence political news coverage today.

Using techniques drawn from the growing field of comparative political communication, an international group of contributors analyse political news content drawn from newspapers, television news, and news websites from 16 countries, to assess what kinds of media systems are most conducive to producing quality journalism.

Underpinned by key conceptual themes, such as the role that the media are expected to play in democracies and quality of coverage, this analysis highlights the fragile balance of news performance in relation to economic forces.

A multitude of causal factors are explored to explain key features of contemporary political news coverage, such as strategy and game framing, negativity, political balance, personalization, and hard and soft news.

Comparing Political Journalism offers an unparalleled scope in assessing the implications for the ongoing transformation of Western media systems and addresses core concepts of central importance to students and scholars of political communication world-wide.

Claes de Vreese is Professor and Chair of Political Communication at the University of Amsterdam, the Netherlands. He is the founding Director of the Center for Politics and Communication (www.polcomm.org). His most recent book is *Political Journalism in Comparative Perspective* (2014, with Erik Albæk, Arjen van Dalen, and Nael Jebril).

Frank Esser is Professor and Chair of International and Comparative Media Research at the University of Zurich, Switzerland. He co-directs the National Research Center on the Challenges to Democracy in the 21st Century (NCCR Democracy). His most recent book is *Mediatization of Politics* (2014, with Jesper Strömbäck).

David Nicolas Hopmann is Professor with special responsibilities at the Centre for Journalism and the Department of Political Science at the University of Southern Denmark in Odense, Denmark.

Communication and Society
Series Editor: James Curran

This series encompasses the broad field of media and cultural studies. Its main concerns are the media and the public sphere: on whether the media empower or fail to empower popular forces in society; media organisations and public policy; the political and social consequences of media campaigns; and the role of media entertainment, ranging from potboilers and the human-interest story to rock music and TV sport.

For a complete list of titles in this series, please see: https://www.routledge.com/series/SE0130.

Journalism in Context
Practice and theory for the digital age
Angela Phillips

News and Politics
The rise of live and interpretive journalism
Stephen Cushion

Gender and Media
Representing, producing, consuming
Tonny Krijnen and Sofie Van Bauwel

Misunderstanding the Internet
Second edition
James Curran, Natalie Fenton, and Des Freedman

Africa's Media Image in the 21st Century
From the 'Heart of Darkness' to 'Africa Rising'
Edited by Melanie Bunce, Suzanne Franks, and Chris Paterson

Comparing Political Journalism
Edited by Claes de Vreese, Frank Esser, and David Nicolas Hopmann

Comparing Political Journalism

Edited by
Claes de Vreese, Frank Esser,
and David Nicolas Hopmann

LONDON AND NEW YORK

First published 2017
by Routledge
2 Park Square, Milton Park, Abingdon, Oxon OX14 4RN

and by Routledge
711 Third Avenue, New York, NY 10017

Routledge is an imprint of the Taylor & Francis Group, an informa business

© 2017 selection and editorial matter, Claes de Vreese, Frank Esser, and David Nicolas Hopmann

© 2017 individual chapters; the contributors

The right of Claes de Vreese, Frank Esser, and David Nicolas Hopmann to be identified as authors of the editorial matter and the authors of their individual chapters has been asserted by them in accordance with sections 77 and 78 of the Copyright, Designs and Patents Act 1988.

All rights reserved. No part of this book may be reprinted or reproduced or utilised in any form or by any electronic, mechanical, or other means, now known or hereafter invented, including photocopying and recording, or in any information storage or retrieval system, without permission in writing from the publishers.

Trademark notice: Product or corporate names may be trademarks or registered trademarks, and are used only for identification and explanation without intent to infringe.

British Library Cataloguing in Publication Data
A catalogue record for this book is available from the British Library

Library of Congress Cataloging-in-Publication Data
Names: Vreese, C. H. de (Claes Holger), 1974– editor. | Esser, Frank, 1966– editor. | Hopmann, David Nicolas.
Title: Comparing political journalism / edited by Claes de Vreese, Frank Esser, and David Nicolas Hopmann.
Description: London New York : Routledge, 2016.
Identifiers: LCCN 2016001725 | ISBN 9781138655850 (hardback) | ISBN 9781138655867 (pbk.) | ISBN 9781315622286 (ebook)
Subjects: LCSH: Press and politics. | Journalism—Political aspects.
Classification: LCC PN4751 .C55 2016 | DDC 070.4/4932—dc23
LC record available at http://lccn.loc.gov/2016001725

ISBN: 978-1-138-65585-0 (hbk)
ISBN: 978-1-138-65586-7 (pbk)
ISBN: 978-1-315-62228-6 (ebk)

Typeset in Times New Roman
by Apex CoVantage, LLC

Contents

List of figures	vii
List of tables	ix
List of contributors	xi
Preface	xiii
Acknowledgements	xv
Praise for this edition	xvi

1 Our goal: comparing news performance   1

CLAES DE VREESE, FRANK ESSER, AND DAVID NICOLAS HOPMANN
WITH TORIL AALBERG, PETER VAN AELST, ROSA BERGANZA,
NICOLAS HUBÉ, GUIDO LEGNANTE, JÖRG MATTHES, STYLIANOS
PAPATHANASSOPOULOS, CARSTEN REINEMANN, SUSANA SALGADO,
TAMIR SHEAFER, JAMES STANYER, AND JESPER STRÖMBÄCK

2 How we did it: approach and methods   10

DAVID NICOLAS HOPMANN, FRANK ESSER, AND CLAES DE VREESE
WITH TORIL AALBERG, PETER VAN AELST, ROSA BERGANZA,
NICOLAS HUBÉ, GUIDO LEGNANTE, JÖRG MATTHES, STYLIANOS
PAPATHANASSOPOULOS, CARSTEN REINEMANN, SUSANA SALGADO,
TAMIR SHEAFER, JAMES STANYER, AND JESPER STRÖMBÄCK

3 The explanatory logic: factors that shape political news   22

FRANK ESSER, CLAES DE VREESE, AND DAVID NICOLAS HOPMANN
WITH TORIL AALBERG, PETER VAN AELST, ROSA BERGANZA,
NICOLAS HUBÉ, GUIDO LEGNANTE, JÖRG MATTHES, STYLIANOS
PAPATHANASSOPOULOS, CARSTEN REINEMANN, SUSANA SALGADO,
TAMIR SHEAFER, JAMES STANYER, AND JESPER STRÖMBÄCK

4 Strategy and game framing   33

TORIL AALBERG, CLAES DE VREESE, AND JESPER STRÖMBÄCK

vi Contents

5 Interpretive journalism   **50**
SUSANA SALGADO, JESPER STRÖMBÄCK, TORIL AALBERG,
AND FRANK ESSER

6 Negativity   **71**
FRANK ESSER, SVEN ENGESSER, JÖRG MATTHES,
AND ROSA BERGANZA

7 Political balance   **92**
DAVID NICOLAS HOPMANN, PETER VAN AELST, SUSANA SALGADO,
AND GUIDO LEGNANTE

8 Personalization   **112**
PETER VAN AELST, TAMIR SHEAFER, NICOLAS HUBÉ,
AND STYLIANOS PAPATHANASSOPOULOS

9 Hard and soft news   **131**
CARSTEN REINEMANN, JAMES STANYER, AND SEBASTIAN SCHERR

10 Cross-conceptual architecture of news   **150**
CARSTEN REINEMANN, SEBASTIAN SCHERR, AND JAMES STANYER
WITH TORIL AALBERG, PETER VAN AELST, ROSA BERGANZA,
FRANK ESSER, DAVID NICOLAS HOPMANN, NICOLAS HUBÉ, GUIDO
LEGNANTE, JÖRG MATTHES, STYLIANOS PAPATHANASSOPOULOS,
SUSANA SALGADO, TAMIR SHEAFER, JESPER STRÖMBÄCK,
AND CLAES DE VREESE

11 Conclusion: assessing news performance   **168**
CLAES DE VREESE, CARSTEN REINEMANN, FRANK ESSER,
AND DAVID NICOLAS HOPMANN WITH TORIL AALBERG, PETER VAN
AELST, ROSA BERGANZA, NICOLAS HUBÉ, GUIDO LEGNANTE, JÖRG
MATTHES, STYLIANOS PAPATHANASSOPOULOS, SUSANA SALGADO,
TAMIR SHEAFER, JAMES STANYER, AND JESPER STRÖMBÄCK

References   184
Index   199

Figures

1.1	News performance in context	5
4.1	The presence of strategic game frames across countries	41
4.2	The presence of strategic game frames according to dominant issues in news items	41
4.3	The presence of strategic game frames according to media outlet type	42
4.4	The relationship between country score on strategic game frame index and national market share of public service channels	44
4.5	The relationship between country score on strategic game frame index and the number of parties in parliament	45
5.1	The relationship between interpretive journalism and newspaper competition	66
5.2	The relationship between interpretive journalism and television market competition	66
6.1	Federalism/decentralization predicting Negativity Index	85
6.2	News production costs predicting Negativity Index	86
6.3	Adspend predicting Negativity Index	86
7.1	Visibility (index of similarity) and impartiality in 15 countries	98
7.2	Visibility (index of similarity) and impartiality across countries	100
7.3	Proportional reduction in error (PRE: $R^2 \times 100$) for 30 linear regressions predicting the relative visibility of political parties in European media outlets	105
7.4	Average favorability of news appearances by politicians, based on aggregated measures per party per news media outlet per country	106
8.1	Percentage of individual actors versus institutions or groups	119
8.2	Relative attention to individual politicians (general visibility)	125
8.3	Relative attention to government leaders	127
9.1	Hard and soft news index by countries	139
9.2	Hard and soft news index by individual medium type	141
9.3	Months from last election and the hard and soft news index across countries	143

viii Figures

9.4 Adspend as a percentage of GDP and hard and soft news index
across countries 143
9.5 Market share of public service broadcasters and hard and soft
news index across countries 144
10.1 Size of news item clusters according to key concepts
in country comparison 164
11.1 Amount of issue-focused hard news coverage per country 170
11.2 Amount of actor-focused news coverage 171
11.3 Amount of issue-focused interpretive coverage 171
11.4 Amount of strategy-focused interpretive coverage 172
11.5 Dimensions of news 173
11.6 Dimensions of news coverage per dimension in the United States 174
11.7 Dimensions of news coverage per dimension in Germany 174
11.8 Dimensions of news coverage per dimension in Norway 175

Tables

2.1	News outlets included in the content analyses by country and type of outlet	12
2.2	International inter-coder reliability, summarized results	18
2.3	International inter-coder reliability, per country	19
3.1	Multilevel framework of factors that shape political news	27
4.1	Presence of strategic game frames in U.S. and European news	38
4.2	Presence of game and strategy frames across countries	39
4.3	Presence of game macroframe and strategic game frames (means) across countries	40
4.4	Correlations between strategic game frame measures, type of media outlet, and national factors related to context, media, and political system	43
4.5	Correlations between game frames, strategy frames, and number of parties in parliament/government	45
4.6	OLS regression of strategic game frame controlled for type of media outlet and national factors related to context, media, and political system	46
5.1	Interpretive journalism in different genres	58
5.2	Presence of interpretive journalism across countries and type of news story	60
5.3	The presence of interpretive journalism in political news items by type of medium	61
5.4	Interpretive journalism by type of medium and country	62
5.5	The presence of interpretive journalism in political news by type of media outlet	63
5.6	Interpretive journalism by type of media outlet and country	64
5.7	The relationship between interpretive journalism, type of media outlet, and media system characteristics (bivariate correlations)	65
5.8	The relationship between interpretive journalism, type of media outlet, and media system characteristics (OLS regression)	67
6.1	Correlations between the four components of negativity	77
6.2	Overview of explanatory variables	78

6.3	Negativity by country	79
6.4	Negativity Index by topic	81
6.5	Negativity by offline and online channels	82
6.6	Negativity by press and TV sector	83
6.7	Bivariate regression models predicting the Negativity Index at the national level	84
6.8	Multivariate regression models predicting the Negativity Index	87
7.1	Linear regressions on political balance in visibility and impartiality across different types of media, with and without dummies for online affiliates	101
7.2	Linear regressions for the relative visibility of party politicians, per news outlet and country	104
7.3	Linear regression on the average favorability of political parties in the news, per party and media outlet	108
8.1	Type of actors in domestic political news	118
8.2	Attention for government actors and ratio of persons versus institutions in government	120
8.3	Attention for political parties and ratio of politicians versus parties	121
8.4	Attention for head of government and head of state	123
8.5	Correlations between general and concentrated visibility, type of media organization, and national factors related to media and political systems	124
8.6	Explanations of general visibility (individual politicians versus institutions)	125
8.7	Explanations of concentrated visibility (presence of government leader)	126
9.1	Presence of hard news indicators in news items across countries	138
9.2	Correlations between hard and soft news index and national-level characteristics	142
9.3	Explaining hard news by medium type and characteristics of the political, economic, and media system context (organizational-level analysis)	146
10.1	Standardized key concepts in comparison – deviations from overall means	155
10.2	Standardized key concepts in comparison per media outlet type	156
10.3	Correlations between standardized key concepts across countries and media	157
10.4	Factor analysis of standardized key concepts across countries and media	158
10.5	Factor structures of standardized key concepts in country comparison	160
10.6	Characteristics of news item clusters based on key concept factor structure	163
11.1	Multilevel framework of factors that shape political news	177

Contributors

Toril Aalberg is Professor at the Department of Sociology and Political Science at the Norwegian University of Science and Technology (NTNU) in Trondheim, Norway.

Rosa Berganza is Professor and Chair of Journalism at the University of Rey Juan Carlos (URJC) in Madrid, Spain.

Claes de Vreese is Professor and Chair in Political Communication at the Amsterdam School of Communication Research (ASCoR) at the University of Amsterdam, the Netherlands.

Sven Engesser is Senior Research Associate at the Institute of Mass Communication and Media Research at the University of Zurich, Switzerland.

Frank Esser is Professor of International and Comparative Media Research at the University of Zurich, Switzerland.

David Nicolas Hopmann is Professor with Special Responsibilities at the University of Southern Denmark, Denmark.

Nicolas Hubé is Associate Professor of Political Science at the University Paris 1 Panthéon-Sorbonne, France.

Guido Legnante is Associate Professor of Political Science at the Department of Political and Social Sciences in the University of Pavia, Italy.

Jörg Matthes is Professor of Communication Science and Director of the Department of Communication, University of Vienna, Austria.

Stylianos Papathanassopoulos is Professor in Media Organisation and Policy at the Faculty of Communication and Media Studies at the National and Kapodistrian University of Athens, Greece.

Carsten Reinemann is Professor and Chair of Political Communication at Ludwig-Maximilians-University Munich, Germany.

Susana Salgado is a researcher and professor of political communication and media and politics.

Sebastian Scherr is Doctoral Candidate at the Department of Communication Science and Media Research at the University of Munich, Germany.

Tamir Sheafer is Professor in the Departments of Political Science and Communication and Vice Dean of the Faculty of Social Sciences at the Hebrew University of Jerusalem, Israel.

James Stanyer is Reader in Comparative Political Communication in the Department of Social Sciences at Loughborough University, UK.

Jesper Strömbäck is Professor of Journalism at Gothenburg University, Sweden.

Peter Van Aelst is Professor in Political Communication at the University of Antwerp in Belgium.

Preface

Comparative research is one of the most rapidly growing fields in communication science. This book brings novel empirical evidence to the study of political journalism. It fills a major lacuna in research that has been identified in the past decade. As Hallin and Mancini (2012) argue, there is a lack of knowledge about media content in a comparative sense. In their chapter for the *Handbook of Comparative Communication Research*, they state that "content analysis across systems, guided by comparative theory, is in our view one of the most fundamental needs in our field" (p. 218). Our book starts to fill exactly this gap. The evidence from 16 countries suggests that economic factors such as strong competition, private broadcast ownership, and heavy dependence on commercial logics are disadvantageous for high news performance. These findings have clear implications for assessing the ongoing transformation of political journalism.

The first goal of this book is to provide a point of reference related to six key concepts of news performance, on which future research can build. The second purpose is to suggest how each of these key concepts should be conceptualized and operationalized. The third goal is to investigate each of the key concepts in newspapers, television news, and news websites in 15 European countries plus the United States. Our endeavor is to find "good news" – in a standardized approach – and to understand why we find that more in some places than others. Overall, we do not find a pervasive and uniform pattern of "bad news" with little political substance. We do find, however, characteristic combinations of news features that create a peculiar news architecture that is increasingly found in Western media.

The book puts forward a unique set of findings and aims to set an example of how comparative political journalism research is conducted. Its contributors are all members of the Network of European Political Communication Scholars (www.nepocs.eu). This group was founded in 2008 and includes one member per European country, and the purpose of this network is to pursue collaborative cross-national comparative research. The group's first joint project investigated "Political Information Opportunities in Europe," and it was published under this title in the *International Journal of Press/Politics* (Esser, de Vreese et al., 2012). The group's next project was a guest-edited special issue on "Studying Political News: Towards a Standardization of Core Concepts" in *Journalism* (Esser,

Strömbäck, and de Vreese, 2012). The group now has completed this book in a truly comparative and collaborative fashion. It is the outcome of many meetings and rounds of revisions over the past couple of years building on the previous works. We thank the institutions that hosted these meetings and those that were able to provide extra funding making the project possible. We also extend a warm thanks to the assistants who were involved in coding and Liza Keezen for her work on the manuscript. Without them, there would be no book.

Claes de Vreese, Frank Esser, and David Nicolas Hopmann
Amsterdam, Zurich, and Odense
January 2016

Acknowledgements

Quotation on Portuguese Television Law in Chapter 7 used by permission of www.anacom.pt.

Praise for this edition

'If there is a single book in recent years that journalism scholars and students should read, *Comparing Political Journalism* is it. The research underlying the book sets a standard for how to conceptualize, operationalize, and investigate news content. The findings are more than revealing—they are laden with implications for the role that journalists play in our democratic life. The authors have given the rest of us a model for how to conduct comparative research, how to engage in cumulative theory building, how to move beyond description to explanation, and how to think about journalists and news systems.'

Thomas E. Patterson, *Bradlee Professor of Government and the Press, Harvard University, USA*

'*Comparing Political Journalism* is methodologically strong, theoretically ambitious, and a significant contribution. With its clear, consistent, and coherent approach, this impressive team effort will be a very influential book in comparative research on journalism and political communication.'

Rasmus Kleis Nielsen, *Director of Research, Reuters Institute for the Study of Journalism, University of Oxford, UK*

'*Comparing Political Journalism* is a fine example of a new generation of scholarship that is using systematic cross-national research to give us new insights into the way systemic factors influence media performance. Using a carefully executed content analysis to compare key characteristics of political news across 16 countries, it provides both a model of how to compare political news across systems and rich insights into the structural factors that influence its quality.'

Daniel C. Hallin, *Professor, Department of Communication, University of California, San Diego, USA*

'*Comparing Political Journalism* sets a new standard in comparative political communication research. Like detectives solving a crime, leading scholars in the field forensically interrogate some of the key concepts in political communication by empirically scrutinising news in 16 countries. In doing so, they question many of the conceptual claims long underpinning political communication scholarship and uncover the diverse ways in which politics is reported cross-nationally. Overall, they identify where and why quality news can flourish, opening up new debates about how political journalism can better serve democracies.'

Dr. Stephen Cushion, *Reader at Cardiff School of Journalism, Media and Cultural Studies, Cardiff University, UK*

Chapter 1

Our goal
Comparing news performance

Claes de Vreese, Frank Esser, and David Nicolas Hopmann with Toril Aalberg, Peter Van Aelst, Rosa Berganza, Nicolas Hubé, Guido Legnante, Jörg Matthes, Stylianos Papathanassopoulos, Carsten Reinemann, Susana Salgado, Tamir Sheafer, James Stanyer, and Jesper Strömbäck

The problem: where is the good news?

Democracy theory expects the news media to serve several roles: informing citizens about political actors and their ideas, interpreting the actions of both politicians and their opponents, scrutinizing those in power, and engaging citizens politically. The extent to which the news media fulfill these functions can be judged by their coverage of politics and society. Whether explicitly or implicitly, most discussions about the media's performance and their democratic role thus focus on political news and political journalism (Benson 2008; Graber 2003; Gurevitch and Blumler 1990; Norris 2000; Strömbäck 2005).

Research on political news and political journalism has grown in the last decade. Both single-country and comparative studies have increased, and the rising prominence of comparative journalism research is especially noteworthy (Albæk, van Dalen, Jebril, and de Vreese 2014; Esser 2008; Hanitzsch et al. 2011; Plasser, Pallaver, and Lengauer 2009; Shoemaker and Cohen 2006; Strömbäck and Dimitrova 2011; Van Aelst et al. 2008; Van Dalen, Albæk, and de Vreese 2011). Single-country and comparative research has generated many important insights into patterns of political news coverage and longitudinal and cross-national differences and similarities.

Much of extant research suggests that, although news availability and supply are proliferative (Esser, de Vreese et al. 2012), the *performance* of news providers is getting worse. In more or less explicit terms, decreasing news quality is seen as having a negative impact on the quality of political life. For example, concerns are voiced about overemphasis on strategy news causing political cynicism and apathy (Cappella and Jamieson 1997), about the media providing too little hard news (Patterson 2003), and about commercialization leading to too much interpretive journalism (Fallows 1996). As Albæk and colleagues observe (2014, p. 5), pessimism pertains to the "dominance in ownership structures, poor content, lack of good journalism, reliance on and misinterpretation of opinion polls, and ill-informed citizens who are losing interest in politics." Judging by much of the current research, we have little reason to be optimistic about today's news media performance, let alone tomorrow's. However, are things really that bad? Is good news, so to speak, really absent from all media environments? By 'good,' we mean in the sense of both news content and positive nodes in the literature. As scholars, we should not accept the pessimistic orthodoxy uncritically. Democratic news media performance is surely not all bad; good news is out there, but it needs to be identified and documented. The fundamental challenge facing scholars, therefore, is finding some good news and not just assuming that things are getting worse.

To address this challenge, solid and comparable evidence is needed. Any optimism needs to be supported by solid empirical evidence. Despite all the progress in recent research on political news, we have only just begun to grapple with some serious challenges that are related to a lack of conceptual clarity, poor comparability across studies, and insufficient cumulativity of findings (Esser, Strömbäck, and de Vreese 2012). These inadequacies hold particularly true for research that focuses on the content of political news. While many scholars use similar theoretical concepts, the conceptualizations and, in particular, the operationalizations often differ. These differences often make it hard to take stock of our current knowledge and to assess whether country differences and over-time developments are real or whether they are a function of differences in conceptualizations and operationalizations.

For example, where is news most focused on politics as a game? And where is it most substantive? Where is news more interpretive, and where less interpretive? And is news in all places equally prone to emphasizing negativity? Or do politicians in some countries receive more balanced treatment than in others? Given the differences in extant research, these questions are tough to answer. We know very little about some concepts, whereas a wealth of (national) information is available about others. But this research is often not comparable. The devil is in the detail! In addition, differences in research make it difficult to build solid theories explaining patterns of political news coverage across time and space. If the goal of social scientific research is to build and test theories, then this problem is a serious one.

In news research, references to 'hard' and 'soft' news are increasing, but they often carry different implications (Baum 2003). In a similar vein, although many scholars in different countries are doing research on the extent to which news journalism frames politics as a strategic game (Cappella and Jamieson 1997; de Vreese 2003; Lawrence 2000a; Patterson 1993; Strömbäck and Van Aelst 2010) and although they largely share the same terminology, there is no agreement on how this framing of politics should be conceptualized and measured. Scholars use various measures, which inhibits the cumulativity of findings. Equally, a mixture of methods hampers efforts to build theories explaining the differences and similarities in how different media, in different countries, at different times, cover politics (Esser, de Vreese et al. 2012). A similar situation holds true for most, if not all, key concepts in research on patterns in political news coverage.

We believe this situation to be highly unfortunate and that researchers investigating news content have a lot to learn from fields where standardization of key variables has progressed further. The best example might be survey research, where a number of standardized core variables are used to investigate political interest and party identification, for example. These variables are standard components of surveys and election studies across the globe, and the academic community has engaged in a long tradition of collaboration to make this standardization possible. National election studies, the European Social Survey, the World Value Survey, and the Eurobarometer are all hallmark examples. Collectively, such surveys provide social scientists with a lens through which to understand public opinion and human behavior. Admittedly, no single variable or set of variables is ideal for all people and all purposes at all times. Undoubtedly, political scientists have wished to change the wording and focus of specific items in various studies – for example, the American national election studies – but the what-ifs are outweighed by the benefits of comparisons and over-time insights. At the end of the day, by standardizing core variables, survey research has made great progress in opening up comparisons across time and space, which has significantly increased our understanding of the phenomena under investigation.

The advantage of standardization is why we – the authors of this book – took the initiative to organize a journal special issue reviewing six key concepts in research on political news journalism. These concepts were *strategy framing, interpretive journalism, negativity, political balance, personalization,* and *soft versus hard news.* The special issue was published in *Journalism* in 2012. The purpose of this special issue was twofold. The first purpose was to review the research and to offer an assessment of the state of affairs vis-à-vis key concepts in research on political news journalism. In so doing, we aimed to provide the scholarly community with points of reference related to each of the selected concepts, on which future research can build. The second purpose was to suggest how each of the selected key concepts should be conceptualized, operationalized, and investigated empirically in order to contribute to their standardization.

In this book, we put theory to practice. We designed a systematic, cross-national content analysis of newspapers, television news, and news websites in 16 Western countries. We investigated each of the key concepts to arrive at conclusions about the nature of political news and the forces driving these patterns.

Six dimensions of news performance

Underlying the quest to understand the nature of political news and the driving forces behind news features is the notion of news quality. Quality, however, is of little practical relevance analytically since it can be meaningfully understood from very different perspectives, ranging from consumers, citizens, and media companies to society as a whole. It makes more sense to consider news performance (McQuail 1992) a guiding concept. News performance is grounded in the notion that media have different functions, which stem from different normative theories. Ceteris paribus, most scholars suggest that news media should provide information, context and analysis, and a platform for – and scrutiny of – power holders (McQuail 1992).

The six concepts that were selected for the special issue and that are examined in this book were chosen because they are all widely used in content analyses of political news, have no standardized operationalizations, and are relevant to democratic news discourse and theories of news production. There are obviously other very important, ongoing discussions about changes in journalism at large and political journalism in particular that are also important and have a bearing on the six concepts. One may think of issues such as political parallelism (which relates to our discussion of political balance) but also of system-level concepts such as journalistic practice and culture and media ownership, which come up in our discussion of explaining why news takes the form it does. At the core of the six concepts is an interest in the role of the media in democracies. As noted, among other things, the media in democracies are expected to inform people, interpret processes with societal and political relevance, scrutinize those in power, and mobilize people politically. Content analyses of political news coverage can make important information explicit about how the mass media fulfill these political roles in divergent national settings.

With respect to their informative role, some national communication systems, compared to others, offer more favorable opportunity structures for relaying political messages comprehensively and neutrally to the public. Some national settings foster a more partisan, depoliticized, or personalized political and reporting culture. With respect to their interpretive role, many democratic news systems have experienced a cultural shift from the media as passive informants to active shapers of public opinion. Some news organizations have pursued an interventionist role, posing as the 'better' public representative compared to elected politicians. While interpretation and analysis can provide an important background for audiences and facilitate a deeper understanding of the issues, an overly interventionist role can become a source of conflict between political actors and media actors, especially if politics is mainly presented as a strategic game. The extent and consequences of interpretive journalism lead us to another political role that is frequently discussed in democratic theory – namely, the media's watchdog function. Here, the media are supposed to guard citizens against undue infringements of their rights by the apparatus of the state and to uncover abuse of power and unfitness for public office. Yet, the media's abuse of the watchdog function may encourage an ideology of negativity and voter alienation.

The discussion surrounding democratic news performance has highlighted several features of political news journalism that have raised particular interest among scholars – notably, the framing of politics as a strategic game, the interpretive journalistic style, media negativity, balance in the news, media personalization, and depoliticization via a focus on soft news over hard news. Collectively, these six dimensions allow us to assess how well news is performing cross-nationally.

News performance refers to the reality of news practices and how they manifest themselves in media outcomes. Of particular interest are the reasons for the differences in news performance that can be observed across types of media systems, news organizations, and journalistic communities. We measure the quality of news performance using six content features – namely, strategy and game framing, interpretive journalism, negativity, political balance, personalization, and hard and soft news. They are related to normative expectations of the news media in contemporary Western democracy (as shown earlier) and have the additional advantage of being closer to the daily routines of news workers than abstract principles such as truth, freedom, solidarity, or order and cohesion. They are also easier to operationalize and are often critically discussed as features of a proliferating yet problematic Western news ideology.

The factors affecting news journalism's conduct and performance are located at the levels of media and political systems, news organizations, and individual journalists interacting with their event environments. Consequently, we consider 'political news coverage' the outcome of three broad and interdependent sources of influence. The first source are the journalists, who engage with political events, actors, and processes according to their professional norms and goals. The second are the news organizations' influences, constraints, and goals (e.g., whether an outlet pursues a public service–oriented or a mass audience–oriented editorial mission). And the third source are the structural influences at the level of the media system (e.g., market competition, market commercialization, and journalistic professionalization) and the political system (e.g., type of party, electoral and government systems) that constitute the contextual environment for the news organizations and the journalists who are employed by them. In combination, these factors affect the editorial processes and actual news outcomes that determine the use of our six news performance indicators. Figure 1.1 offers a simplified visual representation of these relationships.

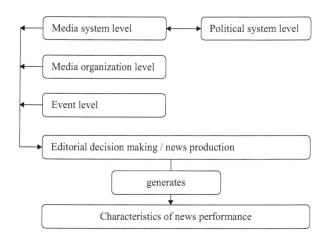

Figure 1.1 News performance in context

A more elaborate specification of our theoretical framework is presented in Chapter 3, where we also derive research questions and concrete hypotheses. Chapters 4 to 9 come next, with in-depth analyses of the six concepts of news performance, following a common structure to ensure readability and coherence. Each of these chapters outlines why the concept is relevant and why a systematic study is needed. The chapters proceed by reviewing the most important theoretical and conceptual foundations, including how the concept has been defined in previous research, and, if appropriate, they discuss different dimensions of the concept. They then outline how the concept fares in news across different countries and the key explanations for the discovered patterns.

Our approach

More than 20 years ago, Blumler, McLeod, and Rosengren (1992) stated that, before comparative communication research can establish itself as a recognized subdiscipline, it must achieve greater cumulativity in findings and interpretation. By explicating concepts in this book, our goal is to contribute an empirically grounded, systematic, and comparative assessment of political news.

At this volume's core are comparative analyses of political news coverage in 16 Western countries with regard to strategy framing, interpretive journalism, negativity, political balance, personalization, and soft versus hard news. Each chapter focuses on one of these concepts (measured collaboratively by an international research network) and compares all countries in relation to common research questions. We also strive to understand what drives the presence of these concepts in the news. In each chapter, we develop research questions and hypotheses about how news content is affected by variables at the (1) event environment, (2) media organization, (3) media system, and (4) political system levels.

The book is based on a unique content analysis of more than 7,500 news stories from newspapers, television news bulletins, and news websites. We examined three newspapers, two television news bulletins, and five news websites from each country over a constructed routine period. Our book speaks to an international literature on news and politics. Only a few publications have addressed this topic in such a systematic manner, but they tend to focus on just one concept (balance, objectivity, bias, domestication, etc.) or explore only a small number of countries (two to five). Some recent projects are more inclusive (e.g., Albæk et al. 2014; Umbricht and Esser 2014, 2015), and some journal articles cover more than 20 countries in a systematic content analysis (see, e.g., Boomgaarden et al. 2013; de Vreese, Banducci, Semetko, and Boomgaarden 2006). But book-length analyses of diverse concepts using large samples of countries are rare exceptions; Pam Shoemaker and Akiba Cohen's *News around the World* (2006) and *Foreign News on Television – Where in the World Is the Global Village* (2013) are perhaps the prime examples. Their focus, however, is very different to ours, and none of the key concepts that we pursue in this book are included in their work. We have also attempted to generate a sample of routine news and to systematize our inclusion

Our goal: comparing news performance **7**

of explanatory variables and are, therefore, well poised to make observations that are general in nature and not confined to specific particularities or to incompatibilities in our design.

We believe that the book is unique because it (1) systematizes national and international research on 6 key concepts in political news, (2) builds on recently developed empirical tools for analyzing these concepts, (3) tests the 6 concepts in a systematic, cross-nationally comparative analysis in 16 countries, (4) develops and tests hypotheses for understanding similarities and differences in the coverage of politics, and (5) brings together a strong team of political communication scholars from different countries. The book is thus not only about investigating the key features of news cross-nationally but also about *explaining* them.

Outline of the book

We outline our methodology and approach in the next chapter. It reviews the choice of countries, media, and periods and details the coding procedures, intercoder reliability, data preparation, analytical strategy, and so on. We opt to keep the methodological information in one chapter so that subsequent chapters merely have to introduce the specific variables of interest (while cross-referencing Chapter 2). In Chapter 3, we explicate our philosophy of trying to move beyond national descriptions and to focus on explanations for the variation in the news coverage. We discuss key works in this tradition, such as those by Shoemaker and Reese (2014), and we identify the most important explanatory concepts for our endeavor. We include macro-, meso-, and micro-level variables, and the chapter outlines the most frequently used explanatory variables, thereby serving as a reference chapter for the empirical concept chapters (Chapters 4 to 9).

In Chapter 4, we take on a key concept in political communication research – game and strategy news framing. Based on the instrument developed by Aalberg, Strömbäck, and de Vreese (2012), the chapter compares the extent to which political news journalism across 16 countries is dominated by game and strategy frames, and equally importantly, it investigates what drives this type of political news coverage. It finds that during regular periods, most political news throughout Europe is not framed as a strategic game (although some issues, typically related to party politics, are more likely to be framed in this way). The use of strategy and game frames is not, as previously assumed, higher in mass-market newspapers and commercial broadcasters compared to upmarket newspapers and public broadcasters. Nevertheless, some of the relatively small cross-national differences may be explained by the market share of public service channels and the number of political parties.

In Chapter 5, we examine interpretive journalism. Based on Salgado and Strömbäck (2012), we examine the operationalization of interpretive journalism and the extent to which political news across 16 countries provides journalistic interpretations. The chapter shows that about a third of public affairs coverage in European and U.S. news media contains interpretive journalism, although there are meaningful differences across countries with respect to its prevalence and the factors that promote it. To give just one example, commercial television news, particularly if integrated in a highly competitive market, provides a highly fertile ground for interpretive reporting.

In Chapter 6, we look at negativity in the news. Although there is an abundance of research on the journalistic tendency to focus disproportionally on negative information, we lack studies that systematically compare theoretically derived indicators of negativity across countries. This chapter draws on a standardized measure of negativity developed by Esser and colleagues (2012), consisting of four highly related dimensions: negative tonality, focus on conflict, focus on incapability, and negative tone towards political actors. The findings show that negativity is highest in media systems with high levels of commercialism and competition and in media organizations that are geared towards commercial goals (as opposed to public service obligations). The tendency to cover politics in negative terms is stronger in the offline than online editions of media outlets and strongest in stories that deal with negatively connoted issues, such as scandals, crises, or conflicts.

In Chapter 7, the focus shifts to political balance. The chapter examines the visibility of politicians and political parties in the news and the neutrality with which they are presented. It follows the article by Hopmann and colleagues (2012) and analyzes to what extent news coverage is politically balanced at the party level. The results show that the visibility of political actors across countries is fairly balanced. Moreover, most appearances of politicians are by far either neutral or balanced, rarely colored in a positive or negative light.

In Chapter 8, we turn to personalization, examining the general belief that the focus of news coverage has shifted from parties and organizations to candidates and leaders. Based on the indicators developed by Van Aelst, Sheafer, and Stanyer (2012), the chapter shows that, in general, individual politicians are more prominent in the news compared to political institutions. The degree of personalized political coverage, however, varies strongly across countries. Two country characteristics are especially important for understanding the variation: the number of TV channels (which represents the competitiveness of the media market) and the degree of federalism (which represents the concentration of power within the political system).

In Chapter 9, we focus on 'hard' and 'soft' news, terms that have become widely used for capturing particular changes in the news. This chapter draws on the recent multidimensional approach to distinguishing harder and softer news developed by Reinemann, Stanyer, Scherr, and Legnante (2012). Findings show that the prevalence of hard and soft news differs strongly between countries. Analysis reveals that the type of medium, a country's political and economic situation, and the state of the media market significantly predict the hard or soft character of individual news items.

In Chapter 10, we survey the different key concepts. The chapter identifies the patterns across the different concepts and countries and offers more general observations about the nature of political news. First of all, we conclude that game or strategy framed news tends to be more interpretive and negative and rather unbalanced and softer. In the same vein, interpretive news tends to be more negative and strategically framed, be less balanced, and carry less hard political information. Negativity and balance are negatively correlated, which makes sense since we would expect a clear and unambiguous negative portrayal of actors to also be reflected in the overall negative tone of a story. And finally, personalization is negatively correlated to hard news such that personalized news tends to have less political substance, whereas news items with more political substance tend to have more institutional actors involved. Second, the chapter identifies two 'meta-dimensions' that summarize and combine the different indicators. One dimension represents the degree of evaluation and interpretation, and the other represents the amount of political substance. Looking cross-nationally, we observe that Belgium, Denmark, the Netherlands, Norway, Spain, and the United Kingdom have the most issue-focused coverage, whereas Austria, Greece, Portugal, and Sweden have the least. News in France, Greece, Israel, Italy, and the United States is the most focused on strategy game coverage.

In the concluding chapter (Chapter 11), we summarize the book's main findings and outline an agenda for future comparative research on political news and political communication. We hold the empirical outcomes against the assumptions about news performance that are embedded in the six key concepts. We also specifically revisit some of the expectations that we had a priori and which turned out to be wrong – or at least, were not supported by the study. We offer a methodological reflection on comparative news analyses and observations on where news is most substantive. At the very end, we identify some key factors that help locate the 'good news' – that is, news that offers citizens a range of choices and provides them with a substantive, rich, and varied information environment.

Chapter 2

How we did it
Approach and methods

*David Nicolas Hopmann, Frank Esser,
and Claes de Vreese with Toril Aalberg,
Peter Van Aelst, Rosa Berganza, Nicolas Hubé,
Guido Legnante, Jörg Matthes, Stylianos
Papathanassopoulos, Carsten Reinemann,
Susana Salgado, Tamir Sheafer, James Stanyer,
and Jesper Strömbäck*

Introduction

The analyses in this book are based on a dataset covering information on more than 7,500 news items and more than 28,000 sources that appear in the news items. How did we gather these news items? In the process of designing a comparative study, numerous decisions have to be made – many of which are not straightforward (Rössler 2012). These decisions relate to the sampling procedure, the construction of the codebook, inter-coder reliability testing, and the strategy of analysis. The goal of this chapter is to provide a technical overview of how we created the main data source for this book and to present the methods applied. In so doing, we intend to provide enough background information for the subsequent analyses that are needed to evaluate and contextualize the data and the results. This chapter does not aim to provide an in-depth discussion or analysis of the methods and strategies applied. Numerous books and articles with extended methodological discussions on cross-country media content analysis have been previously published (e.g., Hopmann and Skovsgaard 2014; Krippendorff 2004; Neuendorf 2002; Peter and Lauf 2002; Riffe, Lacy, and Fico 2005; Rössler 2012). This chapter, by contrast, describes the application of methods.

The chapter proceeds as follows. In the first part, the period of sampling and its various steps are presented, involving countries, news outlets, and news articles. In the second part, we provide a short overview of the codebook. The third part presents our testing of inter-coder reliability, both across countries and within countries. We then briefly explain how our analyses in the subsequent chapters were conducted and why. The chapter's concluding section reflects on some of the advantages and challenges of the data sources and the methods that we have chosen.

Sampling strategies

The more than 7,500 news items analyzed in this book were gathered in 16 different countries. Heading from north to south, the countries are Norway, Sweden, the United Kingdom, Denmark, Germany, the Netherlands, Belgium, France, Switzerland, Austria, Italy, Spain, Portugal, Greece, Israel, and the United States. In short, the country sample covers all larger Western European countries (barring Finland and Ireland) as well as Israel and the United States.

Behind the choice of countries were several considerations. First, we opted for a design that has a set of comparable countries (established Western democracies). Second, the sample of countries captures variance in several dimensions on the media and political systems level, which is crucial for the analyses to be presented in the book (i.e., we decided to cover countries that vary on a number of relevant independent variables, including their media markets and journalistic professionalism). Third, and related to the second consideration, we wanted to include countries that cover the different models of media and politics identified in previous research (i.e., the liberal model, the polarized pluralist model, and the democratic corporatist model, see Hallin and Mancini 2004). The presentation of the key independent variables in Chapter 4 will show how these countries vary with respect to their media markets and political systems. By investigating these 16 countries, we are able to study how these factors correlate with news content. Fourth, we wanted to include newspaper- as well as television-centric countries (Norris 2000; Shehata and Strömbäck 2011). Fifth, the United States was included because of its prominent role in previous news research. In addition, it is seen as a prime example of a liberal media system (Hallin and Mancini 2004). Both Israel and the United States are two countries where public service broadcasting (PSB) has only small market shares (comparable in Europe only to Greece), which is another important reason for their inclusion. Finally, there were practical considerations. The scholars behind this study are based in 14 different European countries plus Israel.

Sampling units

With regard to the choice of news outlets to be included in this study, our goal was twofold. On the one hand, we intended to cover the variation in each country's media market as comprehensively as possible. On the other hand, we aimed for sample equivalency across countries; that is, we wanted to sample comparable units (Rössler 2012, pp. 461–462). A list of all included news outlets is shown in Table 2.1.

With respect to newspapers, we therefore decided to sample the two most popular upmarket outlets in each country and, where possible, one politically left of center and one politically right of center. In most European countries, upmarket (sometimes also called broadsheet) newspapers have a long tradition of being affiliated with specific political camps (see, e.g., the discussions in Hallin and

Table 2.1 News outlets included in the content analyses by country and type of outlet

| Country | Newspaper | | | Television, news bulletin | | Websites | | | | |
| | Upmarket | | Mass-market | Public service | Commercial | Upmarket | | Mass-market | Public service | Commercial |
	Left of center	Right of center				Left of center	Right of center			
Austria	Der Standard	Die Presse	Kronenzeitung	ORF1, ZiB	ATV, Aktuell	derstandard.at	diepresse.com	krone.at	news.orf.at	kurier.at[a]
Belgium	De Morgen	De Standaard	Het Laatste Nieuws	VRT, Het Journaal	VTM, Het Nieuws	demorgen.be	standaard.be	hln.be	deredactie.be	nieuws.vtm.be
Denmark	Politiken	Jyllands-Posten	Ekstra Bladet	DR, TV-Avisen	TV2, Nyhederne	politiken.dk	jp.dk	ekstrabladet.dk	dr.dk/nyhederne	nyhederne.tv2.dk
France	Le Monde	Le Figaro	Le Parisien	France 2, Journal de 20h	TF1, Journal de 20h	lemonde.fr	lefigaro.fr	leparisien.fr	info.france2.fr	lei.tf1.fr
Germany	Süddeutsche Zeitung	Frankfurter Allgemeine Zeitung	Bild	ARD, Tagesschau	RTL, Aktuell	sueddeutsche.de	faz.net	bild.de	tagesschau.de	rtl.de/rtlaktuell
Greece	Tanea	Kathimerini	Espresso	NET, News	Mega, News	tanea.gr	kathimerini.gr	espressonews.gr	ert.gr	megatv.vom
Israel	Haaretz	Ydiot Aharonot[b]	Israel Hayom	Channel 1, Evening News	Channel 2, Evening News	haaretz.co.il	Ydiot Aharonot[c]	israelhayom.com	ynet.co.ilc	mako.co.il
Italy	La Repubblica	Il Giornale	Altri mondi[d]	RAI1, TG1	Canale5, TG5	repubblica.it	ilgiornale.it	quotidiano.net	tg1.rai.it	tgcom24.mediaset.it
Netherlands	De Volkskrankt	NRC Handelsblad	De Telegraaf	NOS, Journaal	RTL, Nieuws	volkskrant.nl	nrc.nl	telegraaf.nl	nos.nl	rtlnieuws.nl

Norway	*Dagsavisen*	*Aftenposten*	*VG*	NRK, Dagsrevyen	TV2, Nyhetene	aftenposten.no	dagsavisen.no	vg.no	nrk.no	tv2.no/nyheter
Portugal	*Jornal de Notícias*	*Público*	*Correio da Manhã*	RTP1, Telejornal	TVI, Jornal das 8	publico.pt	jo.pt	cmjornal.xl.pt	rtp.pt	tvi.iol.pt
Spain	*El País*	*El Mundo*	*20Minutos*	TVE, Telediario de la Noche	Tele5, Informativos	elpais.com	elmundo.es	20minutos.es	rtve.es/telediario	telecinco.es/informativos
Sweden	*Dagens Nyheter*[e]	*Svenska Dagbladet*	*Aftonbladet*	SVT, Rapport	TV2, Nyheterna	dn.se(center)	svd.se	aftonbladet.se	svt.se	tv2.se/nyheter
Switzerland	*Tages-Anzeiger*	*Neue Zürcher Zeitung*	*Blick*	SF, Tagesschau	TeleZüri, ZüriNews	nzz.ch	tagesanzeiger.ch	blick.ch	tagesschau.sf.tv	radio24.ch[f]
United Kingdom	*The Guardian*	*Daily Telegraph*	*The Sun*	BBC, News at Ten	ITV, News at Ten	guardian.co.uk	telegraph.co.uk	thesun.co.uk	bbc.co.uk/news	itv.com/news
United States	*The New York Times*	*Los Angeles Times*	*USA Today*	NBC, NBC Nightly News	PBS, PBS News Hour	nytimes.com	latimes.com	usatoday.com	msnbc.msn.com	npr.org[g]

a We used kurier.at because ATV, the private broadcaster, does not offer an online news site.

b *Yediot Aharonot* is considered a popular newspaper, and its ideology is rather center based.

c Radio was used since the website of the Israeli public television provides only video and not text. Reshet Bet's radio news is part of the Israeli Public Broadcasting Authority, as is Israeli Public Television.

d Given the absence of a mass-market versus upmarket distinction in Italy, we used *Altri Mondi* ("Other Worlds") – a section of the sports newspaper *La Gazzetta Dello Sport*. *Altri Mondi* reports the news of the day and the main political news to its mass audience. It does not have a news website, so we used quotidiano.net, a website pooling news from the national network of locally relevant, mass-market newspapers.

e In Sweden, there is no major left-of-center upmarket newspaper on the national level. *Dagens Nyheter* is considered liberal and slightly right of center but nearer the center compared to *Svenska Dagbladet*.

f The website of Radio 24 was used because TeleZüri does not have a news website.

g We chose NPR because it is a fairer comparison to the much-used MSNBC website.

h For Portugal, we chose the largest news outlets, but the categorization into 'left of center' or 'right of center' does not apply here.

Mancini 2004; Seymour-Ure 1974). Where the leading national upmarket newspapers include newspapers with different political leanings, our sampling strategy included the leading left-of-center and right-of-center newspapers. In addition, we sampled one mass-market (i.e., tabloid) newspaper from each country. Previous research has indicated that mass-market newspapers differ in their news reporting from upmarket newspapers (Albæk et al. 2014). By including both upmarket and mass-market newspapers across all 16 countries, we are able to study the implications of editorial missions and organizational goals for news content. Differences in news content as a consequence of editorial missions or organizational goals are often assumed; the question is whether they can be empirically confirmed.

For a majority of citizens, the most important source for political news continues to be television news (Shehata and Strömbäck 2014). For all countries, we included the most widely watched public service broadcasts and commercial news broadcasts. Except for a few outliers, public service broadcasting (PSB) is widely watched across the sampled countries, and in many countries, public service broadcasters are leading players in the media market (Esser, de Vreese et al. 2012). Previous research has indicated that there are systematic differences between the style of news reporting on public service broadcasters and commercial broadcasters (Aalberg and Curran 2012; Cushion 2012; de Vreese et al. 2006). By including both types of broadcasters, we are able (as was the case with the two types of newspapers) to study whether they differ systematically across countries, and how.

Increasingly, citizens consume news through websites. This trend poses a challenge to comparative research, given the blurred boundaries of website production and the vast differences in consumption at the individual and media-system levels. Since the major news sites in nearly all countries are mostly the online affiliates of established newspapers or television broadcasters (Mutz and Young 2011; Shehata and Strömbäck 2014, p. 107), in Table 2.1, we included the websites of the newspapers and broadcasters chosen. This approach of choosing online sources also has the advantage that they are fairly comparable across media systems. These websites were downloaded on the sampling days to make their content available for subsequent content analysis.

More generally, it is important to note that many of the media outlets analyzed in this study are not centrally archived. We therefore had to tape or download newscasts, buy newspapers at the newsstand, copy websites for offline use, and so on.[1]

Unit of analysis

After having decided which news outlets to include in the content analyses, the next step was to define the unit of analysis – in our case, the news item. Everyone with experience in media content analysis knows that it is anything but easy to define a news item; in particular, a common challenge is deciding when a televised news story ends and a new one begins. The challenge is only magnified in comparative content analysis (Rössler 2012, p. 465). The details of our approach for each type of medium are explained later.

As a general rule, we included only domestically relevant political news items. So, for instance, a short report on some remote country's election result without any reference to domestic politics was not included. In practical terms, this strategy implied searching for news items that verbally or visually referred to at least one domestic political actor (including political parties or political institutions).

Beginning with television, we followed the approach for defining a news item that has been used in previous international comparative studies (e.g., de Vreese et al. 2006; Schuck, Boomgaarden, and de Vreese 2013). A television news item may have several different components, including an introduction by an anchor, a field report, a so-called two-way with a journalist, an interview with a politician, and more. To begin with, we defined a television news item as having one topic. If the topic changes, by definition, a new news item begins. 'Packages' dealing with the same topic (e.g., a field report followed by a two-way with the correspondent) were also treated as two or more different news items. Short teasers or very short news items were not included in the content analysis.

With newspapers, defining a news item is more straightforward since each item is usually clearly graphically separated from the next. The criterion of reference to a domestic political actor was limited to headlines, subheadlines, first paragraphs, and visuals. We sampled only news items appearing in the international or domestic political sections of newspapers; that is, we did not sample news items appearing in sections with a focus on such things as regional, local, cultural, and sports issues. We excluded news articles that were shorter than five lines of text, unless they were major front-page headlines, as is sometimes the case in mass-market newspapers.

Finally, for websites, we treated news items as consisting of text, text with a visual, or text with a video, generally following the same rules as for newspaper article sampling. We did not include very short news items (i.e., less than two sentences) but did include the text introducing a video (the video itself was not content analyzed in any detail). Side stories embedded within a news item that had their own headlines were coded as separate news items, as was also the case with newspaper items.

In a first step, coders were asked to count the number of news items published on a specific day by a specific outlet and to numerate all eligible news items. In a second step, if a specific news outlet published more than five (for websites, three) news items on a specific day, coders had to choose five (for websites, three) random news items that were then included in the content analysis. A randomizer (offered by the website Random.org) drew five random news items from all eligible news items.

Sampling period

We sampled news items during a constructed fortnight (i.e., 14 days in total), stretching from 15 April to 15 July 2012. The main advantage of constructing two weeks from a total period of three months over choosing two consecutive weeks is that special events – even if occurring in only one country – distort the sample (on constructed weeks in content analyses, see Riffe et al. 2005). Special events include major accidents or natural disasters. A special event could still be captured by our sampling procedure if it occurred on one of the days included in the sample, but our strategy ensured that it does not color the entire sample. In other words, in our content analysis, it would remain what it is – a special event.

There were three exceptions to the sampling period: France, Greece, and the Netherlands. In these cases, elections were held in the period mentioned earlier. But, as explained in Chapter 1, one of the goals of this study was to analyze political news coverage in routine times. The sampling was therefore postponed in these countries and took place in the period from 15 September to 15 December 2012.[2]

Codebook

Apart from reviewing the current state of research on a number of key concepts in the political communication literature, the second goal of our 2012 *Journalism* special issue was "to contribute to increasing standardization of how key concepts are conceptualized and, perhaps most important, operationalized and investigated empirically" by suggesting "how each of the selected key concepts should be conceptualized and operationalized" (Esser, Strömbäck, and de Vreese. 2012, pp. 140–141). Each review article included in the special issue presented an overview of how a given concept can be operationalized.

As explained in the Introduction, the goal of the present study is to turn these suggestions into practice. The detailed codebook that was used during the data gathering for the present book was based on this previous review. As shown in Table 2.2, the included variables covered six dimensions on the news item level: formal characteristics (e.g., type of media outlet), strategy versus game framing, interpretive journalism, negativity and style, policy substance, and issue of the news item. For each news item, up to five actors could be coded. On the actor level, we coded formal characteristics (e.g., gender) and the favorability of their appearances.

The attentive reader will notice that we modified and updated some of the measures that were originally suggested in our *Journalism* review of concepts. The changes are hardly surprising. Suggesting a measure in a review is one thing; actually implementing it in a large-scale comparative content analysis is another. Details on the measures used and their derivations will be described in each of the chapters presenting our findings. What is most important is that we applied the same definitions of the variables across all countries. Although one can always discuss whether the operationalization of a concept is too broad or too narrow, the major advantage of this approach is that we can compare levels across countries; that is, our results will inform us about the *differences* between countries.

Inter-coder reliability across countries

Ensuring inter-coder reliability in comparative research is a major challenge – even more so in our study, given the many different languages (see, e.g., Peter and Lauf 2002; Rössler 2012). In this study, we have taken several steps to ensure inter-coder reliability. In a first step, we tested the codebook using English-language material among all authors of the book. The goal was to ensure a common understanding of how to apply the codebook across countries. As Rössler (2012) noted, ensuring a common understanding of the constructs to be measured is especially challenging in comparative research. Based on the results of this initial coding, some variable descriptions and definitions were revised and updated.

In a second step, local coders were recruited and trained. Following suggestions from methodological research on comparative content analyses (Peter and Lauf 2002, p. 826), we recruited native speakers as local coders but whose English proficiency was sufficient to read the codebook in English and to code the first set of coder-training material in English. To ensure a common understanding of concepts across countries, the coder training began with one English-language set of testing material that was used in all countries. In the subsequent third step, the local coders performed the coding of the sampled news items (details are available upon request).[3]

In a fourth and final step, we formally tested the inter-coder reliability based on English-language material after the country-specific coding had been completed. Using five news examples, this test was performed by coders who had participated in the country-specific content analyses.[4] The summarized results of this final test are reported in Table 2.2.

As one can see in Table 2.2, we report two versions of Fretwurst's *lotus* (Fretwurst 2015a, 2015b). The *lotus* coefficient can be applied to categorical, ordinal, or metrical scales and can be reported as both unstandardized and standardized measures of inter-coder reliability. This measure of inter-coder reliability has a number of advantages. The unstandardized *lotus* is directly interpretable, representing the percentage agreement of coders with the most used category by all coders. This approach ignores coder agreement on other categories other than the most used category (Fretwurst 2015a, 2015b). The standardized *lotus* measure is a chance-corrected version; that is, the computation of the *lotus* also takes into account the number of categories used by coders. The reasoning is that the more categories, the more difficult it is to reach an agreement. Finally, comparing countries that have provided information on how they contribute to the overall *lotus* coding results (reported in Table 2.3) is a straightforward task.

What do the results reported in Table 2.2 tell us? Looking at the unstandardized *lotus* first, we see that the coding of formal characteristics achieved good inter-coder reliability scores. With respect to the substantive variables, the results for interpretive journalism, 'policy substance and issue,' and 'strategy and issue

18 David Nicolas Hopmann et al.

Table 2.2 International inter-coder reliability, summarized results[a]

Variable name (coding categories)	Variable group	Fretwurst's lotus	Fretwurst's lotus (standardized)
News item level			
Type of medium (1–4)	Formal characteristics	.94	.92
Type of news item (1–6)	Formal characteristics	.94	.93
Commentary by journalist (0/1)	Interpretive journalism	.80	.60
Consequence speculation by journalist (0/1)	Interpretive journalism	.83	.66
Reasons provided by journalist (0/1)	Interpretive journalism	.73	.46
Conflict (0–3)	Negativity and style	.76	.68
Emotional reporting (1–3)	Negativity and style	.71	.57
Incapability (0–3)	Negativity and style	.66	.54
Negative tonality (0–3)	Negativity and style	.64	.52
Affected groups (0/1)	Policy substance and issue	.83	.66
Decision-making authorities (0/1)	Policy substance and issue	.93	.86
Issue (1–18)	Policy substance and issue	.70	.68
Policy substance (0/1)	Policy substance and issue	.83	.66
Societal actors (0/1)	Policy substance and issue	.84	.69
Media's role (0/1)	Strategy and issue framing	.94	.89
Performance (0/1)	Strategy and issue framing	.71	.43
Public opinion (0/1)	Strategy and issue framing	.79	.57
Strategic macroframe (1–2)	Strategy and issue framing	.87	.74
Strategy/tactics (0/1)	Strategy and issue framing	.83	.66
War/sports language (0/1)	Strategy and issue framing	.70	.40
Winning/losing (0/1)	Strategy and issue framing	.83	.66
Actor level			
Gender (0–2)	Formal characteristics	.97	.96
Function (detailed actor list)	Formal characteristics	.94	.94
Favorability (0–3)	Favorability	.69	.58

a Based on codings from 14 countries.

framing' are also acceptable. The results for 'negativity and style' are somewhat lower. Variables such as 'incapability' or 'negative tonality' are notoriously difficult to code given their evaluative character. On the actor level, we also find good scores for formal characteristics of actors, but favorability of actor appearances was more difficult to code, as one would expect. The chance-corrected *lotus* scores are generally somewhat lower. Again, as one would expect, evaluative variables such as 'incapability,' 'negative tonality,' and 'favorability' towards actors have the lowest scores.

Table 2.3 International inter-coder reliability, per country[a]

Country	Fretwurst's lotus	Fretwurst's lotus (standardized)
Austria	.88	.82
Belgium	.83	.72
Denmark	.78	.60
France	.79	.64
Germany	.86	.76
Greece	.87	.79
Israel	.77	.60
Italy	.73	.53
Netherlands	.80	.67
Portugal	.80	.67
Sweden	.83	.71
Switzerland	.72	.52
United Kingdom	.78	.63
United States	.89	.83
Total	**.81**	**.68**

a Based on the variables mentioned in Table 2.2.

In Table 2.3, we also report the details of the international inter-coder reliability test per country. That is, these results tell us the inter-coder reliability of each country. Low overall scores tell us that a country has had a negative impact on the summarized results reported in Table 2.2. Overall, we see no major differences between countries. Countries such as Israel, Italy, and Switzerland score somewhat lower than other countries. The crucial story to tell from Table 2.3, however, is that despite minor differences between countries, average inter-coder reliability scores across countries are acceptable.

We do want to be explicit that – as in most cases – the inter-coder reliability of our study is open for further improvement. We stress that the test was conducted on identical stories in the project language English, but that the actual coding of the 16-county material was done in the coders' native language. This difference is important as project language tests (such as ours in English) typically yield lower reliability scores and may thus underestimate the quality of the actual coding (see Rössler 2012).

Analytical strategy

After collecting data, the next important question arises – how to analyze the collected data. Our goal was to choose an adequate analytical strategy that readers would find accessible. Therefore, the standard analytical strategy in this book's analyses was to use media outlets ($N = 160$) as the unit of analysis. The rationale behind this strategy was our interest in explaining the *outlets'* news coverage across our sample of countries. As will be explained in Chapter 3, the main independent variables that we were interested in are at the media outlet level (i.e., type of medium) and at the country level (i.e., information on the political and media systems of a given country). In those cases where it was necessary, the unit of analysis was actors, of which we coded more than 28,000. As mentioned previously, up to five actors could be coded per news story. Using actors as a unit of analysis was partly relevant for the chapters on personalization and political balance. Finally, overviews across countries are based on simple country-level means across all news stories (or actors), unless another approach is specified in the presentation of the results.

In short, the six concept chapters and the cross-country analysis in Chapter 7 are mainly based on regression analyses on the news outlet level as well as country means. In the case of regression analysis, we computed robust standard errors (Rogers 1994). By doing so, we aimed to take into account the grouping of cases into country clusters. We did not opt for a multilevel analysis, given the frequent low Ns, for example, on a country level, where we included ten news outlets per country.

Discussion

The starting point of this book was the goal to describe and explain differences in political journalism across established Western democracies. Analyses of news content can take many different forms and approaches, depending on the key questions at stake. Conducting media content analyses in 16 countries simultaneously is anything but easy. Given these comparative ambitions, we had a trade-off by focusing on certain aspects while leaving out more in-depth aspects of the coverage. This lacuna is often the price of working systematically and comparatively. We accomplished our content analysis task through local, native-speaking coders. While the inter-coder reliability across countries could surely have been higher, we are confident that the coding across countries ensured the comparability of the results across countries. Moreover, given the nature of our endeavor – testing multi-item measures for 6 key concepts across 16 countries for the first time – we were willing to relax more stringent requirements in the hope that the work will spark more research that can also improve, in a more focused fashion, certain subfacets. We fully acknowledge that our analysis follows the logic of systematic, comparative content analysis. Using other approaches would have enabled us to go more into depth with particular cases or aspects, and we hope that subsequent research, from a variety of perspectives and approaches, will engage with this work as they further develop their research agendas.

In our previous *Journalism* special issue (Esser et al. 2012), we described the state of the art for a number of concepts that are important in the fields of political communication research and journalism studies. Now the time had come to implement the measures. For this undertaking, we needed additional data from other sources. The next chapter presents the explanatory logic of our analyses and the additional data sources that we drew on (besides the media content analysis described in this chapter). What we found and what we did not find in the 16 media systems included in our study, and how the differences between media systems can be explained, will be presented in the Chapters 4–9.

Authors' acknowledgements

We are indebted to Benjamin Fretwurst for providing us with the necessary tools to compute the *lotus* inter-coder reliability coefficients reported in this chapter. For more details, see www.iakom.ch/lotus.html (last accessed 10 June 2015). Our thanks also go to Sven Engesser for his helpful input.

Notes

1 In a few cases, data were missing or not available: for Denmark, pictures were not included on some websites as the program that was used to download the website was unable to perform certain operations (for example, it could not handle Danish characters in links and references). For Italy, on May 20, it was not possible to download some news from websites; therefore, we performed a new sampling on relevant news of the day. For the U.S., April 26 was replaced with May 4 due to missing data.
2 In the Netherlands, parliamentary elections took place September 12, 2012, implying that the Dutch data covered an immediate postelection period. As in some other European countries, Dutch elections are typically announced only with very short notice, making it difficult to plan accordingly.
3 The content analysis of the U.S. data was conducted by native English speakers residing in the United Kingdom.
4 No Norwegian and Spanish coder was available at the time of the test; these two countries are therefore missing from the results reported in Tables 2.2 and 2.3. In most other cases, one coder per country was asked to complete the test coding.

Chapter 3

The explanatory logic
Factors that shape political news

Frank Esser, Claes de Vreese, and David Nicolas Hopmann with Toril Aalberg, Peter Van Aelst, Rosa Berganza, Nicolas Hubé, Guido Legnante, Jörg Matthes, Stylianos Papathanassopoulos, Carsten Reinemann, Susana Salgado, Tamir Sheafer, James Stanyer, and Jesper Strömbäck

Introduction

Insights gained depend on the questions asked. This chapter describes the why and the how of our study's approach. After outlining some principal research interests of comparative news analyses, we introduce a theoretical hierarchy of influences that needs to be observed in order to understand the construction of media content. In fitting this model to the specific requirements of our study, we emphasize, in particular, the importance of integrating event-centered and media-centered considerations, of incorporating an explicit comparative perspective, and of applying appropriate strategies of data analysis. The main part of the chapter introduces the explanatory factors that are used in this study to elucidate cross-national and cross-organizational differences in journalists' use of the six core concepts of political news. The explanatory factors are systematized according to their level of analysis, and we provide a great many examples to illustrate their use in this study, together with concrete operationalizations. We conclude by situating our own approach in the recent development of explanation-oriented comparative news research.

Research interests

Comparative cross-national news analyses pursue essentially two research questions (Esser and Strömbäck 2012b, p. 314). The first explores the apparent simultaneousness of convergence and divergence in news performance across countries. The second links actual news performance to democratic expectations and explores normative aspects of news coverage. Both perspectives are relevant for this study.

In the first line of research (exploring convergence and divergence in news reporting), convergence is usually explained by concepts of diffusion, integration, and cooperation. Diffusion takes place through the border-transgressing distribution and imitation of news practices that have been successful in the United States (Americanization), integration effects refer to growing 'policy transfer' within the European Union (Europeanization), and mutual co-orientation between national communities of media professionals and transnationally operating media companies has become the hallmark of globalized network societies (globalization). The present study's sample was constructed to account for Americanization and Europeanization tendencies, although our cross-sectional design does not allow for testing long-term processes.

Divergence in reporting patterns is usually explained by major, persistent, and relatively stable differences in the structure of media systems and political systems and in the organizational and professional cultures of distinct types of media. These differences exist despite (and in parallel to) the influences mentioned earlier. Here, the modernization paradigm is an important explanatory concept (Esser and Strömbäck 2012b, p. 314). It acknowledges over-time changes due to external influences but expects these changes to proceed in a path-dependent manner determined by the specific conditions of the institutional and cultural environment in which journalists work. These contextual constellations are said to differ at the national, organizational, and situational levels. The challenge for researchers is to disentangle these factors' effects – located at different levels – in order to explain elements of convergence (such as the emergence of a transnational news logic) and differentiate them from identity-forming elements of divergence (such as the continued significance of distinct national and organizational news cultures). Studying differences in broadly similar systems requires a "most similar systems-different outcome design" (see Esser and Hanitzsch 2012, p. 13), which is precisely what we intend with our own approach.

The second line of research motivating scholars to compare international characteristics of news performance is related to democratic norms. How does the news media fulfill their political role in distinct national settings? Regardless of institutional peculiarities, democratic theory expects the media to provide information that is substantial and reliable, inclusive and diverse, analytical and enlightening, and that serves the public interest, fulfilling the 'watchdog' ideal (see Chapter 1). Against this background, news features such as negativity, bias, personalization, soft news, strategic framing, and interpretive news have given rise to the concern that they may hinder the fulfilment of these functions. Scholars wish to understand which contextual conditions affect news performance and in what ways, as this understanding could provide the basis, where appropriate, for recommending targeted interventions. But scholars are confronted with the same challenge that was mentioned earlier – namely, to disentangle the effects of relevant factors located at different levels of analysis.

Multilevel framework

Several models have been proposed that conceptualize layers of influence – usually hierarchically arranged from macro to micro – for explaining cross-national differences in news (see Donsbach 2010; Preston 2009; Shoemaker and Reese

1991, 2014). Although differing in detail, they regularly include characteristics of political systems and media systems as a whole, the respective media sectors and organizational types that journalists work for, and the journalists' routines and practices when interacting with news events. (This interaction is also guided by influences from the organizational and national spheres.) The multilevel framework by Shoemaker and Reese (1991, 2014) is probably the best known and most refined. It takes a variable-analytic approach to explaining news content in causal terms (see also Reese 2007). It treats content features such as negativity, balance, personalization, game framing, and infotainment as *dependent variables,* with which a number of *independent variables* – located at the 'individual,' 'routine,' 'organizational,' 'institutional,' and 'systemic' levels – are systematically related.

The metaphor of 'peeling an onion' is useful for understanding the concentric layers of influence that surround individual news workers (McCombs and Reynolds 2002, p. 12).

- The *individual sphere*, which lies at the core of the theoretical onion, encompasses the psychological factors that impinge on an individual's work: professional values, personal views, and political attitudes. However, whether journalists allow their attitudes and values to influence their stories depends on the environmental conditions.
- The *routine level* refers to news-making practices. They allow everyday occurrences to be recognized as news events and to be reconstituted as news stories. This level relates to journalistic initiative versus spoon-feeding by sources, news-gathering practices, criteria of newsworthiness, and the logic of news story construction.
- The *organizational level* covers factors such as internal structure, ownership type, economic and professional goals, editorial policy, news philosophy, and the journalistic culture of news organizations.
- The *institutional level* includes influencing factors outside the newsroom: the regulatory media policy environment; the market environment (with advertisers and audiences as revenue sources and other media as competitors); special interest groups and public relations as sources; and also relationships with the market environment, the political environment, and technological development.
- The *systemic level* refers to links between the media system and the prevailing social order of the nation-state. News is filtered through national prisms and cultures and is influenced by broader ideologies that reflect the values inherent in domestic political and economic systems. Only comparative research can help assess the importance of these nation-level differences to news production.

A levels-of-analysis approach requires scholars to be especially clear about the elements that they want to compare and whether they mean the same thing in different contexts. This approach takes the entire context of media production into account when explaining news content (Reese 2007; Shoemaker and Reese 2014). Shifting to such a variable- and causality-oriented perspective in news research has been a real leap forward for conceptual clarification and for the understanding of hypothesized relationships – the hallmarks of explanatory research. The underlying logic is also in line with prominent paradigms underlying social scientific explanations, such as Karl R. Popper's (1963/1994) 'institutional individualism,' James S. Coleman's (1990) 'structural individualism,' and Gidden's (1984) 'structuration' concept. They all focus on explaining the actions of individuals who work within social structures. In contemporary newsrooms, even the most creative journalistic activities are processed through structured rules.

Analytical approaches

News decisions are made based on the available events and sources and their suitability for constructing compelling stories. The event environment (i.e., routines and practices) forms part of our model's routine level, which surrounds the individual sphere (the onion's core). The event environment is relevant insofar as journalists regularly attribute 'news factors' to various aspects of political reality. Nonetheless, the criteria journalists use for considering events as newsworthy (by giving them high 'news value') may differ and are often dependent on factors at the organizational and systemic levels. For example, the news factor 'prominence' is typically attributed a higher news value by tabloids than by broadsheets, and the news value and framing of military events in Iraq depend on how the media outlet's home country is involved in the conflict. It is thus important to integrate event-centered and media-centered considerations when explaining news making (Reinemann and Baugut 2014). Our own study follows this principle.

Over the years, news research has shown that the impact of individual-level factors is constrained by successive factors of influence: in particular, organizational- and systemic-level effects can significantly limit the impact of journalists' personal characteristics (Reinemann and Baugut 2014). Shoemakers and Reese's book, *Mediating the Message*, mirrors our adjustments to the many influences. The first edition, published in 1991, prioritizes the individual level of analysis by discussing it before all other levels, whereas the third edition, published in 2014, moves from an individual-centered to a context-sensitive understanding. It reverses the order of the chapters, beginning with systemic influences and dealing with individual influences only in the last chapter. That said, we agree with Shoemaker and Reese's (2014) position that any argument about the supremacy of one level over another should not be based on any kind of theoretical determinism but on careful empirical analysis. An appropriate way of testing the relative superiority of one set of factors over another is multiple regression analysis. This procedure allows for testing a factor's effect while holding the influence of other factors constant (i.e., controlling for them statistically). Usually, factors are entered as 'blocks' in accordance with the distinct layer of influence to which they belong. We will apply the same strategy of data analysis in our own study.

Although we will not use formal multilevel modeling in our statistical analyses, we will estimate our multiple regressions with robust standard errors to account for the nested character of our data (see Chapter 2 on method).

Working with a multilevel framework of news determinants has the advantage of sensitizing readers to the role of context in understanding the news-making process. Such a framework (see Table 3.1) imposes order onto a multitude of potential factors operating simultaneously. In particular, its context-sensitive and layer-sensitive perspective allows a *comparative* analysis of how, for instance, different organizational or national contexts affect news content. Generally speaking, comparative analysis guides our attention to the explanatory relevance of the contextual environment for media outcomes. It aims to understand how the macro- and meso-level context shapes news practices at the micro-level (see Esser and Hanitzsch 2012). The research is based on the assumption that different parameters of the event and of organizational and systemic environments either promote or constrain the news organizations' and news workers' behaviors, both being embedded in those structures. Recognizing the causal significance of contextual conditions is what makes comparative research exceptionally valuable. In the words of Mancini and Hallin (2012, p. 515), "theorizing the role of context is precisely what comparative analysis is about." Clearly, explanatory logic can be distinguished from mere descriptive comparison, which is considered less mature (Gurevitch and Blumler 2004). Our own study follows the rationale of explanatory comparative analysis by employing one comprehensive comparative design that allows us to vary the influence of assumed independent variables; we study the effect of their presence or absence in 16 contextual settings on the same 6 dependent variables.

Factors of influence: the independent variables used in this study

We consider factors of influence at the four analytical levels that are summarized in Table 3.1 and explained in detail in the following section. The independent variables that are presented in the following chapters are each theoretically grounded and specifically developed for their use. Thus, not all independent variables listed in Table 3.1 are used in each chapter; rather, only those that have a theoretically meaningful link to the news concept in question.

The event level

Our comparative analyses first take the event environment into account. After all, any journalistic behavior occurs in a 'situation,' and journalists' own definitions of news situations are dependent on the 'external' framing conditions set by the event environment.[1] For instance, our analysis of hard and soft news (Chapter 9) takes into account a country's economic situation as an important real-world condition and predicts greater macro-economic problems to correspond with higher levels of hard news. The

The explanatory logic 27

Table 3.1 Multilevel framework of factors that shape political news

Levels of influence	Hypothesized effects on news performance (selected examples)
Event level	
• Bad economic situation	→ More hard news
• Proximity to elections	→ More game/strategy news
• Issue context: e.g., crime and corruption	→ More negative news
e.g., inner party conflict	→ More game/strategy news
Media organizational level	
• Mass-market oriented editorial mission	→ More personalized, soft, strategic,
(e.g., in commercial TV or popular press)	interpretive news
• Public service mission	→ More balanced news
• Online channel	→ More negative news
Media system level	
• High market competition	→ More personalized, negative, interpretive
• High market commercialization	news
• Low competition and commercialization	→ More negative, interpretive, soft news
• High journalistic professionalism and	→ More hard news
independence (i.e., distance to politics)	→ More negative, strategic, interpretive news
Political system level	
• Small number of competing parties	→ More personalized, strategic, negative news
• High number of parties (i.e., need for	→ More hard news
negotiations and coalitions)	
• Majoritarian electoral system	→ More personalized news
• Low federalism, high power	→ More personalized, negative news
concentration	
• Strong party standing in preceding	→ More imbalanced party news
election or current poll standing	

relevant indicator that we use to operationalize the economic situation is the country's harmonized unemployment rate (seasonally adjusted) as reported by Eurostat in May 2012, the time period at which we content-analyzed the news media.[2]

Another event environment factor is the proximity to national elections. The phases immediately before and after polling days are different in nature from routine periods because both the campaign mode before and the honeymoon period after create a climate that causes political actors and media actors to behave in peculiar ways (de Vreese, Lauf, and Peter 2007; Van Aelst and de Swert 2009). The proximity or distance to elections should be relevant for the amount of strategic news (Chapter 4) and hard news (Chapter 9). We operationalize this indicator by using two variables that express the time period (in months) from code start to the last election and from code start to the next election, respectively.

A final indicator of the event environment is the issue context. It is well known from comparative studies that the topical nature of events influences their treatment in the news (see de Swert et al. 2013). In our own study, for example, we expect higher levels of negativity in news reports that deal with negatively con-noted events, such as crime or corruption (see Chapter 6). Similarly, our analysis of strategy and game framing predicts a greater use of such frames in issue contexts that are related to elections and internal party politics (see Chapter 4). We operationalize this indicator with an 18-item list of topic areas that coders used during the content analysis to determine each story's main issue as apparent from the headline and lead paragraph (see Chapter 2 on method).

Given the growing realization in comparative news research that individual journalists matter less than the contextual conditions that guide their practices in characteristic ways, we focus our own analyses on organizational- and national-level factors. In their broad-scope study, Shoemaker and Cohen (2006) discovered an unexpectedly weak and at times negative relationship between journalists' individual views on news values and their actual produced content. Consequently, Weaver and Loeffelholz (2008, p. 8) point to "the importance of studying influences on news content not only at the individual level, but also at the organizational and . . . societal level, as Shoemaker and Reese (1991) have advocated." Contextual conditions and organizational- and national-level factors strongly influence journalists' perceptions of adequate and appropriate behavior in a given news situation. In this regard, the structural constraints within news organizations and home societies and their influence on journalists' socialization processes – including the effects of institutional rules and conditions on the internalization of norms and worldviews – have been particularly emphasized in contributions to so-called multilevel analyses in mass communication research (see Pan and McLeod 1991). That emphasis in the research has shaped our own approach. We follow Shoemaker and Reese's (2014) media-*sociological* perspective (as opposed to an individual-centered, media-psychological perspective) and therefore focus more on the structural *context* than communicators' personal traits.

The media organizational level

Among the factors at the organizational level are distinctions between ownership structures (public versus private), editorial missions (upmarket/elite versus mass market/popular), editorial policy (left leaning versus right leaning), channel type (print, broadcasting, web), and platform (offline versus online). These distinctions refer to a multitude of technological, economic, political, and professional goals of news organizations, all of which have potential implications for media content production. Our analysis of political balance in Chapter 7, for instance, expects public broadcasters to be less biased than newspapers, given newspapers' partisan history in Europe. Similarly, our analyses of personalization, soft news, interpretive journalism, and game framing (see Chapters 4, 5, 8, and 9) expect mass-market oriented outlets, such as commercial television and tabloid newspapers, to exhibit these content features in much more pronounced ways than high-brow media (public broadcasters and broadsheet newspapers). A final example refers to Chapter 6, which expects online editions to carry greater amounts of negativity in the news than their offline counterparts. We incorporated the influence of different organizational types mainly through a targeted selection of media outlets. The stratified media sample, as described in Chapter 2, was constructed according to the differentiations in organizational types mentioned earlier.

The media system level

The extent of competition and commercialization has received much attention in the recent literature on media systems (Aalberg and Curran 2012; Esser, de Vreese et al. 2012; Plasser 2005). Both factors are assumed to shift news criteria from professional and social responsibility–oriented concerns to audience- and profit-maximizing concerns. The literature explicating this connection is extensive (Croteau and Hoynes 2006; Hamilton 2004; McManus 2009; Picard 2004) and features prominently in the chapters that follow. We operationalize competition by the number of television channels available nationwide and by the number of paid-for, nationally available daily newspapers in a media market. The data for the first variable comes from the European Audiovisual Observatory (2011), and for the second variable, from a statistical reference guide of Nordicom (Leckner and Facht 2010). We expect that a higher number of competing TV channels and newspapers will lead to higher levels of negativity (Chapter 6) and personalization (Chapter 8) in political news due to their audience-pleasing and attention-grabbing qualities.

Commercialization, on the other hand, is operationalized by two indicators: the public service channels' small cumulative market share and news providers' high dependency on advertising revenue, measured as percentage of total adspend of the gross domestic product. The data for both variables is again taken from the latest available report of the European Audiovisual Observatory (2011). Theoretically speaking, high competition and higher commercialization indicate a predominance of the 'market model' of news production over the 'public sphere model' – a conflict in logics that Croteau and Hoynes (2006) describe as 'the' major divide in characterizing media systems (see also Aalberg and Curran 2012; Curran, Iyengar, Lund, and Salovaara-Moring 2009). Against this background, we expect high commercial pressures in a media system to lead to high levels of interpretive journalism and negativity (see Chapters 5 and 6). Conversely, we expect that a high market share of public service broadcasters (PSB) and a high number of paid-for national dailies will correspond with high levels of hard news (Chapter 9).

A related factor is the degree of journalistic professionalism. It constitutes a key dimension for comparing media systems (Hallin and Mancini 2004) and is measured in our study by an index constructed from two variables. The first variable measures the extent to which "journalists [in a country] agree on the criteria for judging excellence in their profession, regardless of their political orientation." The second variable measures the extent to which "journalists have sufficient training to ensure that basic professional norms like accuracy, relevance, completeness, balance, timeliness, double-checking, and source confidentiality are respected in news-making practices." These two items – measured with 11-point rating scales from 'untrue' to 'true' – are from the *European Media Systems Survey* by Marina Popescu, and we use this Professionalization Index exactly as constructed by Popescu (2011). Her survey is based on 838 interviews with experts working in communication research, journalism training, and media consultancy from 34 countries. Unfortunately, three of the countries in our study were not represented in this survey – namely, Israel, Switzerland, and the United States. We therefore asked local experts in those three countries for the missing assessments and are grateful for their spontaneous willingness to help.[3]

The emergence of a distinct set of professional norms that guide journalists' daily practices is not so much an indicator of high quality as an indicator of independence from undue political interference as well as a sense of autonomy. News work that is guided strictly by news values as opposed to political values (indicating high professionalism) will likely be more inclined to portray politics in game- and strategy-oriented scenarios (see Chapter 4); it will also be more interpretive (Chapter 5) and negative in nature (Chapter 6). The reason is that these content features meet journalists' professional needs to produce a news product that is rich in strategic interpretation and critical analysis and that signals distance, if not skepticism, from the world of politics (Zaller 1999). For predicting high levels of interpretive journalism, we also use the related concept of journalistic independence (see Popescu 2011 for details on this 5-item index) as an explanatory variable.

A final item from Popescu's (2011) *European Media Systems Survey* is the cost of producing hard news. In countries where experts strongly agree with the statement that "the production costs for hard news content are so high that most news media cannot afford to present carefully researched facts and analyses," we expect to find more negative news (see Chapter 6) and more soft news (see Chapter 9). Both content features represent strategies to maximize audience appeal with minimal newsroom expenses, a behavior perfectly rational within the 'market model' of news production.

The political system level

Political news is the joint product of media–politics exchanges. Therefore Cook (1998, p. 3) considers news to be a 'coproduct' of media and political influences, and Blumler and Gurevitch (1995, p. 26) go so far as to say that media traces and political traces in news messages are "inextricably intertwined." Consequently, the selection, presentation, and discursive framing of political news reflects as much the internal operating logics of the media system as the external framing conditions set by the political system (for a heuristic model of this relationship, see Esser and Strömbäck 2012b, p. 317). In this study, these external framing conditions refer to three key dimensions for comparing Western democracies: electoral system, government system, and party system.

The basic distinction in 'electoral systems' refers to the contrast between majoritarian and proportional visions of democracy. Whereas the majoritarian vision values the concentration of power in the hands of the government party, allowing it to carry out its promises and clarify its responsibilities for the consequences, the proportional vision emphasizes the pluralist principle of minority influences according to their representation in parliament. A key feature of the 'government system' is concentration of power and the sharing of power in different ways – either between actors within the central executive or between different institutions – thereby referring to the basic distinction between centralization and federalism. Both distinctions (majoritarianism vs. proportionality; centralization vs. federalism) feature prominently in Lijphart's (1999) comparative study, *Patterns of Democracy*.

Differentiations within 'electoral systems' are operationalized by a variable that distinguishes between list proportional representation (value 0) and majority or mixed systems (value 1). Drawing on earlier studies, beginning with Swanson and Mancini (1996), one of our expectations is the presence of more personalized political news coverage in majoritarian and mixed electoral systems.

Differentiations within 'government systems' regarding the concentration of power are measured by Lijphart's (1999) Federalism Index, a fivefold classification ranging from a low (value 1) to high degree of federalism (value 5). We expect that political systems that are more centralized and less federalized will be characterized by higher degrees of personalized news coverage, reflecting a concentration on prominent power-holding elites (Chapter 8). Furthermore, because centralized systems have less need to negotiate compromises and balance interests, we also expect a greater likelihood of conflict and critique – and thus of negativity – in the news (see Chapter 6).

A third distinction featuring prominently in Lijphart (1999) is between few party and multiparty systems – an important measure of pluralism in a political system. We operationalize differentiations within 'party systems' by a variable expressing the de facto relevant number of parties in parliament. We expect that systems with small numbers of parties will be characterized by fierce political competition and limited willingness to compromise, fostering a news culture that is more game centered (Chapter 4), more negative (Chapter 6), and more personalized (Chapter 8). A higher number of parties, however, will lead to more hard news coverage (Chapter 9).

Finally, the close connection between political influences and media influences for explaining news content is nicely demonstrated by our analysis of political balance (Chapter 7). It asks whether differences in the visibility of parties can be better explained by a political systems approach (focusing on the parties' preceding electoral vote shares) or a media systems approach (focusing on the parties' current standing in media-sponsored opinion polls). We gathered the data for both these approaches by researching the vote shares of all parties in the national elections preceding our content analysis and by researching the parties' standing in polls around the time of coding.

Conclusion

The still young history of comparative cross-national news research has proceeded through various stages, from initially pursuing solely descriptive goals to developing increasingly explanatory ambitions (de Vreese and Vliegenthart 2012; Esser and Hanitzsch 2012). These kinds of explanatory studies, which are usually based on multivariate regression analyses, are still rare, and their quality is often compromised by low numbers of cases in their country samples. There are a few exceptions, and when designing the present study, we drew inspiration from these exceptional studies. They include, for instance, the study by Schuck and colleagues (2016), which investigated factors explaining the variation in the campaign coverage of the 2009 European parliamentary elections in all 27 European Union (EU) member states. It found that the level of conflict framing in election news was contingent upon the type of medium and the type of electoral system as well as public aversion to the EU. Another noteworthy role model study is by Boomgaarden and colleagues (2013), which investigated predictors for over-time variation in the news media coverage of EU affairs between 1999 and 2009. It found, for example, that the more the national parties were divided about the EU, the greater the increases in EU news media coverage. Our own study follows this same tradition.

The main goal of our 16-country investigation is to explain cross-national variation in news performance (measured using six news concepts) by way of multiple regressions with a total of 20 predictors located at several levels of analysis (see Table 3.1). We are not aware of any other study that has been dedicated to explaining news performance in such a comprehensive manner. It should be noted that not all of the 20 explanatory factors are considered in all chapters but only those that are theoretically relevant to the concept at hand. Chapters 4 to 9 will separately examine strategic game framing, interpretive journalism, negativity, balance, personalization, and hard and soft news before Chapter 10 explores the cross-connections between them.

Notes

1 For a more extensive discussion of the underlying theoretical approach taken towards explaining cross-national differences in news production, see Esser and Strömbäck (2012, pp. 315–317).
2 See Eurostat, http://epp.eurostat.ec.europa.eu/tgm/table.do?tab=table&init=1&plugin= 0&language=en&pcode=teilm020.
3 We extend our sincere thanks to the following colleagues from Israel, Switzerland, and the United States: Meital Balmas, Jonathan Cohen, Zohar Kampf, Lilach Nir, Zvi Reich, Limor Shifman, Yariv Tsfati, Roger Blum, Matthias Kuenzler, Manuel Puppis, Stephan Russ Mohl, Vinzenz Wyss, Randal Beam, Erik Bucy, Matthew Carlson, Stephanie Craft, Ann Crigler, Paul D'Angelo, Daniela Dimitrova, Guy Golan, Marion Just, Spiro Kiousis, Seth Lewis, Patricia Moy, David Tewksbury, and David Weaver.

Chapter 4

Strategy and game framing

Toril Aalberg, Claes de Vreese,
and Jesper Strömbäck

Introduction

The news media's tendency to cover politics as a strategic game has long been a key concern among many political communication scholars (see, e.g., Cappella and Jamieson 1997; Farnsworth and Lichter 2011). When news coverage is focused on winners and losers, politicians' and parties' performances, and campaign strategies and tactics, scholars have argued that these frames 'deprive' the public of quality journalism, which provides political substance and insight into real issues.

Several studies have demonstrated a strong tendency on the part of the news media to frame politics as a strategic game rather than to focus on political issues. Be that as it may, our recent review revealed large variations in how scholars conceptualize and operationalize strategic game frames (Aalberg, Strömbäck, and de Vreese 2012). Most previous research is based on single-country studies, which represents a major problem since different operationalizations make comparisons across time, countries, or studies highly problematic.

Based on the main findings from previous research, we suggested a synthesis of how the framing of politics as a strategic game should be conceptualized and operationalized to increase conceptual clarity and greater comparability across studies and countries. Against this background, the purpose of this chapter is to compare and investigate some of the possible antecedents to the game and strategy framing that dominates ordinary political news journalism across 15 European countries and the United States. The previous lack of systematic comparative research has obscured the more general determinants of strategy and game frames in political news coverage. A major contribution to current research, therefore, is investigating what *drives* this type of political news coverage during ordinary periods across a number of Western democracies.

The strategic game frame

The growing literature about the media's framing of politics as a strategic game typically shares a common theoretical framework. It states that traditional descriptive and issue-oriented news coverage has been replaced by a game-oriented approach (Cappella and Jamieson 1997; Fallows 1997). The rise of the strategic game frame, it is often claimed, can be linked to changes in the political system and the news business. Modern styles of campaigning rely on increasingly sophisticated strategies to manage party political platforms and party images (Esser and Strömbäck 2012a). As strategic political communication has become more professionalized, many news journalists see it as their job to uncover and interpret the strategies behind political actors' words and actions. This line of action is also a defense mechanism against continually being 'spun' by parties or candidates since most journalists want to protect their autonomy and avoid being accused of taking sides politically. By focusing on the strategic aspects of the political game, political reporters maintain an apparent stance of both independence and objectivity (Zaller 2001).

Meanwhile, the rise of television, new technologies, and commercialism may also have increased the focus on politics as a strategic game. Not only does the strategic game frame allow journalists to more easily produce stories on deadline, but it also demands fewer resources than research into the substance of complex public policy debates (Fallows 1997). The proliferation of polling allows news media to cover the state of the 'horse race' quickly and efficiently, and news organizations are consequently among the most important commissioners in the polling business (Brettschneider 1997; Holtz-Bacha and Strömbäck 2012; Sonck and Loosveldt 2008). Moreover, an additional bonus is that a poll provides the news story with a scientific touch and a sense of objectivity compared to a story relying only on the journalist's observations or references to political messages (Lavrakas and Traugott 2000; Strömbäck 2012). Finally, some evidence suggests that a focus on celebrity candidates, their backgrounds, and their successes or failures might draw larger audiences, at least in the case of the United States (Iyengar, Norpoth, and Hahn 2004).

Changes in the political system and the news industry are used to explain the rapid increase in framing politics as a strategic game, and the attractiveness of this frame is additionally related to its newsworthiness. At the most basic level, it fits many of the key news values that have been prevalent in the news business for decades (Galtung and Ruge 1965). For instance, framing politics as a strategic game reflects journalism's enduring focus on drama, conflict, and negativity, typically involving elite individuals or political groups (McManus 1994). Use of the strategic game provides reporters with the currency and novelty that they need for their daily news material and corresponds well with media logic (Skewes 2007), whereas analysis of policy visions and issues may appear stale and repetitive. This framing has thus been linked to the mediatization of politics (Esser and Strömbäck 2014)

One of the most important reasons for people's concern about game and strategy framing has to do with the assumed *effects* of these frames. It is assumed that horse race news – focused on opinion polls and interpretations of who is winning and losing – is distracting citizens from the substance of politics (Patterson 1993). Research shows that the framing of politics as a strategic game (including spotlighting politicians' self-interest) increases political cynicism, depresses knowledge gains about policies and substance, and depresses political engagement (Cappella and Jamieson 1997; de Vreese and Semetko 2002; Shehata 2014), although some evidence suggests that the effects of this particular framing is mixed (de Vreese and Semetko 2002). It is also assumed that 'meta news frames' – focusing on the media's role in politics and on how politicians try to influence the media – worsens public perceptions of politics, the media, and communication professionals (de Vreese and Elenbaas 2010).

One key shortcoming of much research on the game and strategy framing of politics and its effects is the focus on election campaigns. While election campaigns are of key importance in democracies, these time periods are hardly representative, and that observation holds for both media framing and its effects. In fact, our knowledge about the framing of politics and its effects during regular political times is scarce. So what are the main determinants of strategy and game frames in political news coverage? Based on previous research, we have certain expectations in this regard.

First, some issues are more likely than others to be framed in terms of a strategic game, and some news outlets are more likely than others to use this frame. Lawrence (2000a), for example, specified that the game frame (beyond its wide application during election times) is most likely to be applied to public policy issues when they feature in national election news but is less likely when they are discussed either at the state level or during the implementation phase. Based on this research, which complements Cappella and Jamieson's (1997) initial observations, we expect the following:

> H1: The use of game and strategy frames is more frequent with issues that are related to elections, internal party politics, and such, compared to news stories that focus on policy areas, such as the economy, education, and the environment.

Second, we focus on the potentially different use of the strategy and game frames by different media. In Europe, Strömbäck and Van Aelst (2010) found commercial broadcasters to be more likely to use the game frame than their public service counterparts (see also Cushion 2012). One reason is that this type of framing is cheaper to produce and the entertainment value is higher. This observation has also been made of tabloids or mass-market newspapers vis-à-vis broadsheet or upmarket newspapers, although Schuck, Boomgaarden, and de Vreese (2013) found no systematic difference between different outlets during elections for the European Parliament. Nevertheless, based on extant research, we expect:

> H2: The use of strategy and game frames is higher in mass-market newspapers and commercial broadcasters compared to upmarket newspapers and public broadcasters.

While we expect the pattern described earlier to hold across all the European countries and the United States, there is also reason to expect some variation between the different countries included in this study. In this context, we expect that the cross-national variation in the use of strategy and game frames may be explained by factors that are related to the political context, the media system, and the political system.

Our third expectation pertains to the use of the game and strategy frames in relation to a country's proximity to a major election. Cappella and Jamieson (1997), as well as Patterson (1993), found frequent usage of strategy and game frames in the lead-up to elections, and Lawrence (2000a) confirmed a greater likelihood of media using these frames during elections. The evidence from other countries has mostly centered on election periods, but that timing only corroborates our expectation:

> H3: The amount of game and strategy frames is higher the closer in time the country is to a major election.

We next focus on the impact of journalistic culture. Previous research has illustrated that journalists may respond to political professionalism and spin attempts by focusing on political strategies and games (Brants and van Praag 2006; Zaller 2001). Such an approach by journalists is generally seen to be indicative of a professional journalistic culture (rather than, for example, a partisan culture; see van Dalen, de Vreese, and Albæk 2012). Therefore, we expect:

> H4: The amount of game and strategy frames is higher the more professional the national journalistic culture.

Regarding the composition of the media landscape, we believe that the strength of a country's public broadcaster(s) is especially pertinent. As has been documented in several studies (e.g., Aalberg and Curran 2012; Albæk, van Dalen, Jebril, and de Vreese 2014; Cushion 2012), a strong public broadcaster is associated with higher public knowledge levels and higher levels of satisfaction with the media (see also Albæk et al. 2014). It is also clear that, in countries that have a strong public service broadcasting (PSB) news organization, new commercial competitors have tended to base their news products on their public counterparts' successful formulas. This trend leads to an overall expectation that the stronger the role of public broadcasting in a country, the more the news culture is likely to focus on political substance rather than on politics as a strategic game:

> H5: The amount of game and strategy frames is higher, the lower the market share of public service broadcasters.

Turning to the political system, we expect the competitiveness of the party system to be one important antecedent to the framing of politics as a strategic game. On the one hand, if fewer parties take part in elections, the competition is straightforward, and the main focus will be on who is leading the game. On the other hand, if more parties are part of the equation (and if a coalition government is a likely outcome), strategic considerations should be higher. Jointly, these expectations lead to the following hypotheses:

> H6a: The amount of game and strategy frames is higher the lower the number of political parties. Clear-cut, obvious competition will lead to a higher focus on the *game*.
> H6b: The amount of strategy frames is higher the larger the number of political parties. More complex competition will lead to a higher focus on *strategy*.

Conceptualizing and operationalizing game and strategy framing

While research shows that game and strategy frames have become important features of news coverage around the world (Strömbäck and Kaid 2008a), how much they are used and under what conditions they are used remains to be comprehensively investigated. The main reason is that most research on these frames to date is based on single-country studies. Although a small number of comparative studies exist, most include only a few countries. Another barrier to cumulative knowledge within this field is that few studies measure game and strategy in a similar way. This lack of uniformity is one of the reasons why Aalberg and colleagues (2012) suggest that the research community should apply and use a set of standardized variables and coding instructions, not unlike what is done by cumulative survey research (Esser, Strömbäck, and de Vreese 2012). By standardizing, we may compare insights and generate new knowledge from various studies conducted in many countries and over different time periods.

Game and strategy frames belong to the notion of generic news frames (de Vreese 2009), which implies that they can be used in relation to different issues, that they have been identified in different political contexts and media systems, and that they are inherent to the work routines of journalism. Aalberg and colleagues' review (2012) suggested two important dimensions in the study of strategic game frames: the game frame and the strategy frame. The *game frame* refers to news stories that portray politics as a game and are centered around who is winning or losing elections in the battle for public opinion, in legislative debates, or in politics in general; expressions of public opinion (polls, vox pops); approval or disapproval of particular interest groups, constituencies, and publics; and speculations about electoral and policy outcomes and potential coalitions. The *strategy frame* refers to news stories that are centered on interpretations of candidates' or parties' motives for their actions and positions, their strategies and tactics for achieving political or policy goals, how they campaign, and choices regarding leadership and integrity (including personal traits). It also involves different types of media strategies, including news coverage of press behavior.

38   Toril Aalberg et al.

Given that the game and the strategy frames are seen as two equal but separate dimensions of an overall macroframe, we include a variable that taps the dominant framing of politics in a news story, making an overall distinction between strategic game framing and the coverage of politics in terms of substance, issues, or policies. This dominant frame is identified according to the duration, frequency, and order of appearance of the various elements. Moreover, the headline and lead are given extra weight when determining a news story's dominant frame. In addition to this general frame, we also include a set of 2 × 3 items that distinguish the game and strategy frames. The three variables that measure the game frame refer to (1) the coverage of opinion polls, (2) the coverage of political winners and losers, and (3) the usage of the language of sports and wars. To measure the extent to which the media apply a strategy frame, we measure three variables pertaining to references to (1) campaign strategies and tactics, (2) performance, and (3) the media's role in the political process.

In addition to these dependent variables, we also have a set of independent variables. These latter are measures of (1) the topic or issue that was the main focus in the news story and (2) the type of news outlet that the news story was published in (type of broadcaster, newspaper, or webpage). Finally, we have a set of national-level variables that measure (3) election proximity, (4) journalistic professionalism, (5) the market share of public service channels, and (6) the number of political parties in the political system.

Results

Let us start by taking a closer look at the concept of strategic game frames. In Table 4.1, we present an overview of the distribution of the strategic game and issue frames. The total column at the bottom of the table indicates that a minority

Table 4.1 Presence of strategic game frames in U.S. and European news (percentages)

	Macroframe	
	Strategic game	*Issue*
Include game elements:		
Public opinion	28	12
Winning and losing	45	15
Sport language	43	18
Include strategy elements:		
Strategy and tactics	61	18
Performance	62	41
Media	18	8
Macroframe total	22	78
N	1,746	6,047

(22 percent) of the news stories sampled in this study framed politics as a strategic game, whereas a majority (78 percent) focused on issues or issue positions. Thus, we do not find evidence to suggest that an issue-oriented approach in ordinary political news coverage across Europe and the United States has been replaced by a game-oriented approach. Apparently (and unsurprisingly), the level of game and strategy framing is lower during ordinary political news coverage than during election campaign news coverage.

Nonetheless, news stories where the issue macroframe is dominant might also include game or strategy frame elements but typically at a much smaller scale than news stories where the strategic game macroframe is dominant. For instance, 12 percent of the issue-dominated news stories referred to opinion polls, compared to 28 percent of the strategic game–framed news stories.

Looking at our descriptive findings cross-nationally, we see cross-national differences in the degree to which the different game and strategy frame elements are present. Many of them are frequently found in German, Greek, and Swedish news and much less so in Danish, Portuguese, and Spanish news. Looking across the different indicators, we see that references to politicians' performances are by far the most frequently featured element of the strategy frame (see Table 4.2).

Table 4.2 Presence of game and strategy frames across countries (percentages)

Country	(N)	Game frames			Strategy frames		
		Public opinion	Winning and losing	Sport language	Strategy and tactics	Performance	Media
Austria	(477)	11	25	43	50	62	17
Belgium	(487)	8	19	17	27	31	7
Denmark	(483)	14	5	14	5	26	8
France	(534)	22	33	51	46	47	1
Germany	(498)	25	33	18	24	61	12
Greece	(547)	14	32	39	43	61	4
Israel	(519)	16	11	12	23	54	12
Italy	(496)	14	17	25	20	23	21
Netherlands	(475)	33	17	19	16	35	14
Norway	(437)	15	21	21	27	26	2
Portugal	(555)	9	31	30	25	50	5
Spain	(563)	7	4	13	7	50	3
Sweden	(303)	18	18	13	19	63	17
Switzerland	(391)	14	37	12	36	49	7
United Kingdom	(510)	16	21	15	46	39	22
United States	(518)	19	21	27	26	59	8

Our empirical analysis does not support constructing two separate dimensions for game and strategy frames. We therefore move forward with a single game/strategy dimension.[1] A factor analysis (not shown here) indicates that the best dimensional structure is a single index consisting of five of the six game- or strategy-specific variables in Table 4.1. (The 'media' variable has been excluded.) The index yields a Cronbach's alpha of .612. The new index runs from 0 through 1, where 0 indicates that there are no strategic game elements in the news story and 1 indicates that the news story includes all the five frame elements. The average score on this new index is .21 for news stories that were coded as issue dominated and .48 for news stories where the strategic game macroframe was dominant.

If we compare the use of the strategic game macroframe and the score on the strategic game index cross-nationally, we find significant variations across countries (see Table 4.3). The strategic game macroframe is most common in France (47 percent) and Italy (41 percent) and least common in Portugal and Spain (4 percent). The countries that score highest on the strategic game index is France (.40), followed by Austria and Greece (.38). The countries that score lowest are Spain (.16) and Denmark (.13). Interestingly, considering that most research has focused on the United States, the results show that the United States is *not* an outlier.

When it comes to the magnitude of strategic game frames in ordinary political coverage, the considerable differences between the European countries and

Table 4.3 Presence of game macroframe and strategic game frames (means) across countries

Country	(N)	Game macroframes	Strategic game frames
Austria	(477)	15	.38
Belgium	(487)	33	.20
Denmark	(483)	16	.13
France	(534)	47	.40
Germany	(498)	12	.32
Greece	(547)	24	.38
Israel	(519)	16	.23
Italy	(496)	41	.20
Netherlands	(475)	11	.24
Norway	(437)	25	.22
Portugal	(555)	4	.29
Spain	(563)	4	.16
Sweden	(303)	33	.26
Switzerland	(391)	33	.30
United Kingdom	(510)	20	.27
United States	(518)	34	.27

Strategy and game framing 41

the United States are hardly surprising. But the results also show that how the strategic game frame is measured matters for country ranking – and also for the comparison across countries (see Aalberg et al. 2012). The relationship between the strategic game macroframe and the strategic game frame index is illustrated in Figure 4.1.

Let us now turn to our first hypothesis, which predicted that the use of game and strategy frames would be higher with issues that are related to elections, internal party politics, and such like. As Figure 4.2 demonstrates, this hypothesis is

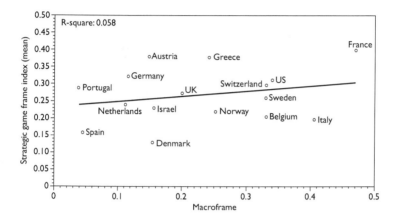

Figure 4.1 The presence of strategic game frames across countries. Percentage of macroframe and mean on strategic game index.

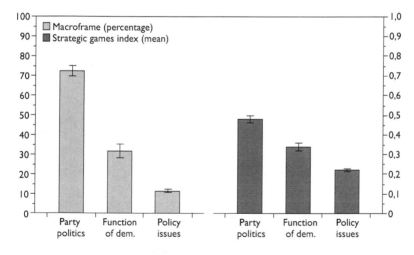

Figure 4.2 The presence of strategic game frames according to dominant issues in news items. Percentage of macroframe and mean on strategic game index. Macroframe: $p < .001$; Strategic game index: $p < .001$.

supported. The framing of politics as a strategic game – regardless of how it is measured – is higher in news stories focusing on issues that are related to party politics and elections and to the functioning of democracy (e.g., state reforms). News stories that focus on issues that are related to policy areas (e.g., the economy, the environment, education) are least likely to frame politics as a strategic game. This finding holds when we look both at the game strategy index and at the macroframe that measures the dominance of issue frames versus strategic game frames, respectively.

Our second hypothesis suggested that the use of strategy and game frames would be higher in tabloid newspapers and commercial broadcasters compared to elite newspapers and public broadcasters. This hypothesis is *not* supported by our data (see Figure 4.3). Generally, we see small variations between types of news outlets, and the only significant difference is between newspapers, where elite papers frame politics as a strategic game more often than mass-market newspapers. This result may indicate that strategy and game frames are primarily for the more educated and very politically interested audience. It is also worth mentioning that this pattern holds across 14 of our 16 countries; Sweden and the United States are the only countries where the mass-market press uses this frame more (cross-national findings not presented here). Within this pattern, there are of course also considerable variations between countries; in several countries, the differences are small, whereas in others, they are extensive.

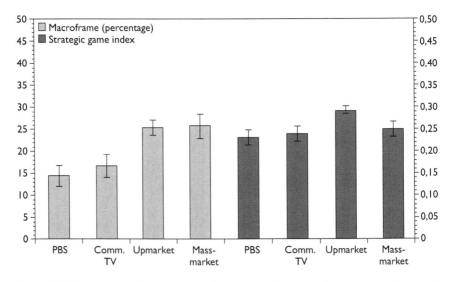

Figure 4.3 The presence of strategic game frames according to media outlet type. Percent of macroframe and mean on strategic game index. Measurements of the broadcasters and newspapers include their websites. The difference between the two types of broadcasters is not significant: macroframe, $p = .209$; strategic game index, $p = .506$. The difference between the two types of newspapers is only significant when measured as a strategic game index: $p < .001$. The difference is not significant for the macroframe measure: $p = .444$.

Table 4.4 Correlations between strategic game frame measures, type of media outlet, and national factors related to context, media, and political system[a]

	Macroframe	Strategic game index
Public service TV	−.067**	−.155*
Commercial TV	−.024	−.066
Upmarket newspaper	.113	.246**
Mass-market newspaper	.053	−.080
Online website	.057	.081
Months since last election	.113	.059
Months before next election	−.068	.085
Journalistic Professionalism Index	−.134	−.091
Public service market share	−.041	−.265**
Number of parties in parliament	−.119	−.350**
Number of parties in government	.96	−.019
N	160	160

a Entries are Pearson's R.
* p < .05, ** p < .01.

Our third hypothesis suggested that the amount of game and strategy frames is higher the closer in time the country is to a major election. We have therefore looked at the relationship between the use of strategic game frames and the number of months both since the last national election and until next national election. In Table 4.4, we present simple bivariate correlations (Pearson's R) on aggregated data across media outlets ($N = 160$). The coefficients do not reveal a systematic pattern providing support for our hypothesis. Only one of the coefficients is negative, as expected; the three other coefficients are positive, suggesting that increased time since the last election or until the next election corresponds with a higher level of strategic game frame coverage. None of these relationships are significant, however.[2] We recall that none of our countries were in campaign mode, but closeness in time to a large national election does not seem to explain much of the cross-national variation in the use of strategic game frames outside of election campaigns. Whether this result means that the closeness to an election does not matter at all or that it has a threshold (e.g., one or two months to the next election) is an open question.

We also expected that cross-national variation might be explained by the national journalistic culture. More specifically, our fourth hypothesis suggested that the amount of game and strategy frames would be higher the more professional the journalistic culture. We assumed that the driving mechanism might be an attempt by professional journalists to avoid being spun by political spin doctors. Comparative data on national professional culture is scarce, but one measurement is provided by Popescu, Gosselin, and Pereira's (2010) elite survey on

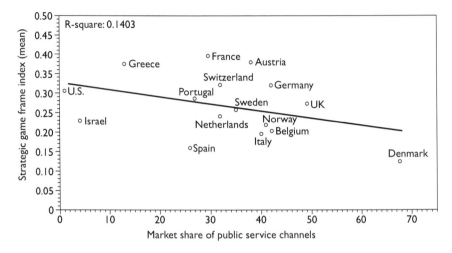

Figure 4.4 The relationship between country score on strategic game frame index and national market share of public service channels.

media systems. In Table 4.4, the correlation between the level of strategic game frames and the Journalistic Professionalism Index is presented. Again, we do not find a significant strong positive relationship as expected. Rather, although this relationship is not significant, it seems as if the strategic game frame is used more in less professional cultures.[3]

Another media system factor that was expected to explain cross-national variance was the public service market share. We assumed that the role of public broadcasting in a country would influence the news culture and increase the emphasis on political substance over a focus on politics as entertainment and a strategic game. When strategic games are measured as an index, the results show a significant negative relationship between the market share of public service channels and the use of these frames (see Figure 4.4 for a visual illustration). The same relationship is not equally evident, however, when games are measured as a percentage of the game versus issue macroframe. Nevertheless, our overall conclusion is that strong public service broadcasting appears to inhibit the use of strategic game frames.

Finally, our last hypothesis suggested a relationship between the use of strategy and game frames and the number of political parties in a country. Therefore, we also ran correlations between our dependent variables and the number of parties in (1) parliament and (2) government. The results presented in Table 4.5 provide somewhat mixed results. Three of the four correlations are negative, but only one is strong and significant.[4] Apparently, there is a consistent negative relationship between the number of parties in parliament and the tendency to frame political news as strategic games. In other words, and as suggested by H6a, the lower the number of parties, the higher the level of strategic game framing. See Figure 4.5 for a visual illustration on the national level.

On the other hand, Table 4.4 revealed one positive (although insignificant when $N = 160$) relationship between the percent of the strategic game macroframe and the number of parties in government (as suggested by H6b). Indeed, we expected that the number of parties might have a different effect on the frequency of the game and the strategy frame. We assumed that the clear-cut competition that occurs more often in political systems with fewer parties would increase the use of the game frame, whereas more complex competition (i.e., with a higher number of parties) would lead to a stronger focus on strategy. Based on the results from our initial factor analysis, we did not construct separate game and strategy indexes, but in Table 4.5, we present the relationship between the separate game

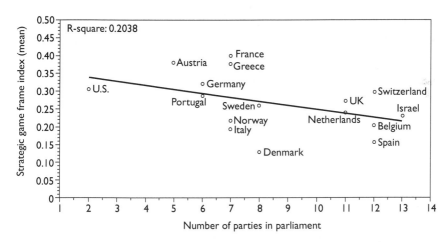

Figure 4.5 The relationship between country score on strategic game frame index and the number of parties in parliament.

Table 4.5 Correlations between game frames, strategy frames, and number of parties in parliament/government[a]

	Game frame			Strategy frame		
	Public opinion	Winning and losing	Sport language	Strategy and tactics	Performance	Media
Number of parties in:						
Parliament	−.106	−.253**	−.512**	−.146	−.202*	−.015
Government	−.061	.064	−.268**	.071	.087	−.100
N		160			160	

a Entries are Pearson's R.
* p < .05, ** p < .01.

46   Toril Aalberg et al.

and strategy frame variables and the number of parties in parliament and in government, respectively.

When it comes to the strategy frames, the pattern is mixed, and there is no general support for Hypothesis 5b. Four out of the six correlations are negative (and only one significant when $N = 160$), indicating that more complex competition with a higher number of parties does not systematically lead to a higher focus on strategy. It is worth noting, however, that there is a weak but positive relationship between two of the strategy frames and the number of parties in government. These relationships were not significant when the analysis was based on media output level ($N = 160$), but they were significant when similar analyses were run on individual news items ($N = 7793$). The results in Table 4.5 confirm, however, that there is a general negative relationship between the number of parties and the tendency to cover politics as a game. This relationship is particularly evident for the use of sports language.

In our final analysis, we model the score of the strategy game index in a regression analysis including the different explanations that we earlier discussed individually. This multivariate analysis (see Table 4.6) shows that the general trends from the bivariate analyses hold up. The coefficients reveal that only upmarket

Table 4.6 OLS regression of strategic game frame controlled for type of media outlet and national factors related to context, media, and political system[a]

	Model 1		Model 2		Model 3	
	B	Robust standard error	B	Robust standard error	B	Robust standard error
Commercial TV	.018	.015	.018	.015	.018	.016
Upmarket newspaper	.063**	.013	.063**	.013	.063**	.013
Mass-market newspaper	.015	.017	.015	.017	.015	.017
Online website			.016	.016	.016	.016
Months since last election					.003	.002
Months before next election					.005**	.002
Journalistic Professionalism Index					−.010	.015
Public service market share					−.001	.001
Number of parties in parliament					−.021**	.005
Number of parties in government					.024**	.007
Constant	.238	.022	.233	.022	.221	.148
R^2	.064		.071		.437	
N	160		160		160	

a Public service TV is used as the reference category.
* $p < .05$, ** $p < .01$.

newspapers are significantly different from public service broadcasters (set as the reference category). In a different model where upmarket newspapers are set as the reference category (not shown here), PSB news, commercial television news, and news presented in mass-market newspapers all differ significantly from news presented in elite papers. When it comes to national-level factors, we see that the distance to the next election has an independent positive impact on the level of strategic games in the news. Similarly, the relationship between the level of strategic game framing and the number of parties in parliament remains negative and significant, while the positive relationship persists between the use of the strategic game frame and number of parties in government.

Discussion and conclusions

This study has revealed that political news across Europe and the United States *is* framed in terms of game and strategy, even in regular time periods that are not characterized by political campaigns. Close to a quarter of the political news covered in this study emphasized the strategic game. Importantly, however, the main focus is on substantive political issues. In that respect, our study does *not* suggest that the European and U.S. publics are deprived of journalism that focuses on political substance and real issues. The traditional issue-oriented news coverage has not been replaced by a game-oriented approach, as some scholars have warned (Cappella and Jamieson 1997; Fallows 1997; Patterson 1993). Notably, however, game and strategy elements do occur in news that predominantly covers political issues. The share of these frames in nonelection news is only half as high as Lawrence (2000a) reported for the United States; while we found that about a quarter of the news carries this framing, she documented between 31 percent and 56 percent. An important and related point is that we did *not* find any evidence to suggest that the United States is a clear outlier in its extensive use of strategic game frames. Indeed, regardless of how this frame was measured, the United States was never on the extreme end of the scale but rather was well-placed in-between the European countries included in this study.

Most common are the frame elements related to performance and strategy, but game elements, such as using sports language and focusing on winners and losers, are also popular. Some topics, typically related to political parties and democracy as such, are more likely to be framed as a strategic game than more policy-oriented topics. This result corroborates Lawrence (2000a), who also suggested that some topics are more prone to game and strategy framing.

Contrary to our expectations, elite newspapers were more prone to frame politics as a strategic game than mass-market newspapers. We found no significant difference between types of broadcasters. The latter finding dovetails with Schuck and colleagues (2013) – who also reported a similar amount of strategy framing in public and private broadcasters – but deviates from other research comparing framing across public service television and commercial television (Strömbäck and Dimitrova 2011; Strömbäck and Van Aelst 2010). Crucially, most previous research has focused on election news, and the dynamics of media framing of politics might very well differ between ordinary political times and election campaigns. The absence of differences between outlets might also be a function of the relatively low levels of strategic game framing in regular political news. Concerning the former finding, however, we tentatively conclude that broadsheet elite newspapers not only typically have longer articles but also cater to an audience that is particularly interested in 'the game of politics' – namely, the more educated and highly politically interested audiences. In fact, in this light, recent research is perhaps not so surprising in suggesting that the politically savvy and knowledgeable, in particular, respond to strategic news framing (Jackson 2011).

The presence of strategic game frames varied somewhat between the 16 countries included in this study. In an attempt to explain this variation, we looked at different contextual factors. What seemed to matter most was the role of public service broadcasting. In countries where the market share of public broadcasting is high, the news culture seems to emphasize political substance more and reduce the focus on politics as a strategic game. Another national-level factor that seems to matter is the number of parties in parliament: the fewer political parties, the greater the use of strategic game frames, suggesting that more clear-cut competition might lead to a stronger focus on the game.

In sum, our study documents only moderate levels of game and strategy framing in ordinary political news. The level of this type of news framing is up to 50 percent less than that found in a nonelection period in the United States almost two decades ago (Lawrence 2000a). While this finding may invite caution about the pervasive nature of this type of political framing, it does not change some of the critical observations regarding election time. Lawrence (2000a, p. 109) reflects on the moderate use of the frame in nonelection time, aptly commenting that a

> less sanguine implication is that news organizations are most likely to approach the political world with the superficial and cynical game schema at precisely those times when public opinion is most likely to be formulated, mobilized, and listened to by politicians: during elections.

Our study has a number of caveats. One of them concerns the lack of empirical support for the hypothesized two dimensions of game and strategy framing. While we have argued in favor of this distinction at a theoretical level, it was not upheld. One reason might be the limited use of the frames, and it is thus conceivable that the two dimensions do appear when investigated during elections. The difference between game frames and strategy frames may be more evident in nonroutine periods. A second caveat has to do with the scope of the study and our analyses. Our explanations are considered at a bivariate and correlational level and in a regression model with robust standard errors. With a larger sample of countries, we could do even more justice to the nested structure of the data (e.g., using multilevel modeling strategies; see, e.g., Boomgaarden et al. 2013), but such techniques typically require additional leverage at the contextual level.

These caveats notwithstanding, the chapter has shed new light on the prevalence and antecedents of one of the most commonly defined types of news frames in the literature on political news. Not least, it has also drawn attention to the danger of generalizing results from particular countries (i.e., the United States) or particular time periods (i.e., election campaigns). From this perspective, this chapter strongly underscores the key importance of comparative research.

Notes

1 The factor analysis did not support that game and strategy should be treated as two separate dimensions. If we do create two indexes, they are highly correlated (Pearson's $R = .62$). Focusing on one single dimension rather than two does not influence the main conclusions of this study. The ranking of countries is quite similar, as is the effect of the explanatory variables.
2 Correlations based on $N = 7,793$ (individual news stories) suggested a significant positive relationship between months since last election and the macroframe, and months before next election and the strategic game index. It is also worth noting that time since last election has a different effect on game and strategy frames. When analyses are run on two separate dimensions (game index vs. strategy index), a strong positive relationship appears between strategy frames and months since last election, whereas the effect is negative but insignificant for game frames.
3 The coefficients were significant when analysis was run on $N = 7,793$.
4 Correlations based on $N = 7,793$ (individual news stories) suggested a significant negative relationship between number of parties in parliament and the strategic game index, whereas the impact of number of parties in government was significant and positive.

Chapter 5

Interpretive journalism

Susana Salgado, Jesper Strömbäck,
Toril Aalberg, and Frank Esser

Introduction

Many observers suggest that the rise of interpretive reporting has been one of the key trends in journalism during the last decades. In Patterson's (1993) view, "facts and interpretations are freely intermixed" in contemporary news. All too often journalists' "interpretation provides the theme and the facts illustrate it. The theme is primary; the facts are secondary" (p. 67). Barnhurst has similarly noted that journalists have increasingly become "makers of meaning" rather than "mechanics of event transmission" (2003, p. 21). Djerf-Pierre and Weibull have even characterized the rise of interpretive journalism as "the most significant change in political journalism" (2008, p. 209).

Claims that journalism has become increasingly interpretive – or that contemporary news coverage is characterized by a high degree of journalistic interpretations – have received support from a number of studies in different countries (Barnhurst and Mutz 1997; Patterson 1993; Reinemann and Wilke 2007; Steele and Barnhurst 1996; Wilke and Reinemann 2001). At the same time, comparative studies show differences across countries (Benson and Hallin 2007; Esser and Umbricht 2014; Plasser and Lengauer 2009; Strömbäck and Aalberg 2008; Strömbäck and Dimitrova 2006; Strömbäck and Luengo 2008; Strömbäck and Shehata 2007). Thus far, however, little effort has gone into trying to *explain* these differences and why interpretive journalism is more common in some countries than in others.

One key problem here is that interpretive journalism has been variously conceptualized and operationalized in previous studies, thus making it difficult to compare results across studies (Salgado and Strömbäck 2012). Another problem is that most research has been done in a limited number of countries, and to the extent that studies have compared across countries, they have usually included only a few countries. A third limitation is that most of the comparative studies have focused on election news journalism rather than ordinary political news journalism. A fourth limitation is that most studies include only one media type – namely, the press. All these circumstances make it difficult to assess whether there is a universal trend towards interpretive journalism and to investigate which factors might help explain the existence and prevalence of interpretive journalism.

Against this background, and building on Salgado and Strömbäck's review (2012) of the conceptualization and operationalization of interpretive journalism and of key findings in previous research, the purpose of this chapter is to compare and attempt to explain the extent to which journalism is interpretive across 15 European countries and the United States. The chapter has five sections. In the first section, we will analyze the concept of interpretive journalism and outline its relevance and how it should be conceptualized. In the second section, we will present our research question and hypotheses before explaining, in the third section, how interpretive journalism was operationalized in this study. The fourth section will present the results. Here, we will begin by mapping the prevalence of interpretive journalism across countries and different media types and media channels, before turning to explanatory analyses and examining the factors that might help explain the prevalence of interpretive journalism. The final section offers conclusions on the main findings.

In summary, one-third of the political coverage analyzed in the 16 countries was found to contain interpretive journalism, with some countries – including France and the United States – making use of it much more than the rest. Indeed, the story genres and the interpretive journalism used in the various countries differ substantially, indicating distinct motives and news cultures. A multivariate analysis conducted to identify the most powerful predictors of interpretive journalism finds that, first, upmarket newspapers and mass-market newspapers are more likely to be interpretive than online news; second, commercial television news is more likely to be interpretive than public service television news; and third, interpretive journalism is further boosted by high competition among television channels. The chapter concludes with a cautionary note warning against overhasty conclusions about the international prevalence of interpretive journalism and the linkage between it and media types or outlets without first examining specific contexts.

Conceptualizing interpretive journalism

The concept of interpretive journalism is both important and complex. It is important since it is often alleged that journalism has become more interpretive, which, if true, would signify changes in both journalism and the relationship between journalists and the sources and events that they cover. More interpretive journalism implies greater journalistic control over news content (Patterson 1993) and thus a higher degree of media interventionism (Blumler and Gurevitch 1995; Esser 2008; Semetko, Blumler, Gurevitch, and Weaver 1991). As suggested by Esser (2008, p. 403), journalistic contribution towards intervention is high when journalists report about politics "in their own words, scenarios, assessments – and when they grant politicians only limited opportunities to present themselves." A high degree of interpretive journalism and media interventionism has thus been linked to, and used as an indicator of, the mediatization of politics (Esser and Strömbäck 2014; Strömbäck and Dimitrova 2011).

On a more fundamental level, increasing interpretive journalism implies a transformation of the traditional journalistic formula that calls for news to focus on what, where, when, who, and why (Salgado and Strömbäck 2012), with a greater focus on why and a weaker focus on what, where, when, and who. A more interpretive journalistic style makes media audiences more dependent on journalists and their interpretations when trying to make sense of the world. Whether this growing reliance is for the good or the bad is a matter of contention and might depend on the actual content of various interpretations. But regardless of normative assessments, a more interpretive journalistic style

> empowers journalists by giving them more control over the news message. . . . The descriptive style places the journalist in the role of an observer. The interpretive style requires the journalist to act also as an analyst. The journalist is thus positioned to give shape to the news in a way the descriptive style does not allow.
>
> (Patterson 2000, p. 250)

This shaping of the news is significant since the rise of interpretive journalism has been linked to, for example, increasing media negativity towards politicians (Djerf-Pierre and Weibull 2008; Farnsworth and Lichter 2011) and the increasing use of strategic game frames with politics (Patterson 1993, 2000).

The concept of interpretive journalism is complex. It touches upon a range of epistemological and ontological questions because journalistic cultures, norms, and values differ between countries and because journalism evolves over time (Benson and Hallin 2007; Esser 2008; Esser and Umbricht 2014; Hanitzsch et al. 2011; Weaver and Willnat 2012). The concept's complexity is also made evident by the many different conceptualizations and operationalizations in previous research (Salgado and Strömbäck 2012), which helps to explain why different studies have reached different results (see, e.g., Benson and Hallin 2007; Patterson 1993). Although different results may follow partly from different units of analysis, conflicting findings highlight the difficulty of assessing interpretive journalism's prevalence when different studies use different conceptualizations and operationalizations.

The most extensive comparative investigation so far of interpretive journalism's long-term development (Esser and Umbricht 2014) examined newspapers from France, Germany, Great Britain, Italy, Switzerland, and the United States from the 1960s to the 2000s for their use of six indicators: separation of facts and opinions; length of politicians' quotations; mixing information with interpretation or with commentary in news stories; use of why reporting; and use of contextualized reporting (addressing causes, consequences, and connections). In all six press systems – led by France, Italy, and the United States – an increase in interpretive journalism could be observed at two levels: a growing use of news analyses and commentaries and a more hybrid character of seemingly 'pure' news items. Esser and Umbricht (2014) trace this development to changes in the journalistic profession and border-transgressing diffusion processes, with the United States as the pioneer in both cases. In the American literature, interpretive journalism is characterized by a disbelief in the notion that facts can be separated from values (Schudson 1978) or that facts speak for themselves. In that sense, interpretive journalism aims at finding out the truth behind the facts and statements and aims at helping audiences understand, not only what is happening, but also why (i.e., how the news should be understood). Particularly at the time of McCarthyism and the White House's lies about Vietnam and Watergate, a growing need was felt among Western journalists for this kind of reporting.

Based on a synthesis of how interpretive journalism has been conceptualized in previous research, Salgado and Strömbäck (2012, p. 154) suggested that interpretive journalism should be defined as

> opposed to or going beyond descriptive, fact-focused and source-driven journalism. On the story-level of analysis, interpretive journalism is characterized by a prominent journalistic voice; and by journalistic explanations, evaluations, contextualizations, or speculations going beyond verifiable facts or statements by sources. It may, but does not have to, also be characterized by a theme chosen by the journalist, use of value-laden terms, or overt commentary.

This conceptualization suggests that interpretive journalism can take different forms in different countries at different times, while at its core, it remains opposed to, or goes beyond, descriptive, fact-focused, and source-driven journalism.

Based on this definition, at least four different facets of interpretive journalism can be identified (see also Salgado and Strömbäck 2012): first, different story types – for example, straight news stories, editorials, columns, analytical commentaries, feature stories, and interviews. Among these, editorials, columns, commentaries, and – in television stories – journalist debriefs (journalist-to-journalist interviews, with journalists acting as news analysts) signal to their audiences that journalistic interpretations can be expected and that the news item goes beyond descriptive, fact-focused, and source-driven journalism. Second, even stories that on the surface appear to offer straight news may go beyond pure factual descriptions by providing explanations or interpretations. A typical example is when a journalist interprets a political actor's motivations for putting forward a certain proposal – for example, claiming that a politician is trying to woo certain voters (Aalberg, Strömbäck, and de Vreese 2012; Cappella and Jamieson 1997). Third, journalists might also include analyses or speculations about the future consequences of events, so-called prospective speculations. Since, by definition, the future is unknown, journalists' statements about the future or their attempts to analyze what might happen as a consequence of an event necessarily entail interpretive journalism, and this kind of interpretive journalism might also occur in stories that appear to be straight news stories. Fourth, the journalist covering a story might also include overt commentary, signaling a more or less explicit expression of opinion – for example, by stating that something is good or bad, true or false, likely or unlikely (provided that his or her commentary occurs without support from verifiable facts). Overt commentary might also include different value-laden terms – that is, terms that are clearly subjective or carry connotations that cannot be considered neutral.

While it is possible to devise other forms of interpretive journalism (for operationalizations in previous research, see Salgado and Strömbäck 2012), this discussion clearly suggests that interpretive journalism comes in several shapes and forms. Any empirical study of the prevalence of interpretive journalism should thus preferably use several indicators. In other words, complex concepts require multiple empirical indicators.

Hypotheses and research questions

The scholarly debate about potential causes of interpretive journalism centers heavily on the United States, where this reporting style has received widespread attention. Referring to key events like Watergate and Vietnam, Patterson (1993, pp. 66–67, 80–81) suggests that the rise of interpretive journalism can be explained by the rise of critical professionalism, skepticism towards official sources, and journalism's striving for independence from outside influences. According to him, there is also a linkage between interpretive journalism; the framing of politics as a strategic game; and media negativity towards political actors, organizations, and institutions. A similar explanation may be deduced from Zaller's "rule of product substitution" (2001), according to which the more political actors try to control the news, the more journalists will try to report something else instead. The degree of journalistic independence and the closeness of the relationship between press and politics are also suggested by Steele and Barnhurst (1996) and Benson and Hallin (2007) as important drivers. McNair (2000, p. 71) agrees that the emergence and increasing use of both political public relations and news management support tendencies towards interpretive reporting. In addition, he emphasizes the commercialization of journalism, meaning the need to construct more compelling news products. This aspect is stressed in Patterson's (1993, 2000) work time and again. Turning our eyes to Europe, we find that several of the northern European media systems have been strongly affected by critical professionalism and media commercialism, whereas southern European media systems are assumed to be still influenced by a history of literary journalism and partisanship that favors commentary and opinionated essays (Esser and Umbricht 2014).

We therefore expect to find that interpretive journalism is quite common in both European and U.S. political news, as would be expected based on comparative research on media systems and journalistic cultures (Hallin and Mancini 2004; Hanitzsch 2011) and interpretive journalism (Benson and Hallin 2007; Strömbäck and Dimitrova 2006). A relevant comparative study recently published by Esser and Umbricht (2014) points to an especially strong affinity to interpretive news in France and the United States. In their study, U.S. and French newspapers exhibited the largest proportion of why reporting in 2006–2007, followed by Italian and British newspapers. An important difference, however, was that U.S. newspapers preferred to mix information and interpretation in their news stories, whereas French papers preferred to run more commentaries and opinion pieces. Other binationally comparative studies suggest that interpretive journalism – particularly around election times – is also commonplace in Great Britain, Norway, and Sweden (Strömbäck and Aalberg 2008; Strömbäck and Dimitrova 2006; Strömbäck and Luengo 2008; Strömbäck and Shehata 2007). From this proposition, we conclude that a cluster of media systems favoring interpretive journalism is emerging (including France, Great Britain, Italy, Norway, Sweden, and the United States) but that any measure of these tendencies should be sufficiently differentiated. The present study, thanks to its wide-ranging country and media sample, offers a great opportunity to test the generalizability of these tendencies. We are thus tempted to pose as a first hypothesis that news media from France, Great Britain, Italy, Norway, Sweden, and the United States will exhibit above-average levels of interpretive journalism. However, if we account for the fragmented nature of the literature and try to avoid overt methodological nationalism, we are better off with an open research question:

RQ1: Across Western news systems, how prevalent is interpretive journalism?

Returning to the importance of media commercialism as a potential explanatory factor (see McNair 2000; Patterson 1993, 2000), we can further expect the prevalence of interpretive journalism to be positively linked with the degree of media commercialism in conjunction with the levels of newspaper and television competition. Following from this expectation – and since previous research indicates that interpretive journalism is less common in public service television news than in commercial television news (Strömbäck 2013; Strömbäck and Dimitrova 2011) – a larger amount of interpretive journalism should be evident in commercial television news than in public service television news. Thus, our next set of hypotheses is as follows:

H1a: There is a positive relationship between the amount of interpretive journalism and the degree of newspaper competition.
H1b: There is a positive relationship between the amount of interpretive journalism and the degree of competition between television channels.
H1c: There is a positive relationship between the amount of interpretive journalism and commercial media market strength.

Related to the difference between public service television and commercial television, we propose two hypotheses:

> H2a: The amount of interpretive journalism is higher in commercial than in public service broadcasting (PSB) news.
>
> H2b: There is a negative relationship between the amount of interpretive journalism and the public service broadcasting market share.

The distinction between public service news and commercial television news raises the issue of whether or to what extent media channels (newspapers vs. television) and media types (upmarket vs. mass-market newspapers, public service television vs. commercial television, and offline vs. online news) matter. Because mass-market newspapers are generally considered more commercialized than upmarket newspapers, and given the link between media commercialism and the prevalence of interpretive journalism suggested by previous research reviewed earlier, we expect interpretive journalism to be more common in mass-market than in upmarket newspapers:

> H3: The amount of interpretive journalism is higher in mass-market than in upmarket newspaper news.

It is less clear whether interpretive journalism can be expected to be more common or less common in newspapers versus television news and in offline news versus online news. Because previous research and theories provide no clear indication whether or not to expect crucial differences across media types, we take recourse to another research question:

> RQ2: Are there significant differences in the amount of interpretive journalism between newspapers, television news, and online news?

As suggested by previous research and theories (reviewed earlier), one key explanatory factor of the variation in interpretive journalism's prevalence might be the degree of journalistic professionalism and independence. The importance of journalistic professionalism and striving for independence has been highlighted by Patterson (1993, 2000) and McNair (2000), among others, and follows the logic of Zaller's "rule of product substitution" (2001). It also follows Hanitzsch's research on the importance of journalistic cultures (2011), where he distinguishes between countries based on the "populist disseminator," the "detached watchdog," the "critical change agent," and the "opportunist facilitator" professional milieus. Hallin and Mancini's research (2004) on different models of media and politics follows a similar track, where the degree to which the media is integrated into politics is one key distinguishing factor between countries belonging to the liberal, the democratic corporatist, and the polarized pluralist models. Based on this research, our next and final hypotheses are as follows:

> H4a: There will be a positive relationship between the amount of interpretive journalism and the degree of journalistic professionalism.
> H4b: There will be a positive relationship between the amount of interpretive journalism and the degree of journalistic independence.

To investigate these hypotheses and address our research questions, we will next explain our methodology and operationalization of interpretive journalism, before presenting the empirical analyses.

Operationalizing interpretive journalism

The analyses in this chapter are based on the comparative content analysis further described in Chapter 2. Following the suggestions by Salgado and Strömbäck (2012), in the present study, interpretive journalism was operationalized using four variables:

1 *Type of news item.* This variable targets the type of news item, distinguishing between news story; reportage, background story or magazine-style report; editorial, column or commentary; portrait; and interview. In the analyses to follow, articles coded as editorial, column, or commentary are collapsed into one group that represents the explicit presence of interpretive journalism, while the remaining categories defined as regular news stories are clustered together in a different group.

2 *Journalistic interpretations of the reasons behind events or actors.* This variable focuses on the extent to which news items include any journalistic interpretations or explanations of the reasons behind the events or actions covered by the news item – providing that these explanations and interpretations are put forward by the journalist without explicit support from verifiable facts or statements by news sources. This variable thus targets the extent to which news items include journalists' retrospective conjectures.

3 *Journalistic speculations about future consequences of events.* This variable focuses on whether news items include any speculations by journalists about things that may happen in the future as a consequence of something that has happened. This variable thus targets whether news items include prospective speculations.

4 *Overt commentary and the use of value-laden terms.* This variable focuses on whether news items include journalists' expressions of opinion without support from verifiable facts (e.g., whether something is good or bad) or their use of clearly value-laden terms (i.e., terms that are clearly subjective or carry connotations that cannot be considered neutral).

58 Susana Salgado et al.

By using multiple indicators, our study covers different facets of interpretive journalism. In addition, we will also include a summary variable that indicates whether or not the news items include any of these forms of journalistic interpretation.

Results: mapping interpretive journalism across countries

Our initial research question (RQ1) asks how prevalent interpretive journalism is across Western news systems. We will address this question by distinguishing first between story types that are explicitly interpretive (e.g., editorials, commentaries, and columns) and news items that do not signal explicitly that journalistic interpretations might be included in the story. The crucial difference is that the first type makes the interpretive content overt and unambiguous, whereas the second type might appear on the surface – and is presumably assumed by many – to be more descriptive and oriented towards facts.

That interpretive journalism is not restricted to editorials, columns, or commentary is clearly borne out by Table 5.1. As expected, almost all news items classified in this group also include at least one of the three types of interpretive journalism (94 percent). However, the most interesting result pertains to the share of regular news stories that includes interpretive journalism, despite the appearance of focusing on straight news and facts. As shown in Table 5.1, 29 percent of all regular news stories include interpretive journalism, including attempts to explain or predict political events, or overt and value-laden commentary by journalists. This supports earlier findings by Esser and Umbricht (2014) that pointed to a long-term change in the discursive texture of seemingly pure news items as one of the most transformative trends in Western journalism between the 1960s and 2010. "The discursive composition of traditional news items," they concluded, "has been geared much more towards analysis (answering why questions) and

Table 5.1 Interpretive journalism in different genres (percentages)[a]

Includes interpretive journalism	News stories[b]	Editorials, columns, and commentary articles
No	71	6
Yes	29	94
Total	100	100
N[c]	6,967	830

a Pearson's Chi-Square test indicates that the differences shown are significant at $p < .01$.
b News stories include regular news stories, reportages, interviews, and portraits.
c Total $N = 7,797$.

contextualizing of political events (addressing causes, consequences, connections)" (2014, pp. 243–244).

While there is no self-evident threshold for what constitutes a large or small amount of interpretive journalism, these results clearly suggest that, on an aggregate level, interpretive journalism is common across Western democracies.

As noted earlier, there are different kinds of interpretive journalism. To further address our research question of how prevalent interpretive journalism is, Table 5.2 shows both how common different kinds of interpretive journalism are and the share of news items that includes some kind of interpretive journalism per country.

If we look at the types of interpretive journalism separately, we see that journalistic speculations about future consequences are least common and only exist in 9 percent of the total news sample (see bottom row of Table 5.2). Both overt commentary and explanations or interpretations of reasons behind events or actions are more common and were found in 16 percent and 17 percent of all news stories, respectively. These types of journalistic interpretations are also, as expected, frequent in news items categorized as editorials, commentary, and columns.

This pattern – where editorials, commentary, and columns are much more interpretive than news stories – holds across the United States and most of the European countries included in our sample. Nonetheless, a few noteworthy differences exist between the various countries.

First of all, if we take a summary view at which news systems come out at the top in the two columns of Table 5.2, we see that, as expected, France, Norway, Sweden, and the United States feature prominently. French and U.S. news media lead the left-hand column ranking of interpretive reporting in 'news stories,' and Norway and Sweden (together with Austria, Greece, and the United States) lead the right-hand column on interpretive content in 'editorials, columns, commentaries.' This result fits in with previous research identifying these countries as particularly drawn to interpretive journalism.

Second, when looking at the differences between the two rankings, it is important to acknowledge how far individual countries observe the distinction between news items and opinion items when providing interpretation. In some countries (e.g., the Netherlands, Norway, and Portugal), this distinction is more evident. In Norway, for instance, 100 percent of stories classified as editorial, commentary, or column included interpretive journalism, whereas only 22 percent of news stories did. But in France and the United States, the distinction between genres is less clear. French and U.S. media provide the most interpretation. The French media do so by way of overt 'commentaries,' and the U.S. media, by way of mixing news with 'explanations' of reasons behind events – a perfect confirmation of earlier findings by Esser and Umbricht (2014, p. 240).

To summarize, the results thus far show that interpretive journalism is common across European and American political news. While it is hardly surprising that interpretive journalism dominates much of the editorials, columns, and commentaries offered by the news media, the fact that 29 percent of all regular news

Table 5.2 Presence of interpretive journalism across countries and type of news story (percentages)[a]

	News stories[b]				Editorials, columns, and commentary articles			
	Speculations	Explanations	Commentary	Interpretive total	Speculations	Explanations	Commentary	Interpretive total
Austria	8	20	22	34	61	86	100	100
Belgium	6	12	6	17	57	71	88	93
Denmark	13	16	20	32	39	41	85	87
France	14	28	31	48	58	54	79	93
Germany	18	9	19	32	82	57	96	96
Greece	8	19	21	33	50	71	92	97
Israel	16	24	10	35	47	81	83	98
Italy	7	13	18	24	68	68	89	93
Netherlands	5	12	10	18	64	85	78	96
Norway	12	10	11	22	74	61	61	100
Portugal	4	4	11	15	40	47	93	93
Spain	5	5	10	12	54	54	78	81
Sweden	4	5	35	36	58	60	97	97
Switzerland	6	26	18	39	80	93	80	93
United Kingdom	6	8	18	25	67	67	85	89
United States	18	38	13	47	77	88	94	97
Total	**9**	**16**	**17**	**29**	**59**	**69**	**87**	**97**

a Total $N = 7,797$.
b News stories include regular news stories, reportages, interviews, and portraits.

stories also include some kind of interpretive journalism is noteworthy. Interpretive journalism is frequent and not restricted to stories explicitly signaling to audiences that journalistic interpretations can be expected.

So what factors explain the prevalence of interpretive journalism in different countries? This question is the central issue in the remaining part of our empirical analysis. In these further analyses, we will exclude editorials, commentary, and columns and focus on news stories only.

Results: understanding interpretive journalism across countries

We begin by investigating the importance of media type. RQ2 enquires whether or not differences between newspapers, television news, and online news are meaningful. The rationale for this open-ended question is simply that no clear arguments point to specific expectations in the literature.

The results demonstrate that some differences between media types exist. As shown in Table 5.3, on the aggregate level, interpretive journalism is most common in newspaper news (34 percent), followed by television news (31 percent) and online news (23 percent).

On this level of analysis, the main difference runs between newspaper and television news on the one hand and online news on the other. However, a closer analysis of differences between media types within countries shows a more varied picture. In eight countries, interpretive journalism is more common in television news, whereas in seven countries, it is more common in newspaper news. Germany is the only country where online news has a larger share of interpretive journalism than newspaper and television news (see Table 5.4).

The comparison between media types within countries also shows that, in some countries (e.g., Portugal and Spain), there is virtually no difference in the amount of interpretive journalism in different media types, whereas in other countries (e.g., Israel, Italy, and Norway), the differences are more pronounced.

Table 5.3 The presence of interpretive journalism in political news items by type of medium (percentages)[a]

	TV[b]	Newspaper[b]	Online[b]
Speculations	11	10	8
Reasons behind events	16	19	13
Commentary	19	19	13
Interpretive total	31	34	23
Lowest N	1521	2655	2791

a A Pearson's Chi-Square test indicates that all differences shown between types of medium are significant at $p < .01$.
b Editorials, commentaries, and columns are not included in this analysis.

62 Susana Salgado et al.

Table 5.4 Interpretive journalism by type of medium and country (percentages)[a]

	TV[b]	Newspaper[b]	Online[b]
Austria	33	37	32
Belgium	15	22*	13
Denmark	24	35	34
France	60***	50	38
Germany	33	26	37*
Greece	23	49***	25
Israel	72***	47	9
Italy	7	43***	17
Netherlands	28***	21	10
Norway	47***	23	11
Portugal	18*	17	10
Spain	15	10	13
Sweden	50***	41	24
Switzerland	33	41	38
United Kingdom	39***	26	17
United States	32	61***	44

a Pearson's Chi-Square tests indicate that all differences shown between type of medium are significant at $* p < .10$, $** p < .05$, and $*** p < .01$.
b Editorials, commentary, and columns are not included in this analysis.

In answering RQ2, we can state that there are differences between media types within countries since, in most cases, interpretive journalism is significantly more common in one medium than another. However, neither the size nor the pattern of these differences seem meaningful enough to draw substantial conclusions from them for the research literature.

Some scholars suggest that one possible explanation for interpretive journalism's increasing prevalence is that it is partly driven by the commercialization of the media industry (McNair 2000; Patterson 1993). Although previous findings have been somewhat mixed, some evidence suggests that public service news is less interpretive than commercial news (Strömbäck 2013; Strömbäck and Dimitrova 2011). Following this line of thought, H3 predicted that the amount of interpretive journalism is higher in mass-market than in upmarket newspapers, while H2a predicted that the amount of interpretive journalism is higher in commercial than in public service broadcasting.

Beginning with H3, on the aggregate level, the results show no significant difference between mass-market and upmarket newspapers (see Table 5.5). However, the kind of interpretive journalism in the two newspaper types shows some

Table 5.5 The presence of interpretive journalism in political news by type of media outlet, by percentages[a]

	Television[b]		Newspaper[b]	
	Public service	*Commercial*	*Upmarket*	*Mass-market*
Speculations	7***	11***	10**	8**
Explanations	10***	17***	18**	15**
Commentary	12***	18***	17	19
Interpretive total	21***	31***	31	31
Lowest *N*	1,392	1,263	2,898	1,414

a Significance on Pearson's Chi-Square tests: $* p < .10, ** p < .05, *** p < .01$.
b Editorials, commentaries, and columns are not included in this analysis.

variation. While upmarket newspapers provide more explanations on potential reasons behind events, but also more speculation about future consequences, mass-market newspapers are more prone to include overt commentary and value-laden language when they cover politics. Despite this variation, the overall conclusion is that H3 is not supported.

Turning to the difference between public service and commercial television news, on the aggregate level, the results support the idea that interpretive journalism is more common in commercial than in public service television news (see Table 5.5), therefore lending support to H2a. Overall, 31 percent of all news stories in commercial broadcasts include journalistic interpretations, compared with 21 percent of all news stories in public service broadcasts. Analyzing differences within countries, the pattern of more interpretive journalism in commercial broadcasting holds in 13 out of the 16 countries included in this study. The only public service broadcasters that provide more interpretive journalism than their commercial competitors are found in Greece, Norway, and the United Kingdom. When it comes to different types of newspapers (H3), the pattern is more mixed. In 8 of the 16 countries, mass-market newspapers provide more interpretive journalism, whereas in the remaining 7 countries, upmarket newspapers include more journalistic interpretations in their news articles than the mass-market newspapers (see Table 5.6).

Thus far, the results show that the factor with most significant explanatory potential appears to be related to whether the news are broadcast on public service or commercial television newscasts. To further investigate potential explanatory factors, we will next examine the bivariate correlations between a number of explanatory factors and the country score on the *total measure* of interpretive journalism, leaving differences in types of interpretive journalism aside. In addition to media types, we will also include a number of

64 Susana Salgado et al.

Table 5.6 Interpretive journalism by type of media outlet and country (percentages)[a]

Country	Television[b]		Newspaper[b]	
	Public service	Commercial	Upmarket	Mass-market
Austria	23	37*	38	35
Belgium	13	23	18	14
Denmark	26	29	31	48***
France	43	58**	46	45
Germany	30	32	31	34
Greece	25	17	41	48
Israel	26	51***	32	32
Italy	6	8	46***	13
Netherlands	11	25**	18	16
Norway	32	23	17	21
Portugal	9	18*	16	13
Spain	4	15***	21***	0
Sweden	40	46	26	45**
Switzerland	19	56***	36	58***
United Kingdom	26	24	18	36***
United States	13	66***	52	55

a Pearson's Chi-Square test: * $p < .10$, ** $p < .05$, and *** $p < .01$.
b Editorials, commentary, and columns are not included in this analysis.

national-level media system factors. The results from the bivariate analyses are presented in Table 5.7.[1]

The results show, first, that there is a negative relationship between television news and interpretive journalism, and second, they confirm that online news is less interpretive than offline news. These results also support our conclusions regarding RQ2; namely, they confirm noteworthy differences in the amount of interpretive journalism across print, broadcast, and web news. And they support our previous rejection of H3 because, again, no significant differences between mass-market and upmarket newspapers can be established.

Turning to the importance of media system characteristics, H1a predicted a positive relationship between the amount of interpretive journalism and the degree of newspaper competition, and H1b predicted the same with respect to the degree of competition between television channels. While the results lend support to H1b, H1a is not supported. To the extent that the degree of competition matters, its importance appears to vary between television and newspapers. H1c predicted a positive relationship between the amount of interpretive journalism and the commercial media market share. Although the correlation is positive, it is not statistically significant.

Table 5.7 The relationship between interpretive journalism, type of media outlet, and media system characteristics (bivariate correlations)

	Correlations
Public service TV	−.191*
Commercial TV	−.110
Upmarket newspaper	.028
Mass-market newspaper	.047
Online website	−.274**
Newspaper competition[a]	−.207**
TV competition[b]	.191*
PSB market share[c]	−.130
Commercial media market strength[d]	.012
Journalistic professionalism[e]	.197*
Journalistic independence[f]	.168*
N	160

a National paid-for dailies.
b Free-to-air national television channels.
c Total market share of public service channels.
d Adspend as percentage of GDP.
e Popescu, Gosselin, and Pereira (2010) index of journalistic professionalism.
f Popescu. Gosselin, and Pereira (2010) index of journalistic independence.
* $p < .05$, ** $p < .01$.

Earlier, the results showed that interpretive journalism is more common in commercial than in public service broadcasting. The bivariate analysis also lends some support for H2b, showing a negative relationship between the amount of interpretive journalism and the public service broadcasting market share. The correlation, however, is not significant.

Two media system characteristics that do matter are the degree of journalistic professionalism and journalistic independence. In both cases, there is a positive relationship with the amount of interpretive journalism, supporting H4a and H4b, respectively. This result further bolsters a well-documented link in the political communication literature (Blumler and Gurevitch 1995; Hallin and Mancini 2004; McNair 2000; Patterson 1993; Zaller 2001).

Two other important media system characteristics are the degree of newspaper competition and the degree of television competition. To take a further look at the importance of these factors, we will next consider how these relationships appear at the aggregate national level. To that end, in Figure 5.1, we present a scatterplot showing the percentage of interpretive journalism and the number of paid-for daily newspapers. This aggregate analysis confirms the existent but weak negative relationship found earlier. Overall, the negative relationship is caused by the somewhat higher use of interpretive news in the few countries

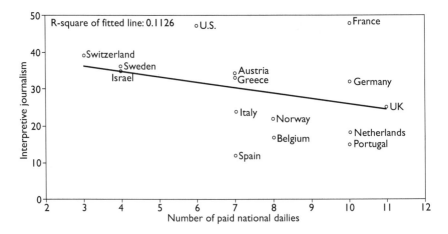

Figure 5.1 The relationship between interpretive journalism and newspaper competition.

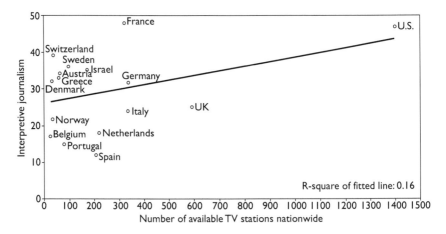

Figure 5.2 The relationship between interpretive journalism and television market competition.

that have a small number of national paid-for dailies (Israel, Sweden, and Switzerland). On the other end of the continuum, we find countries that have a relatively high number of national paid-for dailies. In this group of countries, we find that France has the highest share of interpretive journalism and that Portugal has one of the lowest.

Turning to the importance of competition on the television market, Figure 5.2 similarly presents the aggregate relationship between the share of interpretive journalism in a country and the number of nationwide television channels. This

Interpretive journalism 67

scatterplot unambiguously shows that the weak but positive relationship found earlier is mostly caused by the United States, which is clearly an exceptional case.

Bivariate relationships seldom tell the full story, however. In order to investigate if the potential explanatory factors also have independent effects on the amount of interpretive journalism found in political news coverage, we have included the same variables in a multivariate OLS regression. Table 5.8 presents the results from three models.[2] The first model only includes traditional media. In the second, we also control for online news. The third includes variables that measure the countries' media system and journalistic culture. In these models,

Table 5.8 The relationship between interpretive journalism, type of media outlet, and media system characteristics (OLS regression)[a]

	Model 1		Model 2		Model 3	
	B	*Robust standard error*	*B*	*Robust standard error*	*B*	*Robust standard error*
Commercial TV	.117*	.046	.117*	.046	.117*	.047
Upmarket newspaper	.081	.039	.081	.039	.081	.039
Mass-market newspaper	.092*	.033	.092*	.033	.092*	.034
Online website			−.106**	.035	−.106**	.036
Newspaper competition[b]					−.016	.014
TV competition[c]					.000**	.000
PSB market share[d]					.000	.002
Commercial media market strength[e]					−.031	.130
Journalistic professionalism[f]					.039	.084
Journalistic independence[g]					.012	.083
Constant	.215**	.027	.268**	.037	.230	.147
R²	.004		.116		.227	
N	160		160		160	

a Public service television is used as the reference category.
b National paid-for dailies.
c Free-to-air national television channels.
d Total market share of public service channels.
e Adspend as percentage of GDP.
f Popescu, Gosselin, and Pereira (2010) index of journalistic professionalism.
g Popescu, Gosselin, and Pereira (2010) index of journalistic independence.
* $p < .05$, ** $p < .01$.

68 Susana Salgado et al.

public service broadcasters are used as the reference category, and we see from all three models that commercial broadcasters and both types of newspapers are more likely to include interpretive evaluations in their news. Online news is significantly less likely to include interpretive journalism than public service broadcasters.[3]

In the multivariate analysis, several national-level factors lose some of their effectiveness as predictors for interpretive journalism when simultaneously controlling for the effect of other variables. Only the impact of television competition remains significant, but the effect size is very small. In other words, the cross-national differences we found in the presence of interpretive journalism cannot be fully explained by media system and journalistic culture characteristics, even though the explained variance increased from 11.6 percent to a solid 22.7 percent when these variables were introduced.

Discussion and conclusions

Since previous studies have conceptualized and operationalized interpretive journalism differently, it has thus far been difficult to compare results and make valid inferences about how common interpretive journalism really is or about what might explain the prevalence of interpretive journalism (Salgado and Strömbäck 2012). Extending Esser and Umbricht's (2014) 6-country study further, this 16-country investigation is the largest comparative study on interpretive journalism to date. It tries to both map and explain the presence of this type of journalism in the news and the variations across countries.

A key advantage of comparative research is that it serves as an "essential antidote to naïve universalism," which is the tendency to assume that research findings from one country or setting are applicable everywhere (Blumler and Gurevitch 1995, p. 75). As shown by this study, on average, 35 percent of all political stories – including editorials, columns, and commentary – and 29 percent of regular news stories include journalistic interpretations. While these percentages show that interpretive journalism is common in present-day political news coverage in Europe and the United States, one of this study's other key findings is the great difference across countries. In countries as diverse as France and the United States, close to half of all regular news stories include interpretive journalism, while in countries such as Portugal and Spain, they come to less than 20 percent. This difference is a reminder that one should be careful when making general assumptions.

When we look at different types of journalistic interpretations within regular news stories, the results also show differences between countries. In some countries, such as Great Britain and Sweden, overt commentary or the journalistic use of value-laden terms is the most common type of interpretive journalism. In other countries, such as Israel and the United States, the most common type of interpretive journalism focuses on explanations or interpretations of the reasons behind events, statements, or actions. And in Norway, the most common type of journalistic interpretations are prospective speculations about future consequences of events.

We have seen that one key research result is the significant difference in interpretive journalism between countries regarding its overall prevalence and most common manifestations (types). And, as mentioned earlier, a key lesson is that one should be cautious when making generalizations – for instance, about the facets and origins of interpretive journalism. There are indications that so-called news analyses in the U.S. media are an outgrowth of critical expertise and professional autonomy, whereas the preference for commentary in the French media is a remnant of a partisan, literary journalism (see Esser and Umbricht 2013, 2014). The same caution should be exercised when it comes to the linkage between the prevalence of interpretive journalism and media types or media outlets. As shown by the results, in some countries, interpretive journalism is most prevalent in television news; in others, in newspaper news; and in one case – Germany – in online news. Similarly, in seven countries, interpretive journalism is more common in upmarket newspapers than in mass-market newspapers. The opposite holds for nine countries. The results are less mixed with respect to the importance of commercial and public service broadcasting. Interpretive journalism is more common in commercial television news in all but three countries, but here, exceptions apply, and the differences are not always significant.

The frequency of interpretive journalism, the significant differences among countries in terms of the amount and type of interpretive journalism, and the importance of media and media type are clearly valuable results. The downside of the great variability is the difficulty in establishing clear and unequivocal factors to explain the prevalence of interpretive journalism. Our multivariate analysis suggests only five significant explanatory factors. Using public service television as the reference category, these five factors and the direction of the statistical relationships are commercial television (positive), upmarket newspaper (positive), mass-market newspaper (positive), online news (negative), and degree of television competition (positive). The results are generally the same when we used upmarket newspapers as the reference category. It is important to note that only one of these five significant explanatory factors is related to the national media system.

At this stage, we cannot firmly conclude what explains the presence and prevalence of interpretive journalism, but the results suggest two conclusions that hold across most countries. First, public service television news is less likely to be interpretive than commercial television news, and with respect to television, interpretive journalism is a feature of commercialism, partly driven by the degree of television competition. Second, and compared to public service television news, interpretive journalism is more common in newspapers where it is not, in contrast to television, a feature of commercialism.

The inability to conclusively explain the prevalence of interpretive journalism should not be interpreted as evidence that the explanatory factors that we have examined do not matter. Five explanatory factors are, in fact, significant.

Moreover, different factors could possibly help explain the prevalence of interpretive journalism in different countries. This possibility would suggest that the impact of media type and of various national-level media system factors is conditioned by national-level factors that we have not been able to explore here – such as journalism cultures and traditions within different media in different countries; media system and political system relationships; and the exact nature of, and relationship between, different media within countries. To mention just two examples, in some countries, there are greater differences between commercial and public service television news than in others, and the distinction between upmarket and mass-market newspapers is more clear-cut. In essence, different explanatory factors might be at work in different countries.

While this large-scale comparative study on interpretive journalism has provided many answers, many questions still remain. Until they have been resolved, five key results stand out: interpretive journalism is common across European countries and the United States; there are significant differences across countries regarding the presence of interpretive journalism; there are differences between various forms of interpretive journalism within and across countries; the media and media types in which interpretive journalism is most common vary significantly across countries; and interpretive journalism is less common in public service television news than in commercial television news. Hopefully, these results will serve as an important springboard for further research on interpretive journalism, its antecedents, and its effects.

Notes

1 Results presented here are based on N = 160 (number of media outlets). Correlations based on N = 6,366 (individual news stories) generally result in higher levels of significance. The effects of commercial television, upmarket newspapers, and PSB market share are significant when N = 6,366.
2 Results presented here are based on N = 160 (number of media outlets). Regressions based on N = 6,366 (individual news stories) generally result in higher levels of significance. The effects of upmarket newspapers are significant when N = 6,366.
3 We also ran these models using upmarket newspapers as the reference category. These results (not included here) reveal that commercial television news and mass-market newspapers are not significantly different from upmarket newspapers and that both online news and public service news are significantly less likely to include interpretive journalism than upmarket newspapers.

Chapter 6

Negativity

Frank Esser, Sven Engesser, Jörg Matthes, and Rosa Berganza

Introduction

Few trends are better documented than the news media's inclination to depict political events and actors in primarily negative terms. Yet the concept of *negativity in the news* still lacks an agreed-upon conceptualization and operationalization. Its manifestations are widely divergent, which indicates the concept's complexity and ambiguity (Kleinnijenhuis 2008). Earlier research on the representation of politics in the news – in particular, negative representation – focused predominantly on the U.S. context (Farnsworth and Lichter 2011; Patterson 1993; Sabato 1991; Zaller 1999). So far, European scholarship on negativity in the news is more fragmented and less uniform in its conclusions since it has developed out of a greater diversity of political communication systems and research approaches. This situation makes it hard to say whether negativity is an exceptional U.S. media phenomenon (Schudson 1999) or a generalizable trend across all modern mass democracies. Consequently, the universal validity and applicability of confrontational and negative reporting patterns is still in question (Soroka 2014).

So far, although frequently applied in content analyses, no agreed-upon set of empirical indicators has emerged to measure the concept of negativity in political news reliably in a consistent and comparable way (Ridout and Franz 2008). This disparity has led empirical studies to draw widely varying conclusions about its significance and potential effects. Whereas some stress that confrontational news has important information value, stimulates mobilization, and contributes to healthy skepticism (de Vreese and Tobiasen 2007; Freedman and Goldstein 1999; Norris 2000; Schuck, Vliegenthart, and de Vreese 2016; Weintraub and Pinkleton 1995), others have linked adversarial reporting to a "spiral of cynicism" (Cappella and Jamieson 1997). This latter research relates negative news to a decrease in political engagement (Bennett 2009; Patterson 1993, 2003; Sabato 1991) as well as skepticism and distrust towards political institutions and politicians (Moy and Pfau 2000; Rozell 1996). From scandal coverage to feeding frenzies (Sabato 1991), confrontational and negative political news is thought to have serious repercussions for the way citizens perceive politics, particularly nonpartisans or less educated people (Valentino, Beckmann, and Buhr 2001).

Another shortcoming, in addition to the lack of conceptual consistency, is the scarcity of cross-national research on negativity. The few studies that took a comparative approach focused on the exceptional period of election campaigns, and they often included only a small set of countries (de Vreese 2008; Plasser, Pallaver, and Lengauer 2009). In an attempt to overcome these limitations, this chapter uses a uniform, multidimensional conceptualization to gauge facets of negativity across a wide range of media formats and media systems during phases of routine news – an approach that aims at broader generalizations and a more comprehensive understanding of this key concept.

The chapter will proceed in several steps. After an outline of our conceptualization of negativity, we will discuss several factors that may help explain variations of negativity across outlets and countries. Then we present our operationalizations and methods, followed by an empirical section that provides descriptive and explanatory analyses on the prevalence of negativity in European and U.S. news. The final section will offer conclusions and implications. Our findings show that negativity is highest in media systems with high levels of commercialism and competition, and in media organizations that are geared towards commercial goals (as opposed to public service obligations). The tendency for covering politics in negative terms is stronger in the offline than online editions of media outlets and strongest in stories that deal with negatively connoted issues such as scandals, crises, or conflicts.

Conceptualizing negativity in the news

The ambiguity in research on negativity follows largely from the complexity of the concept. Drawing on a systematic synthesis of the relevant literature, Lengauer, Esser, and Berganza (2012) proposed a multidimensional conceptualization of negativity that distinguishes several components. The *first component* is a negative 'overall tone' towards politics, understood as an aggregated summary of all relevant voices and statements that lends the story a negative framing, irrespective of the topics or actors addressed. The *second component* is 'conflict-centeredness,' understood as an emphasis on disputes and disagreements representing two (or more) sides of a problem. The story may be confrontational, but because both (or several) sides are presented, it is not destructive per se. The *third component* is 'allegation of misconduct,' understood as an emphasis on one-sided criticism, often involving unidirectional accusations of incompetence, illegitimacy, or failure. The *fourth component* is 'actor-related negativity,' understood as unfavorable portrayals of individuals' or collective political actors' (such as candidates or parties) performances.[1] We should add that Lengauer and colleagues (2012) suggest a fifth component – 'pessimistic outlook' – but it has been rarely used in research and has not achieved satisfactory reliability. Hence, it will not be considered further in this analysis.

We will only use overall story tone, conflict-centeredness, and allegation of misconduct (frame-related components of negativity) as well as actor-related negativity (a protagonist-related component) as *key dependent variables* when measuring negativity in the news. For a thorough theoretical discussion of these concepts, we refer the reader to the essay by Lengauer and colleagues (2012) upon which the following empirical analysis is based.

Explaining variations in negativity in the news

Although scholars have offered various explanatory approaches towards negativity in political news, these approaches have rarely been investigated systematically with a comprehensive comparative research design. We will first identify relevant explanatory factors of negativity, embed them into hypotheses, and then examine their relative influence on our dependent variables. Drivers of negativity can be located at various levels of analysis: the micro-level of story contexts, the meso-level of organizational types, and the macro-level of political/media systems (see Chapter 3 of this volume).

Starting at the level of story contexts, it has long been demonstrated (Peter 2003) that journalism is event-driven news and thus contingent on real-world conditions. Should those conditions be 'bad,' journalists will interact with them intensively, which will be reflected in their news coverage. Journalists' built-in attention to negative events follows from their surveillance function as a Fourth Estate in society and from the universality of negativism as an attention-grabbing signal in media, politics, and human behavior in general (Soroka 2014). From a comparative perspective, it is noteworthy that different national event environments will trigger different issue agendas and news selection priorities. Using an identical list of topic categories in all countries, we expect:

> H1: Levels of negativity are particularly high in stories featuring topics that are inherently negative, such as crime, immigration, partisan conflict, political controversy, or corruption.

Moving to the level of types of media organizations, Quandt (2008) showed that, in the case of Germany, online news outlets are more prone to present politics in negative scenarios than print media. He gives the following three reasons: first, online outlets cover politics less intensively and more superficially than their offline counterparts; second, online outlets rely more on news agency material and spend less resources on their own research to check or balance harsh claims made by politicians; and third, online outlets tend to maintain a more skeptical distance from politics in general (preferring other topic areas instead) than the established offline print outlets. This leads us to hypothesize:

> H2: Levels of negativity are higher for the online versions than the offline versions of the news organizations under study.

Another important distinction is between mass-market (popular) and upmarket (quality) news, both broadcasting and print. With regard to broadcasting,

74 Frank Esser et al.

Hanitzsch and Berganza (2012) found, in an analysis of 20 countries, that journalists working for state-owned media are more trustful of, and less critical towards, political institutions (such as the government and political parties) than their colleagues in private media. Strömbäck (2008) finds that, in Swedish election news, commercial television and tabloids use the scandal frame more frequently than quality (or upmarket) newspapers and public television. This finding could lead to the assumption that popular media portray politics more negatively than quality media. However, Takens, van Atteveldt, van Hoof, and Kleinnijenhuis (2013) did not find support for this assumption in their analysis of Dutch election news. Instead, they ascertained that newspapers cover political affairs in a more negative tone than television newscasts. Since the current state of research presents itself so heterogeneously across countries, we confine ourselves to formulating a nondirectional hypothesis that expects general differences between media sectors. More specifically, we predict:

> H3: Levels of negativity differ between upmarket newspapers and public broadcasters, on the one hand, and popular newspapers and private broadcasters, on the other hand.

Taking the step to the systemic level, Hallin and Mancini (2004) and Engesser and Franzetti (2011) proposed various dimensions to differentiate media systems and political systems. Engesser and Franzetti (2011), for instance, suggested freedom, tradition, diversity, and centrality. We outline these factors later, but we disregard the first two because they do not vary enough among the countries under study. Media freedom does not substantially differ among Western European and Northern American systems, as shown by the relevant rankings of Freedom House (www.freedomhouse.org) and Reporters Without Borders (http://en.rsf.org). Western European countries also share the same tradition, as reflected in their stable democratic order, set of Western values, and closeness to the European Union. The dimension of diversity is more interesting. In the political system, diversity can manifest itself as a multiplicity of political parties. Multiparty systems usually coincide with coalition governments, power sharing, arrangements to defend minority interests, and a stronger emphasis on bargaining and compromise at all levels of decision making. Previous scholarship (Strömbäck and Kaid 2008b; Iyengar 2011) gives rise to the following expectation:

> H4: The more political parties there are in a system, the less polarized the political debate and, therefore, the less negative the political news coverage.

In the media system, diversity can manifest itself in a multiplicity of media suppliers (i.e., newspaper titles and television channels). However, a growing number of news providers means a more competitive market environment, which in turn leads to a greater inclination to portray politics in ways that are assumed to be good for business (Blumler and Gurevitch 2001). Consequently, we expect:

H5: The higher the number of newspaper titles and TV channels in a system, the more negative the political news coverage.

The centralization of a political system can be measured by its degree of federalism. Federal systems have politicians who share sociocultural backgrounds with their local constituencies. They are aware of and understand the social divisions in the various regions. They are well-equipped to recognize and articulate experiences and identities that they share with large parts of the population, and this connection will reduce the need to rely on stylized conflicts and critique (Blumler and Gurevitch 2001). We thus expect:

H6: The more federalized a country, the less polarized the political debate and, therefore, the less negative the news.

Hallin and Mancini (2004) proposed further dimensions, of which professionalism and commercialism are particularly relevant. Professionalism refers to the acceptance of a distinct set of common rules for selecting material. The gatekeeping process operates on the basis of universally accepted criteria for determining newsworthiness, and negativity is one of them (Harcup and O'Neill 2001). Obviously, the emergence of distinct professional norms is related to autonomy and the relative influence of outside sources (like politicians) on the news-making process. For every political statement, autonomous journalists – or as it happens, 'critical' journalists – will seek a counter-statement from an opponent (thereby promoting confrontational negativity). They take a skeptical, at times even adversarial, stance towards politicians and politicians' news management techniques in an effort to protect their professional integrity and their public image as an independent institution (Lengauer et al. 2012).

H7: The higher the level of professionalism in a country media system, the more negative the political news.

Commercialization has been defined as basing reporting decisions on economically rather than professionally or public responsibility–oriented concerns (McManus 2009). Cohen (2008) presents empirical proof that economic pressures positively relate to the degree of negativity in the news. Aggressiveness towards political actors seems to serve the news media in fostering a public image of autonomy and thereby legitimacy (Benson and Hallin 2007; Dunaway 2013). In addition to conveying independence from politics, negative news has also economic value in the struggle for people's attention (Soroka 2014). Because negative political news can be presented in dramatic, eye-catching, and easy-to-understand ways, it has an inherent appeal that may be exploited, particularly in commercially oriented media environments. We define a highly commercially oriented media environment by (1) high advertising dependency, (2) low market share of public service broadcasters (PSBs), and (3) a perception among journalists that hard news is expensive to produce. Using these three indicators, we predict:

> H8: The higher the commerciality of a country's media system, the more negative the news.

Operationalizing negativity in the news

Based on Lengauer and colleagues (2012), our analysis will focus on four key dependent variables to measure negativity in the news: overall story tone, conflict-centeredness, allegation of incapability (three frame-related components of negativity), and actor-related negativity (a protagonist-related component). They reflect the consensus of existing work in this area and have proved extraordinarily fruitful in measuring confrontational negativity across media systems, news outlets, political periods, and journalistic cultures (see Lengauer et al. 2012 for details). The first three variables were measured at the story level. Hence, they were coded if the entirety of facts, statements, and interpretations in a story – regardless of where they originated from and who voiced them – conveyed an overall impression that justified the coding. The fourth variable was measured separately for each of the five most important actors in the story and was aggregated at the story level.

Negative versus positive tonality

Indications of 'negative' tonality are the framing of a story as political failure, crisis, frustration, or disappointment, whereas indications of 'positive' tonality are depictions of political success, achievement, improvement, hope, or gain. A coding of -1 was used for predominantly positive, 0 for balanced or neutral, and 1 for predominantly negative tonality.

Conflict- versus consensus-centeredness

The 'conflict' dimension refers to two-sided depictions of disputes, disagreements, or controversies, whereas the 'consensus' dimension refers to depictions of dispute settlements, agreements, or willingness to cooperate and compromise. The codes ranged from -1 (consensus-centered) over 0 (balanced and not applicable) to 1 (conflict-centered).

Incapability- versus capability-centeredness

The 'incapability' dimension refers to depictions of unilateral attacks and critiques due to alleged wrongdoing or incompetence, whereas the 'competence' dimension comprises depictions of capability, competence, and acclaim. The scale went from −1 (capability), over 0 (balanced and not applicable) to 1 (incapability).

Unfavorable versus favorable presentation of actor

Seen from the perspective of the (individual or collective) actor, this variable is coded −1 if the entirety of the facts, quotes, and interpretations presented in a story conveys an overall 'favorable' impression, and 1 for an overall 'unfavorable' impression. The value 0 for 'balanced or neutral' was coded when an actor was allowed to respond to negative coverage (and thus balance the story) or when it could be assumed that the actor appearing in the news story perceived the news story as largely 'neutral' (devoid of any positive or negative connotations). In order to aggregate this component onto the story level, the values for 'unfavorable' presentation were averaged for the five most important actors per story.

These four indicators of negativity in the news are closely related. In fact, their correlations are all statistically significant, as can be seen from Table 6.1. The most encompassing indicator, 'tonality,' is the one most strongly correlated with all others. By contrast, 'unfavorability' occupies a special position of sorts since it is the only indicator directly related to actors; its correlations to the other indicators are therefore slightly weaker. However, these small differences between actor-related negativity and so-called frame-related negativity are not large enough to support a theoretical differentiation between the two (as originally claimed by Lengauer et al. 2012, p. 190). Rather, we take the results in Table 6.1 as a clear call to aggregate all four indicators into one joint average index to represent the multidimensionality of negativity in the news.

The internal consistency of the index is acceptable (Cronbach's $\alpha = .72$). As an additional consistency test, a Principal Component Analysis (PCA) of the four components was conducted. It results in a single component with an Eigenvalue of $\lambda = 2.2$

Table 6.1 Correlations between the four components of negativity[a,b]

	Conflict	Incapability	Unfavorability
Tonality	.47**	.54**	.44**
Conflict		.36**	.24**
Incapability			.34**

a Values are Pearson's correlation coefficients.
b N_{min} = 7,748.
**$p < .01$.

78 Frank Esser et al.

Table 6.2 Overview of explanatory variables

Level	Dimension	Indicator	Source
Story	Topical context	Topics (H1)	Own data
Organization	Platform type	Offline/online (H2)	Own data
	Market position	Upmarket/mass-market press (H3)	
	Ownership type	Public/commercial broadcaster (H3)	
System	Political diversity	Number of parties in parliament (H4)	Own data
	Media competition	Number of national daily newspapers per 1 million inhabitants (H5)	Leckner and Facht (2010)
		Number of national TV channels per 1 million inhabitants (H5)	EAO (2011)
	Decentrality	Federalism/Decentralization Index (H6)	Lijphart (2012)
	Journalistic professionalism	Journalistic Professionalism Index (H7)	Popescu (2011)
	Commerciality	Total adspend (H8)	EAO (2011)
		Production costs of hard news (H8)	Popescu (2011)
		PSB market share (H8)	EAO (2011)

explaining more than half (55 percent) of total variance. A hypothetical second component would only have an Eigenvalue of $\lambda = .8$ explaining a fifth (19 percent) of variance. In addition to these dependent variables, we use a set of independent variables, which are necessary to test our hypotheses and are collected from various sources (see Table 6.2; see also the detailed information in Chapter 3 of this volume).

Findings

How prevalent is negativity in political news? A key finding is that negativity is subject to major cross-national differences and that the assumption of negative news as a universal, transnational constant can hardly be sustained.

Table 6.3 offers a country rank ordered by the values of the Negativity Index. Six countries score top positions, well above the cross-national average value of .21: Austria, Sweden, Portugal, France, Great Britain, and Greece. It is noteworthy that France, Greece, and Portugal – three so-called polarized systems – are amongst the top scorers. During our field phase, these three systems were plagued by disadvantageous real-world conditions affecting their economic performances. Austria is another country with a negative event environment; several

Table 6.3 Negativity by country

Country	Negativity Index [a]		Negativity component				N
			Tonality	Conflict	Incapability	Unfavorability	
	M	SD	%	%	%	%	
Austria	.33	.44	49	58	37	43	476
Sweden	.32	.34	43	44	28	44	303
Portugal	.29	.50	63	54	39	36	555
France	.25	.40	38	48	24	40	534
Great Britain	.23	.32	26	56	17	24	510
Greece	.22	.41	42	46	25	31	547
Israel	.20	.39	36	57	20	30	519
Norway	.20	.44	34	44	34	22	436
Denmark	.19	.38	34	34	19	42	483
Italy	.18	.35	32	28	14	39	496
Belgium	.17	.38	36	32	16	29	488
Spain	.17	.35	31	38	13	31	563
Germany	.13	.36	21	36	16	32	498
Netherlands	.13	.37	25	39	18	31	475
Switzerland	.13	.51	38	44	32	19	391
United States	.11	.36	22	33	17	25	518
Total	**.20**	**.40**	**37**	**44**	**23**	**33**	**7,792**

M, mean; SD, standard deviation.

a Index values range from −1 (positive) to 0 (ambivalent/neutral) to 1 (negative).

widely debated political corruption cases kept the country on edge during the time of coding. Furthermore, in Austria – the highest scoring country in Table 6.3 – journalists perceive themselves as watchdogs of the government (and exhibit greater 'distance to power-holders' in society) to a higher degree than journalists from Greece, Israel, Spain, or Switzerland (Hanitzsch and Berganza 2012). In addition to real-world conditions, we can thus also relate power distance to a greater use of negative news – assuming journalists' attitudes towards public institutions influence the content that they produce. In fact, the country ranking in Table 6.3 is broadly in line with cross-national findings by Hanitzsch and Berganza (2012) on journalists' levels of public trust and suggests that higher levels of power distance correspond with higher levels of negativity in the news.

The relatively high share of negative news in Great Britain can be attributed to the relatively high degree of commercialization and critical watchdog orientation in the British media. At the lower end of Table 6.3, we find countries like Belgium and Switzerland, which are often associated with low levels of polarization and high levels of consensus orientation. Surprisingly, we also find the United States at the bottom of table. We observed the U.S. media at a time when the primaries were over and the general campaign of the 2012 presidential election had not yet started. *The New York Times* and the *PBS News Hour* covered many controversial issues in a critical tone, but other media like the *Los Angeles Times* and *NBC Nightly News* largely refrained from pointed negativity. This reduced negativity may, at least in part, be due to the relative quiet between the finished primary phase and the upcoming general election phase.

With some exceptions, the differences in degrees of negativity seem to follow broader patterns that can be related to contextual conditions. Based on the country-specific information just offered, we can derive that a high degree of political polarization, a real-world environment dominated by negative events, and a high degree of media commercialization provide favorable conditions for above-average levels of negativity in the news.

Exploring the story level

To explore these assumptions further, we had hypothesized that the amount of negativity in the news is influenced by a story's topical context – which, again, is a function of the event environment in a given system. Supporting our assumptions about the inherent negative value of some topics and events (see Hypothesis 1), the results in Table 6.4 indicate that three topics are most prone to negative treatment by journalists: (1) functioning of democracy, quality of governing, occurrence of scandals; (2) crime and judiciary; and (3) immigration and integration. The first topic, functioning of democracy, was especially prevalent in Austrian news (with many allegations of political corruption and misconduct in public office) and in Norwegian and Portuguese news. Immigration was discussed most negatively in Swedish, Norwegian, and Swiss news, and crime most negatively in Austrian and Swiss news.

Another block of topics that were framed in primarily negative terms included unemployment and labor issues, civil rights and freedoms, and party politics and interparty conflict (see Table 6.4). All these issues, together with a fourth (namely, media and communications) received an almost entirely negative treatment in the Greek media. Quite striking were also the negative coverage of party politics in France; unemployment in Portugal and Sweden; civil rights in Israel; and media in Austria, Portugal, and Great Britain. Finally, we note that microeconomics on companies and consumers were painted in especially gloomy colors in the British media, and education, in fairly dismal colors in the Greek media. Hypothesis 1 receives support insofar that negativity in the news seems contingent on real-world conditions and driven by negatively connoted events such as corruption, crime, immigration, and partisan conflict. The especially negative portrayal of the topics mentioned earlier in national contexts can be at least partly explained by a tight presidential election in France, high unemployment in Portugal, high youth unemployment in Sweden, and human rights violations in Israel.

A consistent pattern that we find across all countries is that negativity is most widespread in commentaries, editorials, and other opinion pieces. After all, commentaries often evolve around conflicts and follow a dialectic structure. They

Table 6.4 Negativity Index[a] by topic

Topic[b]	M	SD	N
Functioning of democracy, quality of governing, and scandals	.34	.42	691
Crime and judiciary	.27	.37	566
Immigration and integration	.26	.38	236
Unemployment and labor issues	.24	.41	393
Culture, media, and communications	.23	.39	185
Civil rights and freedoms	.22	.37	337
Microeconomics: companies and consumers	.22	.36	266
Party politics and interparty conflict	.22	.39	1,169
Macroeconomics: taxes, budgets, financial crisis	.20	.40	1,259
Traffic and public transport	.18	.39	230
Education	.17	.40	253
Social affairs (health, pensions, etc.)	.17	.40	535
Defense, terrorism, security	.15	.35	380
Foreign affairs, development, European Union	.11	.42	462
Environment and energy policy	.11	.47	222
Other (disasters, accidents, sports, royalty, etc.)	.05	.38	475
Total	**.20**	**.40**	**7,792**

M, mean; SD, standard deviation. $F_{(17, 7774)} = 13.71, p < .001$.

a Values range from −1 (positive) to 0 (ambivalent/neutral) to 1 (negative).
b Agriculture and housing were dropped due to small numbers.

also give journalists room to fulfill their role as critic or watchdog. Specifically, we find that the Negativity Index for commentaries and editorials, ranging from +1 (very positive) to −1 (very negative), is at an average of $M = .38$. Background and feature stories ($M = .22$) are significantly less negative than commentaries but more negative than straight news items ($M = .18$). Personalized story types, such as interviews ($M = .12$) and portraits ($M = −.02$), are the least negative. This last result could be due to the relatively close personal contact that journalists must establish with those whom they interview. Moreover, in several European countries, the authorization of interviews is common practice, where the interviewee must authorize the final copy of the interview before it is printed.

Exploring the organizational level

In the next step, we move up one analytical level to examine the influence of different organizational types of media. We will start by comparing degrees of negativity in the 80 online and 80 offline editions in our sample. The expectation that the online editions would be more inclined to portray politics in negative terms (see Hypothesis 2) is *not* supported; indeed, the offline editions show slightly higher negativity scores. As can be observed from the *t*-values reported in Table 6.5, the difference

82   Frank Esser et al.

Table 6.5 Negativity by offline and online channels

Negativity measure		Media sector						t
		Offline			Online			
		M	SD	N	M	SD	N	
Negativity Index[a]		.22	.40	4,740	.19	.40	3,052	2.69**
Negativity component	Tonality	.29	.61	4,740	.25	.61	3,052	1.91+
	Conflict	.36	.63	4,740	.33	.64	3,052	1.79+
	Incapability	.16	.53	4,740	.14	.53	3,052	1.19
	Unfavorability	.06	.37	4,706	.03	.36	3,042	3.65***

M, mean; *SD*, standard deviation.

a Values range from −1 (positive) to 0 (ambivalent/neutral) to 1 (negative).
+ $p < .1$, ** $p < .01$, *** $p < .001$.

between online and offline news is statistically significant. There are some variations when looking at the Negativity Index or its subcomponents, but the overall picture is clear: offline news is generally more negative. Four countries are mainly responsible for this overall trend: Belgium, the Netherlands, Spain, and Sweden (whereas just two countries represent the countertrend of greater negativity in online outlets: Germany and Austria). In sum, we do not find support for Hypothesis 2.

Other important differentiations need to be observed; those between upmarket and popular media, between print and broadcasting media, and finally, between privately owned and publicly owned media. Table 6.6 summarizes these differentiations. The vast differences between privately owned media organizations (upmarket newspapers, popular newspapers, commercial broadcasters), on the one hand, and publicly owned broadcasters (the news programs and websites of public service media), on the other hand, are noteworthy. Ownership type and the associated editorial missions seem to play a larger role than other differences in organizational type. As can be seen from the detailed results in Table 6.6, public broadcasters completely refrain from portraying political actors in 'unfavorable' terms and are more hesitant than other outlet types with reproaching political actors of 'incapability' or framing stories in overwhelmingly negative 'tonality.' Hypothesis 3 expected upmarket newspapers to have similar negativity levels to public broadcasters, but that is clearly not the case: public broadcasters form their own camp, and this camp is significantly different from the rest (see F-values and use of superscripts in Table 6.6). This result is consistent with cross-national findings by Hanitzsch and Berganza (2012), showing that journalists working in public service–oriented newsrooms are less cynical and more trustful of public institutions. In sum, Hypothesis 3 is only partially supported as upmarket newspapers and public broadcasters form a less uniform bloc (standing opposite the group of popular newspapers and private broadcasters) than expected.

Table 6.6 Negativity by press and TV sector

Negativity measure		Media sector											F
		Press						TV					
		Upmarket			Mass-market			Public			Commercial		
		M^b	SD	N	M^b	SD	N	M^b	SD	N	M^b	SD	N	
Negativity Index[a]		.22[x]	.40	3,455	.20[x]	.41	1,575	.16[y]	.40	1,445	.21[x]	.39	1,317	8.33***
Negativity component	Tonality	.28[x]	.61	3,455	.28[x]	.63	1,575	.21[y]	.61	1,445	.29[x]	.59	1,317	6.21***
	Conflict	.36	.63	3,455	.31	.63	1,575	.33	.65	1,445	.36	.64	1,317	2.31*
	Incapability	.17[x]	.54	3,455	.15[x]	.51	1,575	.10[y]	.54	1,445	.15[xy]	.51	1,317	6.39***
	Unfavorability	.07[x]	.37	3,437	.06[xy]	.41	1,560	.00[z]	.35	1,439	.03[y]	.34	1,312	13.64***

M, mean; *SD*, standard deviation.

a Values range from −1 (positive) to 0 (ambivalent/neutral) to 1 (negative).
b Means in the same row marked with different superscript letters (x, y, z) differ significantly (Gabriel, Games-Howell, $p < .05$).
* $p < .05$, ** $p < .01$, *** $p < .001$.

Exploring national-level factors

We are now moving to those hypotheses that focus on predictors located at the national level of media systems. As can be seen from Table 6.7, we estimated a series of bivariate regression models to explore the effect of those predictors on negativity levels in the news.

Political diversity. To answer the fourth hypothesis – that a greater variety of political parties leads to a lower degree of negativity in political news – we regressed the number of parties in the 16 national parliaments on our Negativity Index. The analysis reveals no significant effect (indicated by the raw regression coefficient $B = -.004$ and its respective p value $= .541$ in Table 6.7), thereby refuting Hypothesis 4.

Media competition. Our fifth hypothesis expects high numbers of newspaper titles and television channels (calculated per 1 million inhabitants to account for market size) to produce higher degrees of negativity in political news. However, these predictions do not receive empirical support either. We will, however, return to this variable a little later.

Decentrality. Our sixth hypothesis postulates a link between a country's degree of federalism and negativity in the news. To obtain our measures, we draw on Lijphart's (2012) Federalism/Decentralization Index, which captures the degree of federalism contained within a country's constitution and the extent of a political system's decentralization. The corresponding regression model in Table 6.7 reveals strong support, with a coefficient of $-.02$,

Table 6.7 Bivariate regression models predicting the Negativity Index at the national level[a]

Dimension	Predictor	Constant	B	p	R²
H4: Political diversity	Number of parties in parliament	.233	−.004	.541	.03
H5: Media competition	Number of national daily newspapers per 1 million inhabitants[b]	.187	.029	.402	.05
	Number of national TV channels per 1 million inhabitants[b]	.184	.003	.477	.04
H6: Decentrality	Federalism/Decentralization Index[b]	.266	−.022	.052	.24
H7: Journalistic professionalism	Journalistic Professionalism Index	.286	−.015	.310	.07
H8: Commerciality	Production costs of hard news	−.242	.081	.007	.42
	Total adspend	.087	.141	.085	.20
	PSB market share	.188	.000	.663	.01

a $N = 16$.
b Coefficients have to be interpreted with particular caution because the value distributions deviate from normality (Shapiro and Wilk's W-test with $p < .05$).

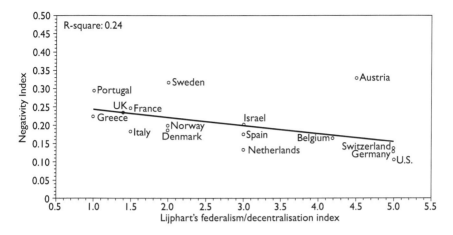

Figure 6.1 Federalism/decentralization predicting Negativity Index.

which verges on the statistically significant ($p = .052$). As further indicated by the negative regression coefficient, the relationship between the two variables is negative. What this result means for the countries in our sample is illustrated by the accompanying scatterplot in Figure 6.1. More centralized political systems with little federalism (France, Greece, United Kingdom) show more negativity in political news coverage, whereas more federal systems (Germany, Switzerland) show lower negativity levels. It confirms our assumption – as articulated in Hypothesis 6 – that federal systems are in a better position to appreciate the people's worries and to tackle the problems of large segments of the population before they can become the basis for media disputes.

Professionalism. The seventh hypothesis predicts high levels of professionalism fostering negative attitudes towards politicians and their activities. For a few countries, like Sweden, this prediction is true. For many others, the opposite tends to be true. These findings are indicated by the negative regression weight ($B = -.015$) for professionalism in Table 6.7, meaning that consensus about basic journalistic norms contributes to somewhat reduced levels of negativity in the news. Nevertheless, Hypothesis 7 is not supported due to lack of statistical significance.

Commerciality. Our measurement of commerciality is based on three components. First, we take a country's total adspend as a share of its GDP (as compiled by EAO 2011); second, we assess the production costs for hard news content by drawing on a corresponding question in Popescu's (2011) European Media Systems Survey ("The production costs of hard news content are so high that most media cannot afford to present carefully researched facts and analyses"; 10-item answer scale); third, we consider the accumulated market share of public service channels as opposed to commercial channels in each system (as reported by Esser, de Vreese et al. 2012). Whereas the last indicator proves unimportant, the expectation of a direct impact of commerciality on negativity is clearly supported with a significant and positive effect of production costs ($B = .081, p = .007$) and a substantial, albeit somewhat weaker and less significant, effect of ad spending ($B = .141$, $p = .085$) on negativity in the news. This relationship is further illustrated by the scatterplots in Figure 6.2 and Figure 6.3, indicating for which of the 16 countries the effects of production costs and ad spending are greatest (e.g., Portugal). Supporting Hypothesis 8, the results underscore the importance of commerciality for predicting negativity in the news.

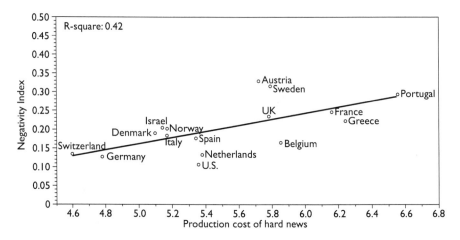

Figure 6.2 News production costs predicting Negativity Index.

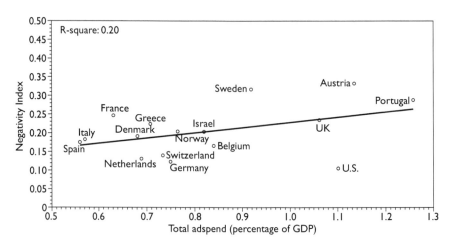

Figure 6.3 Adspend predicting Negativity Index.

Multivariate regression analysis

To enhance the clear implications of our analyses at the organizational and national levels so far, we also used the existing indicators in a multivariate OLS regression. It offers the opportunity to examine potential relationships among the factors and to compare the relative weight of factors located at different levels of analysis. In Table 6.8, we present the results of three models that we constructed. The first model enters a block of three organizational predictors, the second model enters online media, and the third model enters a block of eight national predictors. All

Table 6.8 Multivariate regression models predicting the Negativity Index[a,b,c]

Predictors	Model 1			Model 2			Model 3		
	B	SE	p	B	SE	p	B	SE	p
Upmarket press	.063***	.019	.006	.063***	.020	.006	.063***	.020	.007
Mass-market press	.040 (+)	.024	.115	.040 (+)	.024	.116	.040 (+)	.025	.125
Commercial TV	.052***	.016	.007	.052***	.016	.007	.052***	.017	.008
Online media				−.028 (*)	.014	.068	−.028 (*)	.015	.075
Adspend							.070	.084	.414
Production costs for hard news							.059 (*)	.045	.207
Federalism							−.002	.016	.923
Number of parties in parliament							−.005	.005	.402
Number of national daily newspapers per 1 million inhabitants							.007	.025	.788
Number of national TV channels per 1 million inhabitants							.006 (*)	.004	.214
PSB market share							.002 (*)	.001	.140
Journalistic professionalism							−.006	.015	.669
Constant	.158	.024	.000	.172	.023	.000	−.231	.253	.375
R^2	.052*			.072*			.323***		
F	4.66			4.06			16.97		
p	.017			.020			.000		
N	160			160			160		

a Public broadcasting is used as reference category.
b Robust standard errors clustered in 16 countries.
c Asterisked values indicate the following levels of significance: $+p < .1, *p < .05, **p < .01$; parenthetical superscripts refer to nonrobust standard errors.

models are significant, with explained variance (in terms of R^2) for the first two models at 5 percent and 7 percent, respectively, and for the third model at a solid 32 percent, indicating good model fit. All three models use public broadcasting as the reference category. (A cross-check with upmarket press as a reference category yielded very similar patterns of results.)

One finding is consistently significant in all three models: public television is less negative than the other three types of media organizations (i.e., upmarket press, commercial television, mass-market press). This finding confirms our previous finding from the bivariate analysis (in Table 6.6) and holds up even when controlling for other influences.

In the second model in Table 6.8, another bivariate relationship holds up, although with somewhat reduced strength – the lower negativity level of online news. Even though differences in platform (offline, online) lose some of their effectiveness as predictors for negativity when controlling for the effect of other variables, they are still clearly recognizable.

Moving to the third model in Table 6.8, it emerges that system-level predictors have considerably less explanatory power when entered simultaneously with organizational influences. All the variables in the nation-level block fail to reach standard significance levels.

In summary, Table 6.8's message seems to be the following: the fact that public service broadcasters use significantly less negativity in their political affairs coverage does *not* indicate a deficit on behalf of these channels because media systems with a high market share of public service providers exhibit high negativity levels in total. In systems with high overall negativity (see country ranking in Table 6.3) and high PSB market share (see country ranking in Esser, de Vreese et al. 2012) – including, for instance, Austria and Great Britain – commercial news providers find sufficiently large niches for an alternative program philosophy (transmitting more negativity) to differentiate their offerings from those of public broadcasters (conveying less negativity).

The importance of competition under these conditions can also be clearly seen from the results in Table 6.8. Of all nation-level factors, those related to competition and commercialization contribute the most to predicting negativity in the news – in particular, the combination of many TV channels embedded in a market with a strong public service broadcasting institution.

Another factor that fits the rationale of *commerciality promoting negativity* is ad spending. It proved a powerful predictor in the bivariate regression models (see Table 6.7) but lost its explanatory power in the multivariate models (Table 6.8). Conversely, competition failed to register in the bivariate regression models (see Table 6.7) but left a clearer mark in the multivariate models (Table 6.8). But note that we used different strategies of data analysis in Table 6.7 and Table 6.8.[2] When taking the single results together, we can conclude that, of all the system-level factors discussed here, commerciality and competition affect negativity the most, although the generic character of *negativity in the news* makes it hard to prove.

The influence of story-level and organization-level factors has been much easier to demonstrate.

Discussion and conclusions

At the outset of this chapter, we asked whether the prevailing negativity of news is a typical (and exceptional) U.S. phenomenon or whether a trend towards negative news can be observed across political systems, media systems, and democracies. In order to answer this question, we reported an extensive content analysis of non-election news across 16 countries (Europe and the United States). What's more, we applied a comprehensive conceptualization of negativity that covers four key, highly related dimensions: overall story tone, conflict-centeredness, allegations of incapability, and actor-related negativity. Findings show remarkable differences between countries, which suggests that the trend towards negativity is less universal than previously assumed. In fact, we found that negativity is highest in Austria, Sweden, and Portugal but lowest in Germany, Switzerland, and the United States. The reasons for a lower or higher degree of negativity could be found at the level of news systems, news organizations, and news stories.

At the story level, some clear patterns emerged. Not surprisingly, negativity is highest for topics that are inherently negative, such as functioning of democracy, immigration and integration, crime, and party conflict (supporting Hypothesis 1). It is also higher in commentaries and editorials than in descriptive news stories. The closer journalists get to their sources (e.g., interviews and portraits), the less negative their stories become.

When it comes to the organizational level, we did not find support for Hypothesis 2 that online editions report more negatively than offline editions of leading media outlets, nor could we confirm that popular newspapers report the news more negatively than upmarket newspapers. While online news was more negative than offline news in some countries, it was the opposite in many more. These findings indicate no clear pattern, suggesting that the relationship between negativity levels and online versus offline news is universal. On the contrary, this relation seems to be highly country specific, for which there are certainly many reasons. Another interesting finding on the organizational level is the continued and unabated importance of ownership type. While we did not find a meaningful difference between quality and popular papers (Hypothesis 3a), we found a clear gap between privately owned media (all newspapers and commercial broadcasters) and publicly owned media (websites and news programs of public broadcasters) (Hypothesis 3b). The fact that public broadcasters (both conventional and online editions) report in less negative ways is especially true for Italy and Spain (which seems to support previous research about the close proximity of public broadcasting and political institutions in polarized pluralist systems) and for multilingual Belgium and Switzerland (where public broadcasters have a strong integrative function, creating a shared culture for society).

Finally, nation-level characteristics further added to our understanding of negativity in the news, with media system factors proving more relevant than political system factors. Factors reflecting the degree of commercialization on the national media market (mainly production costs of news), competition (as expressed by the number of TV channels), and the strength of public service broadcasting (as expressed by its market share) turned out to be the strongest nation-level predictors for negativity in the news (supporting Hypotheses 5 and 8). While political diversity proved irrelevant (Hypothesis 4), there is in fact some indication that more federal and decentralized political systems have the potential of reducing negativity in political news (supporting Hypothesis 6). A theoretically interesting factor is journalistic professionalism (referring to consensus about news standards and selection criteria), but the relationship to the generic, all-encompassing concept of negativity proved too distant to register powerfully in our analyses (Hypothesis 7). The loose relationship indicates, however, that media systems with less consensus on news standards will experience higher negativity in the news.

These results provide us with a nuanced and rich picture of the drivers behind negative news. On the one hand, the findings hint at some broader patterns that foster negativity at the country level. This situation is especially apparent in media markets with high competition and commercialization – in particular, where many commercial TV channels compete with a strong public service broadcasting sector and where production costs of hard news are so high that news organizations take refuge in less consequential news formats. In such markets, it is more the offline, rather than the online, variants of privately owned enterprises that show a stronger tendency for covering politics using negative scenarios. Finally, this inclination is most pronounced in stories that deal with political scandals, crises, or conflicts. Such issue-triggers can lead to an immediate increase in negativity, largely independent from the media sector variables and the macro-characteristics of the countries involved.

Our findings allow for three wider conclusions that are relevant to the research literature on negativity. Previous scholarship was largely U.S. centered, adding to the impression that negativity is a peculiar feature of the American news media (see Cappella and Jamieson 1997; Farnsworth and Lichter 2011; Moy and Pfau 2000; Patterson 1993; Sabato 1991). Our results show that this is clearly not the case. Another argument that has been repeatedly made in this strand of literature depicts a paradigmatic and permanent shift in U.S. journalism towards suspicious and deeply negative political reporting following the disillusionment that sprang from lies about the Vietnam War and the Watergate affair (see, in particular, Patterson 1993). Our comparative data finds little evidence that this argument is still relevant. The low levels of negativity in U.S. media and the high levels of negativity in other countries' news hint rather at contextual conditions, which are more complex, more varied, and more international in nature than the two U.S.-specific events in question. Finally, the opposite argument that negativity in the news is a transnational constant – not culturally bound but observable to a similar extent across nations (Soroka 2014) – also seems an overstatement. We have tried to identify contextual factors at various levels, and even if their explanatory power is not easy to pin down statistically, the large variance found in the 16 countries demonstrates that media negativity is triggered by much more than just a universal response of the human brain to alarm signals in the environment (trained by the evolutionary process of natural selection).[3]

Nevertheless, our findings are also subject to some limitations. As already mentioned, we observed negativity of news during a rather short period of time. In some countries, this period was characterized by several inherently negative events. In the absence of a more extensive longitudinal design, it is hard, if not impossible, to separate time-variant from time-invariant drivers of negativity. Furthermore, it is important to stress that we focused on nonelection coverage, which, without doubt, is related to the degree of negativity that we have observed. Therefore, to validate and enrich our findings, more longitudinal comparative research, during both nonelection and elections periods, is warranted.

Notes

1 This last component is conceptually related to bias towards political actors and will be examined in more detail in Chapter 7 on balance.
2 Due to the multilevel structure of the data (stories nested in news organizations nested in media systems), the ideal analysis would include a hierarchical regression model. However, we do not have more than 16 cases on the highest level, and most experts in the field recommend at least 30 cases but better 50 to 100 cases (e.g., Kreft and De Leeuw 1998). So we had to confine ourselves to a "pooled" regression (e.g., Kreft and De Leeuw 1998, p. 27) with robust standard errors, which is considered an acceptable solution in most contexts (e.g., Hox 2002, p. 5). See also Chapter 2 on our method.
3 In fairness, it should be added that Soroka (2014, p. 121) seems to be taking a similar position when he states that negativity biases result from an 'interaction' between humans' built-in negativity biases and negativity in their information environments.

Chapter 7

Political balance

David Nicolas Hopmann, Peter Van Aelst,
Susana Salgado, and Guido Legnante

Introduction

Before every election campaign, the French Conseil supérieur de l'audiovisuel (CSA) publishes detailed rules on how much news coverage candidates are allowed to have vis-à-vis one another in the electronic media to ensure what it calls *pluralisme politique* (e.g., CSA 2011). Also outside election times, the CSA continuously monitors news coverage by electronic media and can sanction broadcasters for not complying with regulations. While, of the modern democracies, France may have the strictest regulations on news media content, other Western democracies also have authorities that monitor and control news coverage (mainly public broadcasters) or have informal rules that determine news coverage of politics (Hopmann, Van Aelst, and Legnante 2012; Kaid and Strömbäck 2008).

Politically defined rules on news content are not necessarily in line with professional journalistic routines and norms on news story selection. Journalists base their decisions on what, whom, and how to cover current affairs on a number of factors, such as news values, practical decisions (e.g., available space and scheduling), audience expectations, and what competitors cover (e.g., Reinemann 2004; Shoemaker et al. 2001; Shoemaker and Reese 1996; Tuchman 1973).

The media in most Western democracies, therefore, face two distinct approaches to balanced news coverage. One is regulative, and the other is based on professional journalism's routines and norms. The crucial research question to be addressed in this chapter is the extent to which news media are in line with these approaches to political balance. The example from the French presidential campaign draws attention to another fact: discussions on media bias typically surface in times of election campaigns. Most scientific studies are on election campaign coverage (for an overview, see Hopmann et al. 2012). Two informative exceptions are the systematic comparisons between election and routine times by Van Aelst and de Swert (2009) and Green-Pedersen, Mortensen, and Thesen (2015). The results from these two studies on the Flemish and Danish news media, respectively, show that the proportion of balanced news items during election campaigns is substantially higher than during routine times. Their findings clearly call for a systematic analysis of political balance in news coverage during routine times.

The current chapter is divided into two parts. In the first part, we follow the preceding chapters and provide an overview of political balance in news coverage in 14 European democracies and the United States and focus more closely on the differences across media types. These analyses show that balance in terms of visibility and tone is a structural feature of political news coverage across countries and outlets. In the second part, we try to explain why some parties get more attention than others across countries and why some parties receive more favorable coverage and others less. We will contrast the regulative approach with the journalistic approach. In this way, this chapter contributes to the scholarly debate on which factors drive the general production of news coverage. Note that unlike the previous chapters in this book, we did not include the Netherlands in this chapter's analyses – hence the 15 countries. The data gathered on the Netherlands covered postelection coalition negotiations and a replacement of government, rendering it difficult to define some of the independent variables used in the analyses. The chapter will end with a discussion highlighting the implications of our findings and sketching directions for future research.

Measuring political balance in the news

Norris (2009, p. 336) has previously noted that "partisanship is . . . often in the eye of the beholder." Indeed, whether news content is perceived as politically biased is largely a question of one's own partisan beliefs. It is common to perceive the media as working to the disadvantage of one's own political point of view and favoring positions with which one disagrees. This tendency has been coined the *hostile media phenomenon.* In their seminal study, Vallone, Ross, and Lepper (1985) showed that partisans tended to recall more negative than positive evaluations of their camp, expecting that this bias could move nonpartisans towards the other camp (see also Reid 2012; Schmitt, Gunther, and Liebhart 2004; Tsfati 2007). In the United States, a recent poll indicated that two-thirds of citizens are convinced that the media are politically biased in their reporting. In the mid-eighties, less than half of respondents agreed with the statement (Groeling 2013, p. 131).

Moving beyond subjective or partisan perceptions of balanced coverage, we need systematic content analyses of news coverage. To interpret these data, however, some benchmarks for what constitutes politically balanced news coverage independent of the political preferences of those investigating news content are a prerequisite. In the United States, where most studies on political bias in news coverage have been conducted, a common approach is to (often implicitly) define political bias in news coverage as deviation from treating the two dominating parties equally. For example, in a study analyzing the coverage of the Democratic and Republican candidates running in the U.S. presidential elections of 2000 and 2004, bias was defined "as the extent to which partisan opponents are given equal prominence and scope to make their cases to the public" (Zeldes, Fico, Carpenter, and Diddi 2008, p. 565).

This definition of political bias in the news faces at least three challenges. First, it assumes that reality – however defined – is balanced fifty–fifty. Needless to say, reality is often not balanced. To mention one example, recent debates in the U.S. media have highlighted the challenge of balancing extreme or outright incorrect positions. Climate change is a fact and by far, most scientists agree that it is, at least partly, caused by humans. Therefore, it makes no sense to treat both sides as equally valid arguments. As to the origins of life, intelligent design is not a plausible alternative theory to evolution; rather, it is superstition (on this debate, see Sullivan 2012). In this case, too, it makes no sense to treat both sides as equally valid arguments. In short, enforcing a balancing rule in debates on climate change or intelligent design is not only highly challenging; potentially, doing so means misinforming the public.

Second, this definition of political bias (i.e., unequal treatment of two parties) does not translate easily to multiparty systems, which are common in most modern democracies. In a two-party system, one party's advantage is the other's disadvantage. The more media coverage the Democrats receive, the less there is on the Republicans. In a multiparty system, the situation is obviously more complicated. This complexity is reflected in the math since more visibility for one party does not necessarily imply less visibility for all other parties. Moreover, more visibility for Party A can actually be beneficial, at least to some extent, for Party B if these two parties join forces in a coalition against Party C.

A third, related challenge is that operationalizations of politically balanced news coverage (based on this definition) cannot be viewed separately to the content indicators that are being measured. If one of two presidential candidates is also the incumbent president during the election campaign, it may make sense to give more coverage to the incumbent since he or she is combining the positions of election candidate and country leader. After all, even during the campaign, the incumbent can make decisions that have direct political consequences (see, e.g., Schneider, Schönbach, and Semetko 1999). Yet, even this conclusion does not guarantee impartiality (tone) towards politicians. If the nonincumbent opponent were leading the polls by a substantial margin, a journalist who aims to reflect the course of the campaign would reject creating the impression that both candidates are faring equally well.

In short, how can political balance be operationalized so that it takes into account the possible 'real' differences between politicians and political parties as well as the complexity of multiparty systems? Moreover, balance operationalizations must be seen in relation to the media content indicators in question. Although 'balance' and 'bias' are used interchangeably, we prefer 'balance' to 'bias.' The main reason is that 'bias' suggests a systematic and deliberate distortion of the news (Groeling 2013), whereas 'balance' is a more neutral term. News that is not perfectly balanced does not necessarily imply a systematic distortion of reality.

In a previous review of the state of research, we argued two basic approaches to defining political balance for different content indicators: a regulative approach and a journalistic approach (Hopmann et al. 2012).[1] The tight regulation of broadcast media content found in France is an example of balance regulation of media content. The French rules demand, broadly speaking, that the parliamentary opposition receive at least as much time as the president, his collaborators, the members of the government, and the parliamentary majority combined (CSA 2009). Another example is the British approach of using the share of so-called party election broadcasts assigned to each party as a benchmark of the visibility that parties should receive during an election campaign – typically divided 5:5:4 between the "major parties of the UK, Labour, Conservatives and Liberal Democrats" (Semetko 2003). In the 2014 European elections, the UK Independence Party was treated as a 'major party' and had to be allocated party election broadcasts in a similar fashion (Ofcom 2014). A third example is found in the Portuguese Television Law. According to Article 64, parties represented in parliament may reply to the government in the same amount of speaking time as was allowed the government:

> Parties represented in *Assembleia da República* [Assembly of the Republic], which do not form part of the Government are entitled to reply in the same programme service to political statements made by the Government in the public television service where such statements directly concern them. . . . When more than one party has requested to exercise the right, . . . the time is divided equally among the different holders of said right, whereas each respondent shall be entitled to a minimum period of one minute.
>
> (Assembleia da República 2011)

Similar regulations are found in other countries (for an overview, see Kaid and Strömbäck 2008, p. 424). In the mentioned instances of French, British, and Portuguese news content regulation, the regulation deals with the visibility (in television, not newspapers) of political actors only. When it comes to the extent of impartiality towards political actors, a regulative approach to news coverage asks for neutral coverage of political actors. In many countries, some politicians still appear to prefer the traditional 'sacerdotal approach,' whereby journalists simply reflect their political messages (Semetko et al. 1991). But we do not argue that politicians would prefer a noncritical party press. Presumably, most politicians in Europe prefer a free and critical press – as long as specific interests are not favored consistently over time and politicians and political parties receive, on average, neutral treatment by the media. Arguably, this preference is also reflected in the frequent references to 'impartiality in news coverage' in media regulations across Europe. Based on this discussion, we can formulate two hypotheses:

> H1a: If news production is guided by a regulative approach, then the visibility of political parties in the news is proportional to their electoral size.
> H1b: If news production is guided by a regulative approach, then the political parties are, on average, covered impartially by the media.

Approaches to political balance in news coverage look different when seen from a professional journalistic point of view. When deciding which political events to report, journalists base their decisions on news routines and news values (O'Neill and Harcup 2009). This approach implies that the news media favor certain stories more than others. According to Hofstetter (1976), such a "structural bias" should be distinguished from partisan bias in the news. For instance, in terms of whose actions to report, the classical preference (or structural bias) is for people with the most political power (Gans 1979). Or put differently, news media favor those who are most important for society and potentially have the largest influence on citizens' daily lives (Hopmann 2014; Tresch 2009). This approach to news reporting implies that incumbent politicians are covered more often than oppositional politicians who, by definition, are less important (Schiffer 2006). Of course, journalists also take into account the current political climate as reflected by the popularity of parties. Party popularity is an indicator of the societal relevance of the different parties (see discussions in Asp 2003, p. 10, 2007, p. 22; Kuhn 2013a, p. 152). If, in an election, a challenger to the incumbent candidate has a good chance of winning, he or she is of course more newsworthy than a challenger with only theoretical chances of winning.

The arguments for the (possible) greater newsworthiness and news visibility of incumbent politicians do not necessarily carry over to how favorably or unfavorably politicians are presented. In fact, previous research even indicates that incumbents may be treated more critically by the media than their challengers (Caspari, Schönbach, and Lauf 1999, p. 272). Treating incumbent politicians more critically makes sense from a journalistic professional point of view (Asp 2007, pp. 33–34) since incumbent politicians are to be held accountable for the current state of affairs, at least more so than oppositional politicians. As Starkey (2007, p. 110) puts it, balance "is particularly problematic when one party has been in office for a long period, as none of the other opposition parties could be reasonably challenged on its own record." He concludes that "[e]venhandedness would require the interviewer to feign an amnesia that would exclude questions about the recent past and so permit no party's record to be examined."

Across the board, journalists are likely to refer to public opinion in their news coverage (Neveu 2002). In consequence, news coverage reflects whether political actors or their policies are popular among citizens. Since we know that negatively colored news coverage affects the popularity of political actors negatively (Fournier et al. 2004; Hopmann, Vliegenthart, de Vreese, and Albæk 2010), it is difficult to say what comes first – negative news coverage or decreasing public support (but see Green-Pedersen et al. 2015). That aside, from the point of view of the individual journalist, increases or decreases in public support reflected in opinion polls are potentially newsworthy. Based on the preceding discussion, we formulate two additional hypotheses:

> H2a: If news production is guided by a journalistic approach, then the visibility of political parties is defined by their incumbency status and status in the polls.

H2b: If news production is guided by a journalistic approach, then the tonality of news coverage of political parties is defined by success in the polls and incumbency status.[2]

In summary, two ways of approaching political balance in news coverage are evident. On the one hand, the regulative approach advocates proportional visibility – which in some countries is explicitly regulated – and (on average) a neutral presentation of political actors. On the other hand, the journalistic approach implies greater visibility of powerful (incumbent) or successful political actors, and its tonality towards politicians reflects the unfolding of events. Clearly, both approaches are not mutually exclusive; they overlap both conceptually and empirically. For example, to some extent, vote shares in a preceding election may capture the same information as current incumbency status. The subsequent analyses will show the different variables' explanatory power, answering the following research question:

RQ: Which approach – regulative or journalistic – better explains news coverage of political parties?

Finally, based on the preceding discussions, it seems reasonable to expect a general difference between public service broadcasting (PSB) and commercial broadcasting. We therefore add one final hypothesis to our list:

H3: Public service broadcasting outlets are more balanced than are other news outlets.

Political balance across countries

In this first part, in line with the preceding chapters, we present the main descriptive results by looking at the differences in political balance across different countries and across different types of media outlets: public service broadcasting versus commercial broadcasting, upmarket versus mass-market newspapers, and offline versus online media outlets. A more detailed analysis of the regulative versus journalistic approaches to balance in the news will be presented in the second part of this chapter.

We use separate indicators for balance in the visibility of, and for the extent of impartiality towards, political parties per country. The indicators relate to the distinction in the partisan bias literature between 'selection bias' and 'representation bias' (Groeling 2013). For visibility, we followed Brandenburg's (2005) analysis of political balance in the Irish media. In his study, he computes the so-called Duncan index of dissimilarity for the visibility of political parties. In this chapter, we reversed the index, creating an index of similarity, or balance. The scale of the index ranges from 0 (no balance) to 100 (perfect balance). The index is computed by calculating the percentage proportion in visibility that one would need to reallocate to achieve perfect balance. The result is then subtracted from 100. If we have two parties with 50 percent electoral support each, but one of them receives 80 percent of media attention – implying that the other one receives 20 percent only – the index value would be 70. That is, one would need to reallocate 30 percentage points of the attention from one party to another to achieve perfect balance in visibility since 80 − 30 = 50 and 20 + 30 = 50. Note that this indicator is not based on the specific regulations on news content that are found in some countries. They vary from country to country, if present, but for this cross-country comparative study, we need an indicator that is not linked to specific countries.

For impartiality, we use a similar index ranging from 0 (perfect one-sidedness, either positive or negative) to 100 (perfect impartiality). Note that we operationalized impartiality from the perspective of the political actor and that being coded as (un)favorable does not imply explicit positive or negative journalist comments. We computed a summary indicator that represents the mean net balance of how parties are depicted in the news. To give an example, if a party is depicted in a media outlet positively 5 times, negatively 4 times, and neutrally or balanced 10 times, the proportion of one-sidedness is 1:19 (the 4 negative instances are cancelled out by 4 positive instances, leaving one positive instance in excess).[3]

Figure 7.1 presents the average scores for visibility and impartiality across countries. The general picture is that of high balance across all the countries that

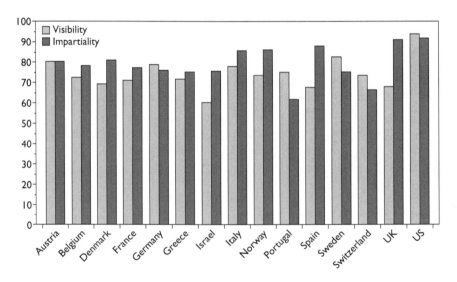

Figure 7.1 Visibility (index of similarity) and impartiality in 15 countries, both scaled from 0 (no balance) to 100 (perfect balance). The proportion of impartiality is the mean proportion of positive (or negative) appearances in excess of negative (or positive) appearances of all appearances. The numbers are country-level averages of each outlet's index value and country-level averages of each outlet's mean impartiality towards parties, respectively (see Note 3 for further details).

we studied, both with respect to visibility ($M = 74$; $SD = 9.9$; $N = 150$) and impartiality ($M = 79$; $SD = 14.3$; $N = 150$). Most political parties get a fair share of attention, which is on average neutral or balanced in tone. In the United States, news coverage is highly balanced. This finding confirms that, in a two-party system, visibility is likely to be equally divided. More surprisingly, the favorability for both parties is also highly balanced. (Note that our sample does not include supposedly more imbalanced outlets such as television shows on the liberal MSNBC or the conservative Fox News.) Other countries score lower on visibility or impartiality. For instance, in Israel, the visibility of parties is less balanced likely because of the strong focus on parties in government and government actors in general (see also Chapter 8 on personalization).

Political balance across types of media

Since the more detailed regulations deal with the visibility of political actors on public service broadcasting, we expect that public television is more balanced than its commercial competitors. Newspapers, however, are rarely strictly regulated. Across Europe, many newspapers have historical and sometimes even current bonds to specific political parties or movements (Hallin and Mancini 2004). Although these traditional ties have largely evaporated, several studies have shown that coverage reflects the favorability towards political actors that is found in the commentary sections and editorials of newspapers (for an overview, see Hopmann et al. 2012, pp. 246–247). This finding can be related to the strong socialization effects taking place in the newsroom (see, e.g., Shoemaker and Reese 1996; Soloski 1989).

In short, there is good reason to believe that we find differences in political balance, both with respect to visibility and impartiality, across different types of media outlets. Given the focus on media outlets in this part of the chapter, we computed summary indicators for the balance in the visibility of, and for the extent of impartiality towards, political parties per media outlet in our analyses ($N = 150$; 10 outlets per country). By computing the indices of balance in visibility and impartiality, we do not have to take into account any assumed left- or right-wing orientation of media outlets; for example, we do not need to model explicitly that the *Frankfurter Allgemeine Zeitung* is right-of-center and the *Süddeutsche Zeitung* is left-of-center. Rather, if types of media outlets, such as upmarket newspapers, show signs of consistent one-sidedness, either with respect to visibility or impartiality or both, our indices would capture this difference in treatment.

Figure 7.2 shows the differences between these types of media. Virtually no differences appear. Public service broadcasting appears to be slightly more balanced than commercial broadcasting, but the differences are small. Balance in newspapers appears similar to television news, with upmarket newspapers being slightly more balanced than mass-market newspapers, but again the differences are minor. The differences between offline and online media outlets are also minor.

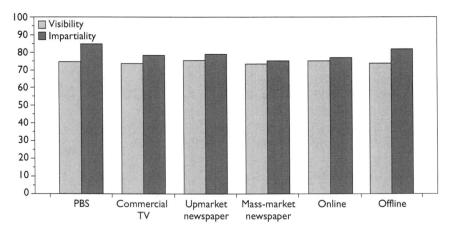

Figure 7.2 Visibility (index of similarity) and impartiality across countries, both scaled from 0 (no balance) to 100 (perfect balance). Scores for PSB, private television, and upmarket and mass-market newspapers include their online affiliates.

To provide a more detailed test, we have computed six regressions with the visibility and impartiality indices, respectively, as dependent variables. Table 7.1 presents the analyses of six regressions with dummy variables covering the different media types included in our analyses: public service broadcasting, commercial broadcasting, upmarket and mass-market newspapers, and their online affiliates. Since public service television is typically regulated most strictly, we use it as a reference category in our analyses. For the analyses on visibility, we included a control variable for the number of parties, assuming that it is easier to achieve balance with fewer parties.

In addition, we have added measures on journalistic professionalism and independence, and on the characteristics of the media market, as done in some of the preceding chapters in this book. What kind of relationships can we expect to find with respect to these indicators? First, professional and independent journalists are not expected to produce systematically imbalanced news. Yet, if certain political actors have a particular news value, professional and independent journalists will focus on them and thus lower the extent of balance in the news, irrespective of what politicians may expect journalists to do. Hence, no clear expectation can be formulated with respect to how journalistic professionalism and independence are related to balance in news content. Second, as we discussed earlier (see Hopmann et al. 2012), there are arguments for both positive and negative relationships between competitiveness of media markets and political balance, depending on whether media outlets aim at maximizing their audience by not turning off possible users or, rather, by catering to specific niches (see, e.g., Hamilton 2004; Mullainathan and Shleifer 2006). Therefore, again, we cannot formulate a clear expectation regarding the media market's relationship with balance in news content.

Table 7.1 Linear regressions on political balance in visibility and impartiality across differ-ent types of media, with and without dummies for online affiliates, regression coefficients with robust standard errors in parentheses[a,b]

Visibility (mean index of similarity)

	Model 1	Model 2 with online dummy	Model 3 with online dummy and contextual variables
Public service broadcasting	Reference category	Reference category	Reference category
Commercial broadcasting	−1.186 (2.155)	−1.186 (2.163)	−1.186 (2.209)
Upmarket newspapers	.841 (1.503)	.841 (1.508)	.841 (1.541)
Mass-market newspapers	−1.120 (1.888)	−1.120 (1.894)	−1.120 (1.935)
Online		.931 (1.517)	.931 (1.549)
Newspaper competition			−1.151 (.631)
Television competition			.013** (.003)
PSB market share			.206 (.161)
Commercial media market strength			10.725* (4.585)
Journalistic professionalism			−2.226 (3.512)
Journalistic independence			2.217 (3.593)
Number of parties	−1.102 (.656)	−1.102 (.659)	−1.035* (.459)
Constant	83.390*** (5.585)	82.925*** (5.594)	72.038*** (8.611)
F	1.27	1.21	16.88***
R^2	.15	.15	.41

Impartiality (mean proportion of balanced appearances)

Commercial broadcasting	−6.544* (2.581)	−6.544* (2.590)	−6.544* (2.645)
Upmarket newspapers	−5.434* (2.223)	−5.434* (2.231)	−5.434* (2.278)
Mass-market newspapers	−9.719* (3.423)	−9.719* (3.435)	−9.719* (3.508)
Online		−4.472* (1.969)	−4.472* (2.011)

(Continued)

102 David Nicolas Hopmann et al.

Table 7.1 (Continued)

Visibility (mean index of similarity)			
	Model 1	Model 2 with online dummy	Model 3 with online dummy and contextual variables
Newspaper competition			−.640
			(.711)
Television competition			.020***
			(.004)
PSB market share			.206
			(.118)
Commercial media market strength			−14.627
			(7.498)
Journalistic professionalism			−8.960
			(4.969)
Journalistic independence			6.468
			(5.322)
Constant	84.841***	87.077***	105.367***
	(2.548)	(2.339)	(10.495)
F	5.19*	9.02***	57.71***
R^2	.05	.07	.31

a Robust standard errors are clustered in countries ($N = 15$).
b $N = 150$.
* $p < .05$, ** $p < .01$, *** $p < .001$.

As one could expect from Figure 7.2, there are no significant differences with respect to balance in visibility across media outlet types. There are differences with respect to impartiality, however. Public service television is more balanced than other types of media, as expected (H3). This finding indicates that public television news still uses a more sacerdotal approach and is more careful in covering political actors in an outspokenly positive or negative manner. Note also that the media appear to be more balanced if the (television) media market is more competitive. However, recall that our sampling strategy focused on larger media outlets and not niche outlets catering to more specific segments of the public. In addition, Table 7.1 does not show that higher journalistic professionalism, or journalistic independence, is correlated with more political balance. In this chapter, we have argued that journalistic professionalism might imply focusing on those political actors who are the most newsworthy, which is not captured in the analyses presented in Table 7.1. We will return to this discussion in the second part of the results section. Overall, we see that adding the contextual variables increases the proportion of explained variance substantially. This finding makes sense when comparing Figures 7.1 and 7.2, showing that the variance across countries is much larger than across media types.

Note also that, as part of our sampling strategy, we included two upmarket newspapers in each country, with the goal of including one based on the left of the political spectrum and one based on the right. Historically, at least in Europe, upmarket newspapers were often characterized by their affiliations with certain political parties or movements. Given our strategy of analysis, we do not need to model such affiliations explicitly. If media content in a given media system were to be characterized by such affiliations, our results would show patterns of imbalance. The results indicate that little is left of these affiliations, at least in the way that politicians are covered. The results reported in Table 7.1 show that upmarket newspapers have a tendency to cover political parties less neutrally than public service broadcasting (see also Figure 7.2). Based on the standard deviations of the favorability that parties receive by media outlets, we also analyzed whether certain types of media outlets cover political parties differently consistently (results not shown here). The results largely confirm the results shown in Table 7.1. Public service broadcasting shows the lowest level of deviation between parties, but there are no significant differences between upmarket newspapers, on the one hand, and mass-market newspapers or commercial television broadcasting, on the other hand.

In short, our analyses leave the impression that journalists across countries are guided by the same principles when deciding whom to cover and how. Therefore, in the next section, we try to *explain* the factors that drive coverage of political parties beyond specific outlets. That is, we analyze the data on the party level rather than presenting figures aggregated on the publication level.

Regulation versus news values

To obtain a general picture of how political parties are covered by European and U.S. media outlets, we analyze to what extent we can best explain the visibility of politicians and political parties by a regulative approach or a journalistic approach. In our previous review paper (Hopmann et al. 2012), we listed a number of possible ways to operationalize these two approaches. We are limited by the data that are available to us for all countries, so we opt for the following operationalization (see Note 3). The regulative approach is operationalized by the preceding electoral vote share of parties, and the journalistic approach is operationalized by political parties' current standing in the polls and their incumbency status.

Table 7.2 provides a first look at the results of our analyses. Here, two linear regressions are shown, both with the relative visibility of a party per media outlet as the dependent variable. That is, for each domestic party and its representatives, we have computed how visible they are relative to other domestic parties and their representatives.

As shown in Table 7.2, vote shares of parties in the preceding elections help explain the composition of news coverage. Simply put, larger parties in parliament receive more attention than smaller parties. Additionally, from a news value standpoint, there is a clear correlation between the standing of parties in the polls and their visibility in the media; the more popular you are, the more visible you are. We see that incumbency status is also directly correlated with visibility in the news (except for the head of state status). Moreover, from a general point of view,

104　David Nicolas Hopmann et al.

Table 7.2 Linear regressions for the relative visibility of party politicians, per news outlet and country, regression coefficients with robust standard errors in parentheses[a]

	Regulative approach	Journalistic approach
Vote share in preceding elections	1.164***	–
	(.025)	
Standing in opinion polls	–	.690***
		(.025)
Incumbency: party of head of state (= 1)	–	.665
		(1.315)
Incumbency: party of prime minister (= 1)	–	24.869***
		(1.670)
Incumbency: party in government coalition (= 1)	–	7.184***
		(.631)
Incumbency: party supporting government (= 1)	–	2.157**
		(.642)
Constant	−2.292***	−1.183***
	(.347)	(.261)
F	2,180.00***	808.80***
R^2	.67	.81
N	1,070	1,070

a　Standard errors are clustered in outlets; N = 150 clusters (10 outlets in 15 different countries).
** $p < .01$, *** $p < .001$.

the fairly simple linear regressions presented in Table 7.2 can explain two-thirds or more of the variance in the visibility of political parties and their representatives across European and U.S. media outlets. We see that the journalistic approach is better at explaining the variance in the visibility of politicians and parties than the regulative approach (81 percent explained variance vs. 67 percent). That is, the combined current standing in the polls and incumbency status of political parties have more explanatory power than preceding election results of the parties alone. Both approaches, however, are not mutually exclusive, as discussed earlier. Indeed, if we combine the vote shares with the incumbency indicators, our model explains slightly more – 83 percent (results not in table).

How do the patterns look if they are disaggregated by country? Would we find that the journalistic approach is again somewhat better at explaining the visibility of political parties when looking at each country individually? In Figure 7.3, we have plotted the results from 30 linear regressions – one regression for the regulative approach per country and one regression for the journalistic approach per country.[4]

Figure 7.3 confirms that we are fairly good at explaining the relative visibility of political parties across European and U.S. media outlets by taking into account

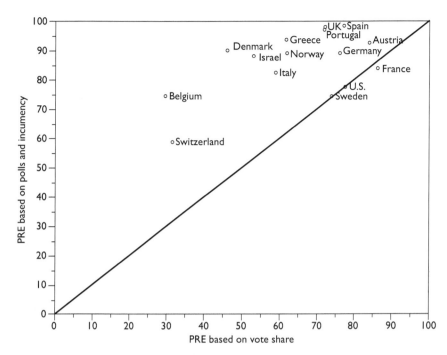

Figure 7.3 Proportional reduction in error (PRE: $R^2 \times 100$) for 30 linear regressions predicting the relative visibility of political parties in European media outlets based on a regulative approach (x-axis) and a journalistic approach (y-axis) per country (for more details on the regressions, see Table 7.2).

the parties' popularity and their incumbency status. As the aggregated results in Table 7.2 have already shown, we are somewhat better at explaining the relative visibility of political parties by taking into account their current standing in the polls and their incumbency status (journalistic approach) rather than their preceding election result alone (regulative approach). This finding confirms yet again that professional journalistic norms seem to be crucial when attempting to explain how often political parties are visible in the news.

Looking at the individual countries, we see that the relative visibility of parties in Germany, France, Austria, and Spain is fairly highly predictable. At the same time, we see a group of countries where both approaches are substantially less good at explaining the relative visibility of political parties. Belgium's and Switzerland's complicated federal political systems might explain why news coverage here is less predictable. Switzerland has neither a majoritarian government nor a prime minister but has extensive direct democratic elements, and Belgian politics are fragmented across its linguistic divides. These peculiarities apparently render the composition of news coverage less predictable, at least when judging by fairly simple models of news production. Moreover, Belgium and Switzerland may be more difficult to integrate in cross-country analyses precisely because of the institutional peculiarities; that is, the differences in the results may in part be attributed to the chosen strategies of analysis. For Belgium, only Flemish parties and news outlets are included in the analyses. Similarly, for Switzerland, only German-language media outlets have been included in the analyses.

Summing up our analyses of the relative visibility of politicians representing political parties across European and U.S. media outlets, we find that we can explain two-thirds or more of the variance in the data by taking into account political parties' popularity and incumbency status. Moreover, we also found that we are generally better at explaining the visibility of political parties by following a journalistic approach (referring to professional journalistic criteria for producing news coverage) rather than a regulative approach (the visibility of political parties is to be in line with their vote share in the preceding elections).

We know that visibility of politicians has an effect on media users' party preferences, and so does the favorability of their media appearances. Figure 7.4 shows the average favorability of news appearances of politicians on the party level. The average favorability per country is based on the average depiction of parties and their representatives per news outlet, where negative appearances were coded −1, neutral or balanced appearances 0, and positive appearances +1. Unlike our indicator of impartiality, this measure documents the direction of the average tonality of the depictions – that is, whether, on average, they are favorable or unfavorable. Note, therefore, that the interpretation of Figure 7.4 is not that news coverage of politicians and parties in general, in for instance Portugal, is more favorable than

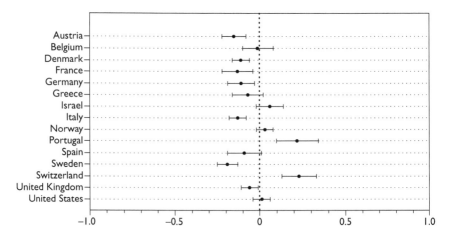

Figure 7.4 Average favorability of news appearances by politicians, based on aggregated measures per party per news media outlet per country (95 percent confidence intervals).

unfavorable. Rather, the interpretation is that the averaged depiction of *parties* (and their politicians) is more positive than negative, treating all appearing parties alike irrespective of their electoral size or number of appearances in the media.

The results show that politicians, on the party level, are depicted in the news in a predominantly neutral manner. This finding confirms the results for impartiality that are shown in Figure 7.1 and is in line with a regulative approach. From a politician's point of view, this finding must be comforting – although most politicians would be likely to dismiss it, arguing that, in any case, they are presented less favorably than their opponents. Indeed, on average, parties and their representatives are more often depicted in a negative light than in a positive light when appearing in the news, as indicated by the negative signs of most of the measures in Figure 7.4. This finding makes sense if one of journalism's goals is to hold political parties and their politicians accountable and to scrutinize the actions of those in power (see, e.g., Asp 2007; Deuze 2002). However, it is also noteworthy that the confidence intervals differ across countries, indicating that parties are treated more differently within some countries than in others. For instance, Portuguese media outlets, on average, depict parties more positively than negatively, yet at the same time they treat the individual parties more differently than elsewhere (see also Table 10.1, which reports additional balance analyses).

The results presented in Figure 7.4 as mentioned do not differentiate between different parties; they are all treated alike. Following the journalistic approach to news coverage, we have argued that journalists will depict those parties that have momentum in the polls more favorably while depicting politicians who are in office more critically and, hence, less favorably. In Table 7.3, we show to what extent favorability towards politicians correlates with changes in public opinion and politicians' incumbency status. The model shown in Table 7.3 addresses the direction of favorability of news coverage by using the mean favorability of news media appearances by party representatives per outlet as dependent variable.

The results are mixed. There are indications that changes in public opinion do influence average favorability. Unsurprisingly, parties that do well in the polls receive slightly more favorable news coverage. Clearly, the prime minister's party – the leading party in government (recall that government mentions are coded as the prime minister's party) – is discussed less favorably than other parties. This finding suggests that journalists take a more critical stance towards those in power. This effect, however, does not include all parties in government. Overall, the model presented in Table 7.3 is not good at explaining how favorably or unfavorably politicians are depicted in the news; only 3 percent of the variance in the dependent variable is explained.

Summing up our discussion on impartiality towards politicians, the depiction of politicians in a consistently favorable or unfavorable light is the exception rather than the norm, in line with the regulative approach to news coverage. At the same time, we have seen that the explanatory power of changes in public opinion and incumbency status (as suggested by the journalistic approach) is limited

Table 7.3 Linear regression on the average favorability of political parties in the news, per party and media outlet, regression coefficients with robust standard errors in parentheses[a]

	Average favorability of appearances
Change in public opinion since last election[b]	.007***
	(.002)
Party of head of state (= 1)	.043
	(.024)
Party of prime minister (= 1)	−.153***
	(.026)
Party in government coalition (= 1)	.049
	(.028)
Party supporting government (= 1)	−0.094*
	(.036)
Constant	−.022
	(.023)
F	9.56***
R^2	.03
N	843

a Standard errors are clustered in outlets; N = 150 clusters.
b Change in public opinion is the change in electoral support from the preceding election to an opinion poll taken shortly before our period of sampling began.
* $p < .05$, ** $p < .01$, *** $p < .001$.

when explaining why some parties are depicted in a less favorable light than other parties. Thus, more concrete and context-related variables (e.g., locally relevant events) are necessary to explain such variation.

Discussion and conclusions

In this comparative study, we looked at the presence of political parties in the news from a balance perspective. Does every party get a 'fair' share of the news? We analyzed both the amount of attention and the impartiality of the coverage. Our results show limited differences between countries and types of media outlets. There are some indications of public service television generally depicting politicians in a more neutral fashion than other types of media outlets (partly supporting H3). Overall, our findings imply that coverage of political parties is guided by a more systematic dynamic that influences political news across countries and media outlets. The share of coverage for each party can, to a large part, be explained by the vote share in the most recent election (supporting H1a). However, taking into account the current popularity and incumbency status of political parties improves our explanatory model (supporting H2a). This finding means that journalists do not merely reflect the political *status quo* but rather that their coverage is also guided by their professional criteria. To answer our main research question (RQ1), we can conclude that, when it comes to visibility of political actors, the journalistic approach appears to trump the regulative approach.

When it comes to the extent to which political parties are depicted in a favorable or unfavorable light in the media, our study showed that the majority of appearances is neutral or balanced (supporting H1b). This finding is more in line with the regulative approach. When trying to explain the extent of impartiality of depictions based on changes in polls and incumbency status, we find a mixed picture (only partly supporting H2b). These two indicators of what may guide journalists in their decision making when producing news appear to have only limited explanatory power. In sum, the journalistic and the regulative approaches in combination structurally determine the visibility and impartiality of political parties in the news.

This study differs in two important ways from most of the literature on balance and bias in the news. First, we did not focus on election campaigns but rather on routine periods, which makes defining and explaining balance less obvious. Elections are contests between parties and persons about conflicting plans and ideas for future policies, whereas routine periods are more about actual policy implementation. During routine times, ministers and parties in government are much more central actors, which is reflected in the news (Green-Pedersen et al. 2015; see also Van Aelst and de Swert 2009). Our study confirmed that the incumbency status of political parties is a strong predictor of media coverage. This focus on government actors probably stems not only from the journalistic approach but also from the watchdog perspective, which states that journalists should scrutinize the works of those in power. The more unfavorable coverage for the prime minister and his or her party seems to be in line with the watchdog perspective.

A second innovative feature of this study is its comparative character. We showed that, in countries with a more fragmented and complex political system, the attention for political parties is harder to explain. For instance, the federal structure of Belgium (where the country's largest party is currently not part of the federal government) makes it difficult for journalists to simply follow the trail of power. Also, the specific features of the Swiss system lower the explanatory power of the classical indicators of newsworthiness. Future studies need to address to what extent the Belgian and Swiss results indeed are a result of their specific design of their political systems or are a result of the difficulties of grasping these particularities in a comparative analysis as presented in this chapter.

The comparative and broad scope of our news study also has some limitations. First, it is important to stress that we were interested in general features of political news journalism across European and U.S. media. Therefore, we did not engage in studying single countries in great detail and are unable to detect clear examples of partisan bias. Our results, for instance, do not tell us whether French *Le Figaro* has a tendency to favor right-wing politicians (and the reverse for *Le Monde*). Our results do document, however, that the French media, like the media in other countries, should not be characterized as generally lacking in balance. In addition, more detailed analyses at the level of individual politicians could include personal characteristics, such as gender or specific political position (prime minister, cabinet minister, party leader etc.), and provide additional insights into antecedents of the visibility and favorability of politicians in the news.

Another limitation of our study was that we were not able to include more dynamic elements in our models, such as issues or time. The attention that is given to parties probably depends partly on the types of issues in the news. In a recent study, Green-Pedersen and colleagues (2015) showed that the saliency of issues can strengthen (less salient issues) or weaken (more salient issues) the incumbency bonus of parties in the news. Returning to our opening example of France, the rules set out by the French CSA for the 2012 presidential elections had ensured a virtually equal amount of speaking time for Nicolas Sarkozy and François Hollande in the broadcasting media, but they did not prevent Hollande's probable advantage, which consisted of the issue coverage being more favorable to him (Kuhn 2013b p. 11). This aspect of balance remains difficult to explain and likely needs a more in-depth country approach (see, e.g., Hopmann et al. 2012; Walgrave and Van Aelst 2006). In a similar way, real-world conditions might influence the tonality of the news towards politicians in power. For instance, if the economy is doing well, this fact will most likely influence the way in which the government is discussed in the news (Schiffer 2006).

Finally, in line with our review of the literature on political balance in news coverage (Hopmann et al. 2012), this chapter focused on political balance, not bias. Putting balance center stage has two advantages. First, we believe that this strategy is more in line with the formal and informal rules in many countries. In those cases where explicit rules on media content exist, they define balance, not bias, in the news. Second, by focusing on balance and defining it, we hope to contribute to the development of explicit benchmarks in the analysis of news coverage that can be used across studies and countries – a prerequisite for cumulative empirical research. Although U.S. studies on (partisan) media bias have developed several, sophisticated, empirical measures for bias and subjectivity (see Groeling 2013), their application in a comparative setting remains challenging – or simply impossible. We hope that our across-the-board approach to balance in the news places the more in-depth country studies on bias into perspective.

Authors' acknowledgements

The authors are highly indebted to Gunnar Thesen and Christian Bächler for their very helpful comments on a previous version of this chapter. The chapter, in particular its theory section, is based on and extends our previous work in this area, in particular Hopmann and colleagues (2012) and Hopmann (2014).

Notes

1 Note that, in Hopmann and colleagues (2012), we depicted a 'political system perspective' against a 'media system perspective.' For the sake of clarity, we here suggest a 'regulative approach' and a 'journalistic approach,' highlighting the points of view expressed by these approaches (regulators vs. journalists).

2 The argument is that, if politicians were to define explicit rules on their visibility, then the electoral shares of political parties in preceding elections seem to provide a good numerical benchmark, and the argument is that, if they were to define rules on tonality, then neutrality over the long-term appears to provide a good numerical benchmark for impartiality with respect to tonality (see also Hopmann et al. 2012).

3 Note also the following details for the subsequent analyses. Mentions of the government are coded as the party of the prime minister (in the case of Switzerland, a country without a prime minister, as the party of the head of state). Independent politicians are excluded (e.g., during the time of analyses the Italian government consisted of non-partisan technocrats). Heads of state were only included if they were politicians (e.g., monarchs were not taken into account). Foreign (i.e., not domestic in a given country) politicians are excluded. Generic mentions of 'the parliament' or 'the opposition' and the like are excluded. For Belgium, figures refer to Flanders as we only coded Flemish news media; Walloon parties are excluded. The Flemish prime minister is included and mentions of the Flemish government are coded as the party of the Flemish prime minister. As mentioned and explained in the introduction of this chapter, the Netherlands is not included in the analyses. Some minor parties are excluded. For the analyses in the second part, only cases for which both election results and opinion polls are available are included to ensure comparability across the analyses. In this vein, the computation of change in electoral support is obviously only based on those parties for which both election results and opinion polls results are available.

4 Given the particular nature of the data, the results from linear regressions are to be read as indicative only. For example, party mentions are clustered in publications, but obviously the same parties are included for (nearly) all publications within one country, which the used clustering does not take into account. Moreover, in some cases of the presented analyses, the Ns are fairly low.

Chapter 8

Personalization

Peter Van Aelst, Tamir Sheafer, Nicolas Hubé, and Stylianos Papathanassopoulos

Introduction

Is political news about individual politicians or rather about political institutions? This question is guiding the growing literature on the personalization of media coverage, a hot topic in both political science and communication science. Several studies indicate that the degree of personalization in the news affects both ordinary people and politicians. First, personalized news coverage might influence the general public's perceptions about who the central players in politics are. From a normative perspective, personalization might be seen as a threat to parliamentary systems where traditionally the party, not the candidate, stood at the center of the political process (Shenhav and Sheafer 2008). More generally, literature on personalization suggests that the political system is presented as the domain or battlefield of individual actors, and as a consequence, the public gets little insight into more fundamental power structures (Bennett 1996, p. 51). Furthermore, some authors studying presidential systems (France and the United States) have identified that more visibility is given to actors at the expense of issue coverage (Gerstlé, Davis, and Duhamel 1991). Other scholars, however, have argued that this trend does not necessarily imply a shift away from substantive news coverage in parliamentary regimes; just because the news features individual politicians does not mean that issues are discussed less (Oegema and Kleinnijenhuis 2000). Rather, individual politicians are the spokespersons of the parties' ideas. Second, as has been shown in the Israeli case, more personalized news coverage can affect politicians' behavior. As journalists focused more on individual politicians, these politicians, in turn, showed more personalized behavior (i.e., a focus on other individual politicians) in parliament (Rahat and Sheafer 2007). In short, the degree of personalization in the news is not merely a question of presentation.

Besides the debate about the consequences of personalized news coverage, an empirical debate on the degree of personalization in the news is also ongoing (Van Aelst, Sheafer, and Stanyer 2012). A lack of conceptual clarity, however, and an absence of common operationalization mean that no definitive conclusions can be reached on this issue. In general, the consensus is that 'personalization' refers to the growing importance of a select number of individual politicians at the expense of such institutions as political parties or governments. However, as we argued elsewhere (Van Aelst et al. 2012), in order to improve our understanding of personalization and its antecedents, it can be useful to study the degree of personalization at a certain moment in time (i.e., cross-sectionally). Scholars have mainly studied the visibility of leading politicians, as opposed to institutions, during election campaigns (e.g., Rahat and Sheafer 2007; Reinemann and Wilke 2007). The findings of these country studies are hard to generalize since they are strongly determined by the national context and even the specific characteristics of the campaign under study. As far as we know, comparative studies on personalized media coverage have been the exception (but see Gerstlé et al. 1991; Schönbach, De Ridder, and Lauf 2001), and scholars have gone beyond country borders only recently (Balmas and Sheafer 2013; Boumans, Boomgaarden, and Vliegenthart 2013; Kriesi 2012; Zeh and Hopmann 2013). These studies have given us more insight into the factors that might explain country differences in the degree of personalization of news coverage. Most of these studies, however, involve only a limited number of countries (between two and six), making it difficult to generalize the effects of systemic factors.

In this chapter, we address this shortcoming by a comparative study of routine political news in 16 Western countries. We focus on the visibility of individual politicians (versus institutions) in general and on the 'concentrated' visibility of political leaders in particular. Both types of personalization are conceptually different and should be analyzed separately (Balmas, Rahat, Sheafer, and Shenhav 2014; Van Aelst et al. 2012). After presenting and discussing these indicators of personalized news coverage, we also try to explain the differences between outlets and countries using meso-level variables (type of media organization) and different political and media system–level characteristics. First, we elaborate on the concept of personalized news coverage and the findings of previous comparative studies on media personalization.

Personalized political news in comparative perspective

In discussions about the changing features of politics in advanced industrial democracies, personalization is considered one of the key developments (Blumler and Kavanagh 1999; McAllister 2007). Individual politicians, it is argued, have taken a more central position in politics at the expense of other political institutions, in particular, traditional political parties. The concept of personalization is used in relation to the behavior of voters, political actors, the media, and institutions (Adam and Maier 2010; Karvonen 2010). First, voters may increasingly base their electoral choices on the individual attributes of candidates and of leaders, in particular (e.g., Aarts, Blais, and Schmitt 2011; Bittner 2011; Elmelund-Præstekær and Hopmann 2012). Second, personalization can be linked to the changing behavior of candidates and parties. Parties have become electoral-professional organizations; office holders are displaced by professionals with both technical and political skills, emphasizing their personal role in party governance and strategy (e.g., Negrine, Holtz-Bacha, Mancini, and Papathanasso-polous 2007). Politicians may act and campaign more as individual actors and less as party members (Zittel and Gschwend 2008). Third, the media may represent politics more as a confrontation of individuals rather than of collectives. This chapter focuses solely on how the media present individual politicians and political institutions. We will not examine the behavior of voters or political actors but acknowledge that they influence media coverage.

Since the concept of personalization has a clear temporal aspect, most of the discussion has concentrated on how political news and election coverage has changed over time. The general impression – that the focus of news coverage has shifted from parties and organizations to candidates and leaders – is sometimes, but certainly not always, supported by empirical studies (for an overview, see Van Aelst et al. 2012). These studies, however, give us some insights into the factors that explain changes in the degree of personalization. For instance, Rahat and Sheafer (2007) show that, in Israel, a growing degree of media personalization is mainly driven by institutional changes in the political system. These changes led to a more personalized coverage, which, in turn, influenced politicians' behavior. Since political system characteristics are crucial to understanding personalization, we need comparative studies to better understand the determinants of personalized news coverage.

Kriesi (2012) compared the election coverage in six European countries over time. The study did not find a general trend towards personalization but rather observed large country differences in the degree of personalized coverage. The most outspoken difference in media coverage was between France (characterized by its semipresidential system) and the five other countries (United Kingdom, Netherlands, Germany, Austria, and Switzerland). The importance of the presidential system is also underscored by Gerstlé and colleagues (1991). Kriesi (2012, p. 841) attributed these differences to the "institutional arrangements of the respective political systems, with the overall regime type and the electoral system accounting for most of the differences." In most countries, he found the same levels of personalized coverage across media outlets.

The study also distinguished between general visibility of politicians and the concentration of media coverage on a few top leaders. Both types of personalization are related but far from identical (see also Balmas et al. 2014). For instance, the general share of individual politicians (compared to institutions) was only slightly higher in the United Kingdom compared to the Netherlands. The focus on a limited number of political leaders, however, differed substantially, with the degree of concentration being much higher in the United Kingdom. This finding is confirmed by the two-country comparison by Boumans and colleagues (2013). In particular, when it comes to the prime minister's role, both countries differ. The study shows that, in the United Kingdom, attention has been increasingly focused on the political leader, whereas in the Netherlands, the prime minister even loses visibility in comparison with other ministers; indeed, he is highly visible only in campaign periods but far less during routine periods. Schönbach and colleagues

(2001) found a clear difference between the election coverage of political leaders in Germany and the Netherlands – the Dutch Prime Minister being relatively less visible in comparison to the German Chancellor. According to the authors of both two-country studies, the reason for these differences is likely the media system (higher degree of commercialization, journalistic culture) interacting with a political system where power is more or less concentrated.

Based on the literature on personalization and insights from previous comparative studies, we formulate eight hypotheses that can be used to explain differences in the extent of personalized coverage. The first three hypotheses deal with country variation and focus on the main distinctions between media organization types. The next five hypotheses relate to systemic characteristics that can account for differences between countries.

In general, television is seen as a driving force behind the personalization of politics (Hart 1992; Meyrowitz 1985). In particular, because persons are better suited to be visualized than institutions, we expect television news coverage to be more personalized compared to newspapers. In addition, we expect that the greater the commercial pressure, the more personalized the media coverage of politics will be. This expectation follows from the general idea of news values (O'Neill and Harcup 2009). News about persons is expected to be more easily understood and more attractive for the audience (Luhmann 2000). In particular, commercial television channels are supposed to be more oriented towards, first, their audience and, second, towards celebrity politicians (Bourdieu 1998; Darras 2005). Along the same vein, we can expect that popular or mass-market newspapers are focused on persons, looking at their gestures more than at their policies. They therefore explain political institutions to their readers by focusing on the central role of leading politicians (Karvonen 2010).

H1: Television coverage is more personalized than newspaper coverage.
H2: Commercial television covers politics in a more personalized way than public television.
H3: Mass-market newspapers cover politics in a more personalized way than upmarket newspapers.

In line with the idea of commercial pressure, we can expect that, on a media system level, more competition can lead to more personalized coverage. This expectation can be measured by the number of television channels with a media market or by the number of national dailies. It seems plausible that, in media-saturated democracies, journalists and political actors are trying to gain readers and visibility by personalizing (and even more, by intimating) politics (Stanyer 2013).

H4: The higher the number of national television channels, the higher the degree of personalized coverage.
H5: The higher the number of paid national dailies, the higher the degree of personalized coverage.

Previous studies have referred to the political system to explain country differences but have been unable to identify what exactly drives personalized coverage. We can expect that news coverage of politics reflects a country's political power structures to a large extent (Wolfsfeld 2011), meaning that, in countries with more political institutions (multilevel of governance, multiparty system, etc.), the chance is higher that coverage is less personalized. In their comparative study of international news coverage in six countries, Balmas and Sheafer (2013) found that the coverage of countries with a two-party system is more personalized than those with multiparty systems. In the same line, we argue that, in federal countries, which are characterized by some form of multilevel government, attention to institutions is higher. In these countries, power is shared among multiple actors and not concentrated in the hands of a few individuals. The degree of federalism relates to one of the two central dimensions in *Patterns of Democracy*, the seminal work of Lijphart (1999, 2012), distinguishing between countries where power is centralized and countries where power is shared. The electoral system is an important feature in Lijphart's study and may also play a role in news coverage. The main distinction in the literature is between majoritarian systems (the candidate who wins the highest number of votes 'takes it all') and proportional representation systems (Lijphart 2012, p. 130). More personalized coverage may be expected in countries with majority electoral systems, where the greater focus is on single candidates, than in countries with proportional representation, where emphasis may be placed more on the different parties. Also, countries that have a mixed-member electoral system, such as Germany, have a higher degree of personalization (Zittel and Gschwend 2008), which might lead to more personalized media coverage. The electoral system has a clear impact on the number of parties, with proportional representation leading to more parties in parliament overall (Farrell 2001). More parties mean a greater division of power, spreading it over more actors, and may lead to less personalized coverage.

> H6: The more centralized (or the less federal) the political system, the higher the degree of personalized coverage.
> H7: The level of personalized coverage is higher in majoritarian or mixed electoral systems compared with systems that have list proportional representation.

Data and methodology

We carry out comparative content analyses of the political news in 16 countries. Our data set contains a selection of news items from newspapers, television news, and online news sites in routine periods. For more information on the data, see Chapter 2.

For each news item, the first five actors were coded. We used an elaborate code scheme for all types of actors, including domestic and international political actors as well as nonpolitical actors. Furthermore, each actor had to be mentioned at least twice in the news item. In this way, we ensured that the political actors who were included in our analyses were prominent in the news item and not merely mentioned on the side. In total, almost 29,000 actors were coded. Our analyses will focus almost exclusively on the 60 percent national political actors.

In an attempt to explain the extent of personalized coverage in each country, we have constructed two main dependent variables. The first measures individualized coverage of politics, with a focus on the general visibility of politicians versus all institutions. This variable is the sum of the number of individual politicians mentioned in the news item (between 0–5) minus the number of institutions mentioned in the news item (0–5). The second variable deals with concentrated visibility; that is, the relative focus on the head of government or the head of state. Because the number of leaders is limited to one or two, it is impossible to construct this variable as the first. Hence, it represents a simple ratio of the number of items that mention the leader out of the total items that were analyzed.

In line with the previous chapters, we test for three independent media variables: television type (commercial vs. public), newspaper type (mass-market vs. upmarket), and online news. As main indicators of market concentration and competition orientation in the media system, we use the number of paid national dailies and the number of national television channels.

Three independent political variables were used. The first one is the effective number of parties in the parliament as an indicator of *pluralism* in the political system. The second explores the level of *federalism* in countries. This variable is based on the index (range 1–5) developed by Lijphart (2012). It distinguishes between political systems where the national governments are sovereign relative to their territorial units (1) and full federalism, which are systems where responsibilities are shared between national authorities and semiautonomous regional units (5). The third is a nominal variable that represents the electoral system. It distinguishes between list proportional representation systems (0) and majority or mixed systems (1).

The unit of analysis is the media outlet within a country. As there are 10 outlets within each of the 16 countries analyzed here, the N is 160. Since media outlets are nested within countries, we conduct linear regressions with robust standard errors (see Chapter 2). Before we turn to the explanatory analyses of personalized news coverage, we discuss the descriptive results showing the attention that is focused on politicians and on the main institutions across countries.

Descriptive results

Actors in the news

In general, we see that about 8 percent of actors are nondomestic. This low number is mainly a consequence of our focus on national political news; we only selected those stories that included a domestic political actor (see Chapter 2 for details). As a consequence, these results tell us little about the share of international actors

118 Peter Van Aelst et al.

Table 8.1 Type of actors in domestic political news

	International (%)	National (%)		Total number of actors
		Nonpolitical	Political	
Austria	10.8	27.5	61.8	1,847
Belgium	4.2	40.6	55.3	1,631
Denmark	6.3	31.4	62.3	1,792
France	2.9	28.2	68.9	2,098
Germany	13.7	30.0	56.3	1,933
Greece	11.3	9.3	79.5	1,822
Israel	4.8	50.8	44.4	2,008
Italy	7.2	18.7	74.1	1,659
Netherlands	8.9	26.6	64.5	1,776
Norway	3.2	34.6	62.2	1,591
Portugal	7.7	39.4	52.9	2,011
Spain	8.9	39.2	51.8	2,090
Sweden	4.4	29.6	66.0	1,062
Switzerland	8.5	35.0	56.4	1,370
UK	12.8	34.4	52.8	2,012
US	7.1	43.6	49.3	2,136
Total	**7.8**	**32.8**	**59.4**	**28,838**

in the news since few 'real' international news stories were included. In some cases, the high number of international actors is related to the country's economic situation (e.g., Greece). In such news items, international institutions, including the European Union and the International Monetary Fund (together 6 percent), are often present. Politicians in other, larger countries such as the United Kingdom and Germany seem to play more prominent roles on the international scene, and therefore, more foreign news is domesticated. In France, the low presence of international actors can be related to the process of new government formation and to several domestic issues that dominated the news (e.g., gay marriage).

We coded the first five actors in the news, and not all domestic actors are political. Almost one-third of actors are nonpolitical actors, including ordinary citizens, companies, civil servants, and police officers. Again, we see large country variation in the presence of these nonpolitical actors. For instance, in Israel, ordinary (nonorganized) citizens (13 percent) and police and military forces (8 percent) are much more prominent compared to other countries. In Greece, to the contrary, the percentage of nonpolitical actors is low, which might be a reflection of the fiscal crisis that expanded into the political world. In the remainder of this chapter, we will mainly focus on the largest category of domestic political actors, including both individual politicians and political institutions (government, parliament, parties, and ministries).

General visibility: individuals versus institutions

In general, in most countries, a small majority of actors are individuals (54 percent), and this share grows when we include political actors only (61 percent). These figures mean that the news coverage of political actors is more personalized than the news coverage of all actors that are featured in political news stories (e.g., interest groups, companies). With six out of ten political actors being persons, political news is indeed personalized, but institutions and groups[1] still play a visible role. The most important institutions are political parties (43 percent of all references to national political institutions) and government institutions (35 percent).

As shown in Figure 8.1, the variation in the degree of personalization between countries is extensive. Clearly, in countries such as Italy and the United Kingdom, the news is most personalized, with three out of four political actors being an individual. The news is mostly about politicians and not so much about parties and governments. The opposite is true in Switzerland and Spain, where political institutions are more present than individual politicians. In the case of Switzerland, this result has partly to do with the absence of a real prime minister and the government working as a collective unity. Kriesi's longitudinal study (2012) also showed that campaign coverage is generally less personalized in Switzerland compared to other countries. In Spain, it is remarkable that the news often

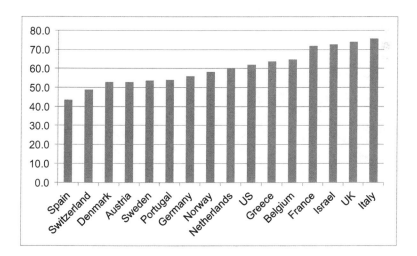

Figure 8.1 Percentage of individual actors versus institutions or groups.

120   Peter Van Aelst et al.

refers to specific ministries but less to the responsible minister. For instance, the Ministry of Social Affairs is twice as often an actor in the news as the minister (90 versus 46 mentions). Given the United States' presidential system, it is often considered a highly personalized country, but this belief is not supported by our data. The general visibility of persons versus institutions in the US media is unexceptional compared to other European countries.

Most attention in domestic political news is devoted to the executive. In general, government actors receive about 40 percent of all the attention paid to national political actors (see Table 8.2). In countries such as the United Kingdom, Israel, and Portugal, government actors represent even more than half of the actors in the news, and in Spain, the attention paid to the government is three-quarters of all actors.

The degree of personalized coverage of government actors is calculated by dividing the attention given to persons who are active in the government by the attention given to government institutions. Again, the variation of countries is large and mainly in line with the general level of personalized coverage. In

Table 8.2 Attention for government actors and ratio of persons versus institutions in government

	Attention for all government actors[a] (%)	*Ratio government person/institutions*
UK	58.4	4.85
Italy	28.1	3.86
France	37.0	3.50
Belgium	42.4	2.78
Israel	53.4	2.64
Greece	36.1	2.42
Germany	32.2	2.41
Netherlands	31.2	2.28
Austria	26.9	1.98
US	42.3	1.69
Denmark	38.2	1.47
Norway	44.6	1.45
Portugal	56.1	1.14
Sweden	23.2	1.01
Switzerland	25.5	1.01
Spain	74.1	.88
Average	40.7	1.91

a $N = 17,147$.

countries such as Italy, France, and the United Kingdom, the media focus more than three times as much on persons in government rather than on the government in general or government ministries. In Spain, Switzerland, and Sweden, government is as much or more about institutions than about the people leading the government.

Besides governments, political parties are also central players in Western democracies. Although political parties have been challenged by growing voter dealignment and decreasing membership, they have maintained a strong position, particularly in multiparty systems (Dalton, McAllister, and Wattenberg 2000; Van Biezen, Mair, and Poguntke 2012). This established position is reflected in most countries' news coverage – in particular, the Nordic countries and central European countries, such as the Netherlands and Austria. In the United Kingdom, the United States, and Israel, parties have a remarkably low share of media attention. In general, politicians are almost four times more visible than parties. In the United Kingdom, the United States, and Israel, references to politicians happen about ten times as often as references to parties (see Table 8.3). In the United Kingdom and the United States, this overrepresentation can be related to the low number of parties (two and a half and two, respectively).

Table 8.3 Attention for political parties and ratio of politicians versus parties

	Attention for parties (%)	Ratio politicians/ parties
Israel	6.0	12.12
UK	7.3	10.14
US	7.3	9.35
France	11.5	6.24
Italy	14.2	5.34
Portugal	14.0	3.86
Germany	14.9	3.75
Spain	12.7	3.42
Belgium	19.1	3.39
Norway	17.8	3.27
Sweden	29.7	3.25
Greece	22.4	2.84
Netherlands	22.2	2.71
Denmark	24.6	2.15
Austria	26.1	2.03
Switzerland	15.0	1.80
Average	**16.5**	**3.72**

Concentrated visibility: focus on leaders

To what extent is the news focused on a few leading politicians? In most countries under study, the prime minister or president is the most powerful political actor and therefore also the most visible person in the news. Again, the degree to which the head of government[2] dominates the news varies strongly across countries. The visibility of the government leader is compared to the visibility of all domestic political actors most outspoken in the United States, United Kingdom, and Israel. Barack Obama (19 percent), David Cameron (17 percent), and Benjamin Netanyahu (17 percent) are even more visible than the French president, François Hollande (12 percent). This lower visibility probably has to do with the division of governmental power in France, which is shared between the president and the prime minister. When both are taken into account, the concentrated visibility of France rises to 18 percent (see Table 8.4). Still, this result is much lower than Kriesi (2012) found in his comparative campaign study, where the semipresidential system of France was far more personalized than those of other countries. This difference might be related to the extreme focus on the main candidates in French presidential elections. Additionally, Hollande's intention at the beginning of his presidency to be a less 'omnipresent' president (compared to Sarkozy) might have influenced news coverage. And at the time of the analysis, the major opposition party (UMP) was in a leadership crisis after internal elections. Italy, which showed the highest degree of personalization in general, had slightly lower concentrated visibility scores. This lower focus on the leader might be partly due to the specific prime minister at the time under study; Mario Monti was not elected but was leading an expert cabinet.

As shown in Table 8.4, concentrated visibility is lowest in traditional consensus democracies such as Switzerland, Austria, and Belgium.[4] These countries have fragmented multiparty systems and high levels of federalism, leading to a greater division of power over multiple actors. The extremely low score in Switzerland is due to the government coalition and rotating leadership that are specific to it, which means that there is actually no real prime minister. Observing the number of articles dealing with prime ministers or heads of state reveals a more contrasted picture. In traditional majoritarian countries such as France, the United Kingdom, and the United States, a more than one-third of the articles cover this actor, whereas the articles number less than one out of ten in some of the typical consensus democracies.

Explanations of personalized coverage

To *explain* the extent of personalized coverage, we use two main dependent variables: (1) general visibility, which is the relative focus on individual politicians out of the total coverage of individual politicians and political institutions, and (2) concentrated visibility, or the relative focus on government leaders. We introduced

Table 8.4 Attention for head of government and head of state

	% that head of government or state[3] is an actor (on total of all political actors[a])	% that head of government and state are actors (on total of all political actors[a])	% of articles[b] with head of government as actor
US	18.8	18.8	43.9
UK	17.0	17.8	37.1
Israel	16.8	20.2	37.9
France	12.0	18.0	34.1
Italy	10.7	14.4	26.6
Germany	9.1	11.7	22.1
Netherlands	9.1	9.4	24.1
Greece	8.6	9.7	23.0
Spain	7.8	8.4	16.8
Norway	7.7	8.8	18.2
Portugal	6.9	11.2	14.4
Denmark	6.4	6.6	16.1
Sweden	4.8	4.8	12.6
Belgium	3.7	4.5	8.6
Austria	2.6	3.9	6.7
Switzerland	1.3	1.3	2.9
Total	**8.6**	**10.4**	**22.2**

a $N = 17,147$.
b $N = 7,106$.

several possible explanations earlier for the extent of personalized coverage. We use media organizational variables to clarify intracountry differences (H1–H3) and then introduce characteristics of the media system (H4–H5) and political system (H6–H7) to explain differences between the 16 countries. Before we turn to our multivariate analyses, we have a brief look at the bivariate correlations between the relevant variables. In general, Table 8.5 shows that outlet variables are hardly correlated with either type of personalized coverage, whereas the country variables seem much more relevant. Both media and political system variables are strongly correlated to general visibility and concentrated visibility in the news. The correlations for both types of personalization show a similar, but not identical, pattern. They have a bivariate correlation of .60. Next, we turn to our regression analyses for a more rigid test of their importance.

124 Peter Van Aelst et al.

Table 8.5 Correlations between general and concentrated visibility, type of media organization, and national factors related to media and political systems[a]

	General visibility	Concentrated visibility
Public service TV	.009	−.083
Commercial TV	.033	.058
Upmarket newspaper	−.165*	.009
Mass-market newspaper	.160*	.014
Online website	−.007	−.023
Number of national TV stations	.306**	.635**
Number of paid national dailies	.096	.173*
Level of federalism	−.237**	−.159*
Electoral system	.310**	.536**
N	160	160

a Entries are Pearson's R.
* $p < .05$, ** $p < .01$.

General visibility: individual politicians versus institutions

The focus on individual politicians (versus political institutions) is the most basic measure of personalized media coverage of politics. First, we expected that television news would be more personalized than newspaper and website coverage. Individual actors are indeed slightly more present in television news (64 percent) than in newspapers (60 percent), but the difference is not significant (not in table). Newspapers favor individuals before institutions, and television news, in turn, devotes substantial attention to the main political institutions. When we further distinguish between media organizations, we see that the difference in degree of general visibility between commercial (65 percent) and public television (62 percent) is also modest and not significant. The difference between mass-market newspapers (66 percent) and upmarket newspapers (58 percent) is more discernable. Our regression Model 1 in Table 8.6 confirms that broadsheet newspapers differ significantly from the other media types (H3). We do not find support for Hypothesis 2 regarding type of television ownership. Model 2 points out that online media are neither more nor less personalized than traditional media. This finding is in line with recent studies showing that websites do not change the form of the news, whether in the direction of more commercialization or less (Benson et al. 2012).

When entering the country variables in Model 3, we see that only one variable is significant – the level of federalism. The number of national television stations and the number of newspapers in a country – important indicators for the degree

Personalization 125

Table 8.6 Explanations of general visibility (individual politicians versus institutions)[a,b]

	Model 1 B	Model 1 Robust standard error	Model 2 B	Model 2 Robust standard error	Model 3 B	Model 3 Robust standard error
Commercial TV	.028	.060	.028	.060	.028	.061
Mass-market newspaper	.174	.090	.174	.090	.174	.090
Upmarket newspaper	−.126*	.054	−.126*	.054	−.126*	.055
Online website			−.008	.083	−.008	.085
Number of national TV stations					.000	.000
Number of paid national dailies					−.038	.053
Level of federalism					−.158*	.065
Electoral system					.380	.307
Constant	.542***	.114	.546***	.104	.716	.493
R^2		.038		.038		.269
N		160		160		160

a OLS regression with robust standard errors.
b Public television is the reference category for the media type.
* $p < .05$, ** $p < .01$, *** $p < .001$.

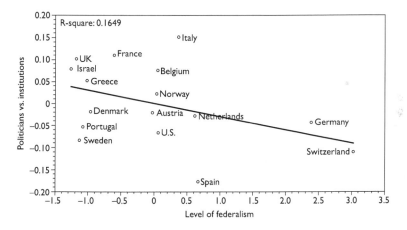

Figure 8.2 Relative attention to individual politicians (general visibility). $N = 16$; $R^2 = .16$ for the level of federalism.

of commercialization of the media system – turn out not to be significant. The impacts of the number of national television stations (H4) and of the electoral system (H7) go in the expected direction but are not significant.[5] Figure 8.2 presents a partial plot ($N = 16$ countries) that demonstrates the impact of the level

126 Peter Van Aelst et al.

of federalism on the dependent variable while holding the other independent variable constant. As can be seen in the regression line in Figure 8.2, the more federalist a country, the lower the personalized coverage. This finding might be mainly related to the higher number of institutions that are part of multilevel governance structures. Yet, the countries are clearly not comfortably aligned around the regression lines; other central effects on personalized coverage appear not to be accounted for in our analysis.

Concentrated visibility: the focus on government leader

As in the case of individual politicians versus institutions, the media outlet variables prove to be relatively unimportant in explaining the attention given to the government leader (which is a common operationalization of concentrated media personalization). Only commercial television presents more personalized coverage compared with public television (H2). Turning to the country variables, we see that a combination of politics-related and media-related variables is at work. As can be seen in Table 8.7, at the national level, the variable found to account best for variations within the dependent variable is, again, the level of federalism (H6). The

Table 8.7 Explanations of concentrated visibility (presence of government leader)[a,b]

	Model 1		Model 2		Model 3	
	B	Robust standard error	B	Robust standard error	B	Robust standard error
Commercial TV	.037*	.016	.037*	.015	.037*	.016
Mass-market newspaper	.025	.016	.025	.015	.025	.016
Upmarket newspaper	.023	.017	.023	.017	−.023	.017
Online website			−.006	.013	−.006	.013
Number of national TV stations					.000***	.000
Number of paid national dailies					−.002	.013
Level of federalism					−.033**	.010
Electoral system					.057	.042
Constant	.193***	.026	.196***	.024	.179	.104
R^2		.008		.009		.538
N		160		160		160

a OLS regression with robust standard errors.
b Public television is the reference category for the media type.
* $p < .05$, ** $p < .01$, *** $p < .001$.

number of national television stations (H4) also has a significant impact on the dependent variable. Again, the hypotheses on the number of newspapers and the electoral system are not supported (although the hypothesis on the effect of the electoral system is supported when excluding outliers). We will elaborate on this finding in the conclusion.

Similarly to the first figure, Figure 8.3 presents partial plots ($N = 16$ countries) that demonstrate the impact of each of the two significant national-level independent variables (the level of federalism and the number of national television

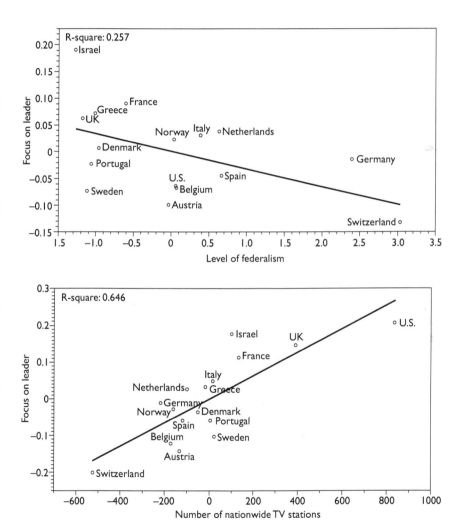

Figure 8.3 Relative attention to government leaders. $N = 16$; $R^2 = .30$ for the level of federalism; $R^2 = .66$ for the number of national television stations.

channels) on the dependent variable while holding the other independent variable constant. As can be seen in the regression lines in Figure 8.3, the more federalized a country, the lower the personalized coverage, and the larger the number of television channels in a country, the greater the focus on national leaders. These figures show us the effect of both centralization (Israel, France, Greece, and the United Kingdom in the first graph) and competition for large nationwide audiences (mainly the United Kingdom and the United States) on the mediatization of top leaders. As earlier, the graphs clearly show that the impact of the dependent variables on the relative focus on government leaders still leaves much to be desired.

Discussion and conclusions

Our comparative news study shows that, in general, individual politicians are more prominent in the news compared to political institutions. The degree of personalized political coverage, however, varies strongly across countries. For instance, in Italy and the United Kingdom, in three out of four cases, the central actor in the news is an individual politician. Conversely, in Spain and Switzerland, this figure is less than half. When we focus only on government leaders, similar (but not identical) variation among countries emerges. The United States demonstrates the difference between both types of personalized coverage. It is characterized by an average degree of general visibility but has the highest degree of concentrated visibility. This result shows that it is important to distinguish between general and concentrated visibility when studying personalization in the news.

It appears that both political and media system variables account for such differences, but identifying the central variables that explain variation in a systematic way continues to be difficult. Our study shows that at least two country characteristics matter: the number of television channels and the degree of federalism. Clearly, political features also influence the degree of personalized coverage. Our analyses show that the degree of federalism helps to explain country differences. Federalism is one of the two central dimensions in Lijphart's work (2012) and distinguishes between countries where power is centralized and those where power is shared among multiple actors. Our study suggests that, in typical federal systems (Belgium and Switzerland), news is less personalized than in centralized and presidential systems (e.g., France and the United Kingdom). The electoral system correlated positively with both types of personalized coverage. Although this variable's impact did not prove to be significant in the general regression models, its impact became significant whenever outlier cases were excluded from the analysis. Probably the explanatory impact of the electoral system is more obvious when studying election campaigns. This reason might explain why, for instance, the visibility of the French president was high, but not in the exceptional way it was in Kriesi's (2012) campaign study.

Second, it is apparent from our analyses that the number of television channels within a country plays a central role in explaining the centralized form of personalized political coverage. (As noted, the impact of this variable was found to be significant on general visibility after excluding outliers from the analysis.) Is television, therefore, a medium that is more prone to coverage of a few 'political celebrities'? While this assumption sounds logical (one would expect television to prefer individuals over abstract organizations), the data does not necessarily support it. In ten countries, television's focus on the main political leader (prime minister or head of state) is higher than in the other six, but the difference is only significant in Norway. In the six other countries, concentrated visibility is higher in newspapers compared to television, but again the effects are insignificant. Rather than the medium, therefore, the competition among television channels may be the force that drives personalized coverage. Or, put differently, in more competitive media environments, news organizations might be more inclined to use personalized coverage to attract a larger audience.

We also note that, in the case of France, Israel, and the United Kingdom as well as Switzerland, these relationships seem to be cumulative. Media systems and political systems must certainly be considered together (Strömbäck and Dimitrova 2011). Neither the media system nor the political system is solely able to explain the variation of actors' personalization in political news coverage. The precise interplay of these system characteristics, however, remains unclear. For example, there is little evidence that Hallin and Mancini's media system classification (2004) explains the variation. The most personalized and competition affected news coverage is coming from a variety of countries. But as we previously argued (Van Aelst et al. 2012), following Hallin and Mancini's seminal, explanatory study, we still need additional studies to explore the determinants of personalization. We believe that at least two paths of further research are worth developing. First, better indicators are necessary to explain country variation. The number of institutions likely plays a role but so do their magnitude or political impact. For instance, we lack a measure of the actual strength of the institutions that take part in the political process, such as political parties. Second, our study focused on 'normal' political news in routine periods. This focus is in contrast to most previous work dealing with campaign periods. Combining both periods in a longitudinal perspective would surely serve to improve our understanding of their different dynamics.

Notes

1 Also, references to a collection of individual politicians such as 'members of parliament' or 'several politicians of the opposition' were considered as a group.
2 Also, mentions of the prime minister in his/her function as party leader are included. In some countries (e.g., the Netherlands), this happens frequently.
3 In most countries the Prime Minister is considered as the head of government, except for Switzerland, France and the United States where we have taken the president as the main political actor.

4 In Belgium, the visibility of the French-speaking prime minister, Elio Di Rupo, is also low since we only included the Flemish (Dutch-speaking) media in our study.
5 When outlier cases are excluded from the analysis (using Cook's D statistics; seven outliers where found and excluded), the impact of the number of national television stations and of the electoral system become significant and in the expected direction in line with H4 (the higher the number of national television stations, the greater the personalized coverage) and H7 (the level of personalized coverage is higher in majoritarian or mixed electoral systems compared with systems that have list proportional representation). The impact of the level of federalism continues to be significant in that analysis.

Chapter 9

Hard and soft news

Carsten Reinemann, James Stanyer,
and Sebastian Scherr

Introduction

In recent years, the seemingly dichotomous distinction between hard and soft news has become widely used to capture developments of news coverage in various countries around the world. Some scholars see the softening of news as an example of the damaging effects of commercialization on the quality of journalism, and they fear negative consequences for democratic discourse. In contrast, others point to possible positive effects of soft news, such as the inclusion of audiences usually less interested in political affairs (for a synoptic account, see Reinemann, Stanyer, Scherr, and Legnante 2012). However, despite the concept's popularity, no consensus exists on its definition, and internationally comparative research and large-scale systematic comparisons are few and far between. Due to these problems, the factors that determine the character of news items remain obscure. Against this backdrop, this chapter investigates the character of the news using a multidimensional approach inspired by Reinemann and colleagues (2012). They use three dimensions to distinguish harder from softer news: (1) the political substance of the matter covered (*topic dimension*), (2) specific aspects of emphasized events or topics (*focus dimension*), and (3) the way events or topics are presented (*style dimension*). Moreover, they argue that the topic dimension forms the bedrock on which the other dimensions rest. This chapter seeks to explain differences in the character of news between countries and news outlets drawing on this model. It starts by examining the relevant literature to identify the factors that may help to explain the hard or soft character of political news across the media outlets and countries investigated here.

Explaining the character of news

Media output is shaped by a series of interconnected factors. Existing models mostly distinguish between characteristics of culture, nations, political or media systems (*macro-level*), media organizations or journalistic working routines (*meso-level*), and individual journalists (*micro-level*) (e.g., Hanitzsch and Donsbach 2012; Shoemaker and Vos 2009). Past research has found that factors of all levels may influence news work and news output (e.g., Esser and Strömbäck 2012b; Pfetsch and Esser 2014). However, prior research has also clearly shown that contexts beyond the individual limit the impact of personal characteristics to a very large extent (see, e.g., Reinemann and Baugut 2014). Because of that limitation, we will concentrate on macro- and meso-level factors.

Some authors, however, have pointed out that patterns of news coverage cannot be fully explained on the basis of stable structural factors. Instead, they argue that these factors only shape the way journalists *typically* see the world when making decisions. These factors, therefore, represent the more or less *stable* or *structural criteria* relevant for news production. But besides these criteria, actual events and real-world developments with their specific characteristics (*news factors*) have to be taken into account when explaining news coverage at specific points in time. What coverage looks like in a certain country or news outlet, then, depends upon the specific *interaction* of stable criteria and situational contexts. One concept describing this interaction is the *two-component model of news making* that integrates situational, event-centered (*news value theory*) and media-centered explanations of news making (*news bias, gatekeeping theory*) (Kepplinger and Ehmig 2006; Reinemann and Baugut 2014). The concept of *event-driven news* draws on a similar idea. Here, typical patterns of coverage might be overturned during extraordinary events, which, for example, might open up windows of opportunity for nonelite actors that typically do not get heard in the media (Lawrence 2000b; Shehata 2007).

Structural factors

On the meso-level of news outlets, the few comparative studies show that commercial television and mass-market newspapers (tabloids) generally carry more soft news topics than public service television and elite-oriented, upmarket newspapers (broadsheets) (Aalberg, Van Aelst, and Curran 2010; Brekken, Thorbjørnsrud, and Aalberg 2012; Curran, Coen, Aalberg, and Iyengar 2012; Curran, Salovaara-Moring, Coen, and Iyengar 2010). These differences also hold true for the framing of news. Overall, elite newspapers and public service broadcasting (PSB) newscasts were found to offer more thematic news, whereas tabloids and commercial television contained more episodic news (Brekken et al. 2012, pp. 76–77). The main reason for these differences is that media differ in their target audiences or regulatory requirements to provide more, thematically oriented, detached, and rather complex political news. Media that are not obligated to provide a lot of hard news, or whose audiences are not politically interested, focus more on softer issues, or they use more episodic, personalized, and emotional ways to present the news.

Besides these differences, some open questions remain. First, it is not clear from extant research whether television news generally produces softer news than the press. Second, we do not know whether there are systematic differences between offline and online media. On the one hand, some scholars argue that the unlimited space in online media may give journalists the opportunity to produce more high-quality background reporting that cannot be printed offline. On the other hand, the character of the Internet as a pull-medium might be an incentive for online editions to publish more tabloid, easy-to-consume, immediate-reward news. However, studies directly comparing online and offline media are scarce, include few media, and come to contradictory conclusions (e.g., D'Haenens, Jankowski, and Heuvelmann 2004; Quandt 2008). That said, one recent comprehensive study of German television newscasts, newspapers, magazines, and email news did not find systematic differences between online and offline editions (Oschatz, Maurer, and Haßler 2014, pp. 37–38). According to the authors, financial restrictions in online newsrooms, common working practices across departments, and similar audiences of online and offline editions are responsible for this high degree of similarity.

At the macro-level, some scholars argue that the amount of media regulation may affect the character of news because regulation often refers to measures establishing and keeping alive public service–oriented media, which then provides a harder news diet. Aalberg and colleagues (2010) and Brekken and colleagues (2012) found support for these assumptions. In addition, media market structures might affect news organizations' reporting because the media system as a whole constitutes the environment for media competition and journalistic co-orientation. Market structure might therefore affect not only news standards within journalism but also audience expectations as to what news should be like and what it should cover. Thus, a commercialized media environment dominated by soft news could lower the level of hard news in elite or public service media, too. In contrast, strong PSBs might positively affect the amount of hard news in a given media system because they contribute to a political information environment that favors hard news standards of reporting and molds expectations of news audiences accordingly. Again, Brekken and colleagues (2012) found support for these assumptions. They concluded that, in countries with strong PSB and low media commercialization, people get more hard news. Along the same lines, a high importance of the press, and particularly the quality press, in a given country might foster a general preference for hard news among audiences. And finally, a very straightforward connection is likely between the general cost of producing hard news and the amount of such news in media coverage in a country. The more costly the production of hard news, the more incentives the media have to refer to easy-to-produce stories that do not need too much time, money, and personnel.

Environmental factors

Large N comparative studies usually look for rather general patterns that tend not be affected by specific events occurring in the time period under investigation. However, when it comes to hard and soft news, it seems necessary to also take into account the situational, real-world contexts of the countries, especially when the contexts differ considerably and for a longer time. The reason is that exceptional circumstances might overthrow the usual patterns of reporting and confine the influences that would usually guide media reporting across media systems or within certain media. The present study takes into account some of these real-world factors, such as the economic crisis that affected some countries more than others. We included some basic indicators of a country's economic situation to control for its possible impact on the amount of hard versus soft news. In addition, we also included two measures of the situational political context. First, prior research has shown that the character of news might vary over the course of the electoral cycle. More specifically, politicians are more active in pursuit of publicity immediately before a general election, and journalists are keen to report the latest political negotiations in its aftermath. Therefore, before and immediately after elections, media coverage is usually more intense than in periods further away from elections (e.g., Walgrave and Van Aelst 2006). We controlled for the time lag between our study period and the most recent general election in each country. Second, we draw upon an argument put forward by Nir (2012) and others concerning possible effects of the number of parties in parliament. She suggests that a higher number of parties increases political competition and leads to more communicative efforts by the parties. This situation might result in higher shares of hard news in the media. Taking Nir's argument on board, we controlled for the number of effective parties in parliament (ENP).

Research questions and hypotheses

As the literature review shows, any explanation of differences needs to explore an array of variables at the organizational and national levels and the relationships between them – including structural factors and more changeable factors reflecting important aspects of a country's political and economic situation. Insights from the literature were crucial in helping us formulate a series of hypotheses. First of all, we wanted to know whether there were systematic differences between newspapers, television, and websites. Here, we were especially interested in whether news in the online environment is harder or softer than news in offline media. Good arguments support differing views on this question. On the one hand, the online environment might provide the unlimited editorial space that is needed to do in-depth reporting of political issues. On other hand, the patterns of media use in online environments might be an incentive for journalists to focus even more on the softer side of politics because the speed of users' decisions favors 'immediate-reward' items (Reinemann et al. 2012). Based on the latter argument, we hypothesize:

> H1: Offline versions of newspapers and television news will report more hard news than their online versions.

The next set of hypotheses regards possible influences exerted at the organizational level. In line with the existing literature and findings, we argue that the commercial character of a news outlet, its orientation towards certain audiences, and the editorial space available affect the amount of hard news reporting. We therefore propose the following hypotheses:

> H2: Quality or upmarket newspapers and PSB broadcasters report more hard news than tabloid mass-market newspapers and commercial broadcasters.
> H3: Elite upmarket newspapers report more hard news than mass-market newspapers.
> H4: Public service broadcasters (offline/online) report more hard news than commercial broadcasters (offline/online).

At the macro-level, we suggest that various country characteristics might have an impact upon the amount of hard news. Here, we differentiate between more stable characteristics of the media system and indicators that reflect the countries' current political and economic situations. More specifically, on the basis of the literature reviewed, we hypothesized that three characteristics of the media system will help to explain media preferences for hard or soft news:

> H5: The lower the production costs of hard news in a country, the more hard news will be reported in that country's news media.
> H6: The higher the number of paid-for daily newspapers in a country, the more hard news will be reported in that country's news media.
> H7: The higher the audience share of public service broadcasters in the television market of a country, the more hard news will be reported in that country's news media.

Moreover, we investigate another set of hypotheses that are related to possible effects of the political and economic situation vis-à-vis organizational and media system factors. These factors can also be located at the macro-level but are more situational than the rather stable organizational and media system factors.

> H8: The more negative the economic situation of a country, the more hard news will be reported in that country's news media.
> H9: The closer the sampling period to a national election, the more hard news will be reported in that country's news media.
> H10: The more intense the political competition in a country, the more hard news will be reported in that country's news media.

Method and operationalization

To test our hypotheses, we conducted a comparative content analysis of the leading news media in 16 Western democracies. We analyzed political news items in the main sections, excluding regional, local, motor, fashion, sports, science, travel, and culture (for details, see the methods chapter, Chapter 2).

Operationalizations

While most existing studies used a single dimension to differentiate hard from soft news, the present study uses the multidimensional approach recommended by Reinemann and colleagues (2012). We concentrate on two dimensions – namely, the topic and the style dimensions. In this chapter, we exclude the *focus dimension*, given insufficient reliability scores for this dimension. In line with Reinemann and colleagues (2012), in the *topic dimension*, we differentiated between different degrees of political relevance. In terms of the *style dimension*, we distinguish between reports that included verbal or visual emotion-arousing elements and reports that did not include such elements. More details can be found in Chapter 2.

Dependent measure: hard and soft news index

For a continuous measure of the hard versus soft character of news items, we calculated an index variable that represents both the topic and style dimension of a given news item. Five variables were included in the index: the mention of (1) political actors, (2) decision-making authorities, (3) policy plans, and (4) affected groups (each coded as 0 = not present or 1 = present) and whether an article was predominantly unemotional (coded as 0), balanced (1), or predominantly emotional (2). As a first step, we applied a Principal Component Analysis, in which items were retained if their component loading was .40 or higher on one, and only one, factor (Principal Component Analysis with Promax rotation; variance explained = 47.3%; KMO = .719; Bartlett's test $p < .001$). Overall, PCA showed a single component structure of the hard and soft news index. Thus, we transformed all indicators of a hard or soft news story into an additive index. The index theoretically ranges from 0 ("story contains no hard news indicators") to 6 ("story contains all hard news indicators"). Bearing the large-scale comparative context of this study in mind, the index shows an overall acceptable internal consistency indicated by a Cronbach's alpha of .65.

Independent variables

For the independent variables, we used media system- and political system-level indicators, together with media organization- and event-level characteristics. They were collected from various sources (for details, see the chapter on independent variables, Chapter 3). At the event level, we included the number of months from the date of coding to the last national election and the unemployment rate. At the media system level, we included the number of paid-for daily newspapers per 1,000 adults, PSB share, and adspend as a percentage of GDP. At the media organization level, we included the production costs of news and whether an outlet was online or not, whether it was public service channel or not, and whether it was an upmarket newspaper or not. At the political system level, we used the number of parties in parliament.

Data analysis

The first part of the analysis provides a descriptive overview of hard and soft news in the 16 democracies under investigation. We differentiate between the share of hard and soft news for public service broadcasters and commercial broadcasters, for online and offline media, and for broadsheet and tabloid newspapers. We then test our correlational hypotheses using bivariate analyses. Finally, we include selected organizational and macro-level characteristics in a lean, stepwise linear regression model in order to predict the hard and soft character of different news outlets.

The presence of hard and soft news in Western democracies

Taking a look at the presence of the five hard news indicators, it becomes apparent that political reporting is mostly factual, with the share of detached, formally unemotional reporting accounting for an average of almost two-thirds of all news items across countries. However, the four other indicators of political substance are less visible in political coverage. For example, on average, political authorities are mentioned in 63 percent of the news items, political actors in 62 percent, the substance of a policy plan or program in about half of the news items, and the groups actually affected by a plan or decision in not more than 39 percent of news items. Moreover, political coverage looks significantly different in the countries under investigation with respect to all five indicators.

Especially interesting is the emphasis placed on the different aspects of politics in each country's media. Four groups of countries can be distinguished on the basis of a cluster analysis. Denmark, Norway, Switzerland, and Spain put an above-average emphasis on all indicators of political substance but give especially high attention to the substance of decisions and the groups affected. Austria, the Netherlands, Portugal, and the United Kingdom stand out because of their special focus on actors and their above-average attention to decision-making authorities. Belgium, France, Germany, Greece, and Sweden make up the average group, with no single aspect standing out in comparison to the cross-country averages. Finally, Israel, Italy, and the United States rank especially low in addressing all of the four indicators of political substance. Most notably, the groups affected by political decisions are only mentioned in one-fifth of the articles or less (Table 9.1).

But what do the results look like when we analyze the indicators of hard and soft news together? First of all, the average index value for all items analyzed was $M = 3.79$ ($SD = 1.68$), with individual news items spanning the whole range of index values. Three percent of news items had no indication of hard news whatsoever, whereas 18 percent reached the full value of the hard and soft news index. Overall, hard news is more likely to be found in certain kinds of journalistic formats, whereas other formats are more likely to carry soft news. A one-way

138 Carsten Reinemann et al.

Table 9.1 Presence of hard news indicators in news items across countries (percentages)

	(N)	Topic dimension				Style dimension
		Authorities mentioned[a]	Societal actors mentioned[b]	Substance of decision mentioned[c]	Affected groups mentioned[d]	Unemotional reporting[e]
Austria	(476)	59	86	62	39	75
Belgium	(488)	65	54	59	42	92
Denmark	(483)	73	43	69	58	82
France	(534)	40	39	52	40	60
Germany	(498)	53	61	44	34	69
Greece	(547)	44	50	51	20	48
Israel	(522)	70	58	31	14	62
Italy	(496)	36	28	35	20	82
Netherlands	(475)	56	80	33	33	85
Norway	(437)	87	81	70	61	48
Portugal	(555)	96	93	40	38	94
Spain	(563)	84	70	80	77	94
Sweden	(303)	45	47	59	37	55
Switzerland	(391)	70	76	75	50	68
United Kingdom	(510)	72	74	60	39	74
United States	(518)	47	48	23	19	86
Mean[f]		62	62	53	39	73
SD[f]		18	19	17	17	16

SD, standard deviation.
a $\chi^2 = 1026.92, p < .0001$, Cramer's $V = .363$.
b $\chi^2 = 1129.84, p < .0001$, Cramer's $V = .386$.
c $\chi^2 = 848.422, p < .0001$, Cramer's $V = .330$.
d $\chi^2 = 916.931, p < .0001$, Cramer's $V = .343$.
e $\chi^2 = 1320.103, p < .0001$, Cramer's $V = .412$.
f Means and standard deviations are based on country percentages.

ANOVA demonstrated statistically significant differences between various types of news stories; portraits and miscellaneous news items were often softer than editorials and background stories, with the latter being softer than typical, factual news stories and interviews ($F(5, 7787) = 68.29$, $MSE = 2.70$, $p < .001$, $\eta^2 = .04$). Interestingly, when politicians are interviewed, the degree of political substance is the highest. However, when they are personally covered in great detail by journalists, the result is the softest kind of coverage.

Moreover, hard news is more frequent in certain topic areas than in others. Among the 'hardest' topics were education, labor, and unemployment as well as

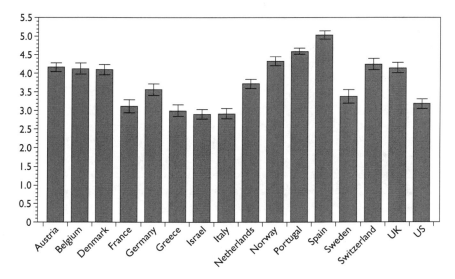

Figure 9.1 Hard and soft news index by countries, ranging from 0 = "story contains no hard news indicators" to 6 = "story contains all hard news indicators."

macroeconomics and taxes. Reports on the functioning of democracy and party politics were significantly 'softer' ($F(17, 7775) = 134.90$, $MSE = 2.18$, $p < .001$, $\eta^2 = .23$). Comparing the size of effects, it is obvious that topics exert a bigger influence on the hardness of news items than the news story type. This finding supports our decision not to operationalize the hardness of news either on the basis of topics or on the basis of news item types – which has frequently been done in prior studies of hard and soft news (Reinemann et al. 2012).

When comparing the democracies, huge and significant differences become apparent. A one-way ANOVA ($F(15, 7777) = 91.23$, $MSE = 2.39$, $p < .001$, $\eta^2 = .15$) showed that while the media in France, Greece, Italy, and Israel provided audiences with the softest news diet, the media in Portugal and most notably Spain had a strong preference for hard news in the period under study. Indeed, political coverage looked very different with respect to the way political discourse, decisions, and processes were reflected in the different countries' news media (Figure 9.1).

The presence of harder and softer news in different types of media

Hypothesis 1 suggested that online media would have more soft news than their offline versions. Having investigated this question on the level of individual news items, we do indeed find a small significant difference between offline and online versions but not in the expected direction. Taking the different kinds of newspapers and television programs together, online versions provide a slightly harder news diet than their offline counterparts. The respective means were $M = 3.74$ ($SD = .80$) for offline and $M = 3.83$ ($SD = .71$) for online versions. However, a small $\eta^2 = .003$ indicates that these differences are tiny and may be only due to the large variance in the sample. Despite the small effect, Hypothesis 1 is not supported because it points in the opposite direction to the one that we expected.

In Hypothesis 2, we proposed that the upmarket press and public service broadcasters would generally display a higher share of hard news than commercial television and the mass-market press. To investigate this hypothesis, we put together news items that were produced by public service news organizations and broadsheet newspapers, on the one hand, and commercial stations and tabloid newspapers, on the other hand. In the analysis, we see that upmarket newspapers and public service broadcasters generally have harder news than mass-market newspapers and the commercial media. Hypothesis 2 is therefore supported, although again, the effect size is modest. Comparing the various types of media in more detail, it becomes obvious that PSB newscasts and PSB websites as well as upmarket newspaper websites score significantly higher on the hard and soft news index than mass-market newspapers, while upmarket newspapers, commercial television, commercial television websites, and mass-market newspaper websites range in between. This rank order is surprising, especially with respect to the printed versions of the upmarket papers, which we would have expected to rank higher on the hard/soft scale. However, only upmarket newspaper websites provided significantly harder news than commercial television news and its websites. As may be expected, it is the public service broadcasters that provide the highest share of hard news and hold the top position in the hard and soft news index.

Hypothesis 3 stated that upmarket papers and their websites would display a higher intensity of hard news than mass-market papers and their websites. Indeed, broadsheets have a higher amount of hard news offline and online than tabloid newspapers. This difference is significant at the .05 level and represents a small-sized effect of newspaper type on the amount of hard and soft news. Hypothesis 3 can therefore be supported. Hypothesis 4 compared public service broadcasters and commercial broadcasters (for both their offline and online news). It was hypothesized that PSB programs display a higher share of hard news than those of commercial broadcasters. Our analysis on the level of media outlets shows that public service broadcasters provide their audiences with harder news than their commercial competitors. The difference is significant at the .05 level and represents a small-sized effect on the amount of hard and soft news in PSB programs and on websites. Hypothesis 4 is therefore supported.

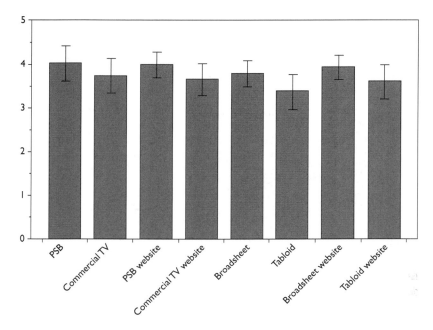

Figure 9.2 Hard and soft news index by individual medium type (level of analysis: outlet). For all scales, higher scores are indicative of more extreme responding in the direction of the construct assessed. Hard and soft news index ranges from 0 = "story contains no hard news indicators" to 6 = "story contains clear hard news indicators."

Macro-level characteristics and harder and softer news

In the next step of our analysis, we explore the different level characteristics shown in Chapter 3. Hypotheses 5 to 10 all suggest that there will be significant correlations between these characteristics and the intensity of hard versus soft news reporting. To test these hypotheses, we calculated bivariate correlations between the hard and soft news index and the various indicators on the level of individual news outlets. For all but two indicators, we find significant small to moderate correlations in the expected direction ($r < .34$). The characteristics of the political and media systems and of the event level – namely, the current political situation – show the highest correlations with the hard and soft news index. There are positive correlations between the share of hard news and PSB strength in the television market and the number of parties in the parliament. In addition, the share of hard news articles is negatively correlated with the number of months that have passed since the last election. One characteristic of the economic context, adspend as a percentage of GDP in a given country, also correlates positively with the share of hard and soft news. Moreover, the number of paid-for

142 Carsten Reinemann et al.

Table 9.2 Correlations between hard and soft news index and national-level characteristics[a]

Dimension	Indicators	Organization level[b]
Event level (environment)	Months from last election	−.287**
	Unemployment rate	.083
Political system	Number of parties in parliament	.183*
Media system	Adspend as percentage of GDP (2010)	.140*
	Number of paid-for daily newspapers	.216**
	PSB share	.329**
Media organization	High production cost of hard news	.001

a Table entries are correlation coefficients (Pearson's R). Hard and soft news index ranges from 0 = "story contains no hard news indicators" to 6 = "story contains clear hard news indicators."
b N = 160.
* $p < .05$, ** $p < .01$.

daily newspapers seems to be connected to our hard news index. Production costs of hard news, however, and the unemployment rate do not seem to influence the presence of hard news. These results support Hypotheses 6 to 10 and but do not support Hypothesis 5 (the lower the production costs of hard news, the more hard news is produced; see Table 9.2).

To get an impression of how national characteristics and the hard and soft news index interact on the national level, we plotted the highest correlating media market, economic, and political context indicators against the hard and soft news index. With regard to the political context, Figure 9.3 shows that the number of months since the last election is associated, to a certain extent, with differences in the countries' news reporting. However, we also see a broad range of hard/soft news reporting in countries in which the last election only happened a few months previously and also stark differences between countries in which the last election was held years ago. Obviously, the differences in the character of political reporting between these countries can only slightly be attributed to the elapsed time since the last election (Figure 9.3).

Figure 9.4 illustrates the correlation between adspend as a percentage of GDP and the intensity of hard news reporting. It shows that countries that were most hard hit by the economic crisis (Greece, Italy, Portugal, and Spain) did not witness similar levels of hard and soft news. As one can see, news items in Greece were much softer than news items in Spain or Portugal, although all three countries were heavily affected by the financial crisis. On the other hand, adspend as a percentage of GDP was considerably higher in Portugal compared to Spain, Italy, or Greece (Figure 9.4).

Hard and soft news 143

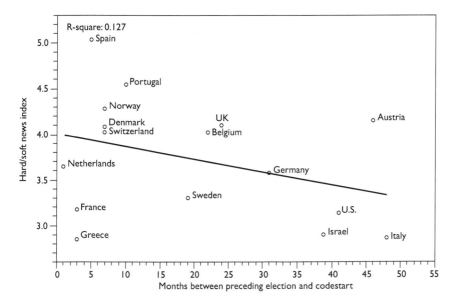

Figure 9.3 Months from last election and the hard and soft news index across countries.

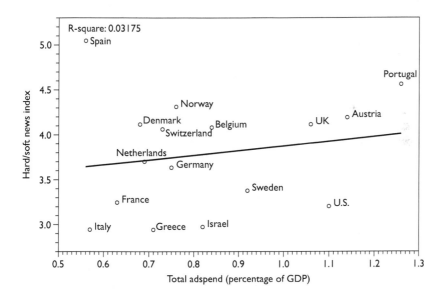

Figure 9.4 Adspend as a percentage of GDP and hard and soft news index across countries.

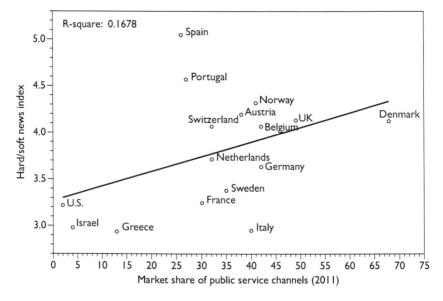

Figure 9.5 Market share of public service broadcasters and hard and soft news index across countries.

Figure 9.5 shows the relationship between PSB market share and the hard and soft news index. We see that the hard and soft character of political news differs in countries such as Italy and Spain where PSB reaches a similarly sized audience. But we also find a difference between Denmark, where PSB channels have the highest market share in Europe, and Portugal, where PSB market share is less than half that of Denmark.

Taken together, we found that media system-, political system-, and event-level indicators perform well when differentiating hard and soft news between countries. That said, the difference between countries can be large for some national characteristics, while the correlations between these indicators and the hard/soft news are not necessarily large. The majority of findings are in line with the theoretical expectations, which make hard and soft news basically amendable to national-level economic, media market, and political information factors. The findings also suggest that the concept is worth further investigation. What remains to be seen, then, is how these different level characteristics work together to explain the degree of hard and soft news.

Explaining hard and soft news by country and medium level characteristics

For a more detailed exploration of hard and soft news across 16 Western democracies, we performed 3 stepwise linear regression analyses in order to identify macro- and meso-level factors associated with the hard or soft character of news in the 160 media outlets under investigation.[1] In line with the earlier analyses, the average hard and soft news index calculated for each news organization was used as the dependent variable. In order to account for characteristics of media organization, we differentiate between commercial television and PSB as well as tabloid and broadsheet newspapers, including their news websites. In our regression models, public service broadcasters are the reference category because they showed the highest degree of hard news reporting in the earlier comparisons of the different media types. Moreover, we differentiate between online and offline media in separate regression models that include both television and newspapers. As for the country-level characteristics, we reused the information on the political and economic situations and the media markets already utilized in the earlier bivariate analyses.

A total of three models were calculated to test the influence of these factors. The first model only included the type of media outlet. The model itself explains only 5.6 percent of the observed variance, with commercial TV ($B = -.301$, $p < .05$) and mass-market newspapers ($B = -.526$, $p < .01$) contributing strongest to soft news. In the second model, a differentiation between on- and offline media was entered. It led to almost no improvement in the model regarding explained variance (Model 2 $R^2 = .06$). In the third model, information was included on the political system (months between coding and last election, number of parties in parliament); on the economic situation, which also influences the media system (unemployment rate, adspend as a percentage of GDP); and on the media market itself (production cost of hard news, number of paid-for daily newspapers, market share of all PSB). The findings are depicted in Table 9.3. Obviously, the inclusion of these context variables in Model 3 leads to an increase of explained variance, up to 48 percent – a remarkably high figure, bearing in mind that the research focused on political news. Taking a look at the individual predictors, it becomes apparent that news organization characteristics significantly affect the hard or soft character of news. Across our countries, political news is softer when it is published in a mass-market newspaper ($B = -.526$, $p < .01$) or on commercial television (including their respective websites) compared to PSB television ($B = -.301$, $p < .05$). In contrast, there is no across-the-board effect on news items published in broadsheet newspapers or in online media ($B = .084$, $p > .05$). This result means that news items in prestigious newspapers are not harder per se than items on PSB television and that there is no general difference between offline and online media – which is opposite to the prediction of H1. However, the amount of variance explained by medium type does not exceed 6 percent, which is small when compared to the variance that is explained by macro-level factors (see Models 1 and 2 in Table 9.3).

Among macro-level factors, economic and media market variables were especially useful predictors of the hard or soft character of news. Other political factors, such as the number of parties in parliament, did not exert a significant influence when controlling for other characteristics ($B = .049$, $p > .05$). The factor with the strongest effect was adspend as a percentage of GDP, which was included as an indicator of the general economic situation in a country. The positive and high value of the coefficient ($B = 2.536$; $p < .001$) indicates that the better the

146 Carsten Reinemann et al.

Table 9.3 Explaining hard news by medium type and characteristics of the political, economic, and media system context (organizational-level analysis)[a,b]

Variable	Hard and soft news index					
	Model 1		Model 2		Model 3	
	B	SE[c]	B	SE[c]	B	SE[c]
Constant	4.010***	.155	3.967***	.179	4.583**	1.230
Commercial television (and website)	−.301*	.129	−.301*	.129	−.301*	.132
Upmarket newspapers (and website)	−.147	.117	−.147	.118	−.147	.120
Mass-market newspapers (and website)	−.526**	.168	−.526**	.169	−.526**	.173
Online website			.084	.095	.084	.097
Months between code start and last election					−.016*	.006
Number of parties in parliament					.049	.035
Unemployment rate (May 2012)					.054	.031
Adspend as percentage of GDP (2010)[d]					2.536***	.459
High production costs of hard news					−.742*	.287
Number of paid-for daily newspapers					.023	.042
Accumulated market share of all public channels					.018*	.006
R^2	.056		.059		.48	
F	3.69		4.38		15.65	

a $N = 160$.
b Public service television is used as the reference category.
c Robust standard errors are reported.
d Mean imputation of missing values of adspend as a percentage of GDP.
* $p < .05$, ** $p < .01$, *** $p < .001$.

economic situation in a country, the more hard news coverage is to be found. This result runs counter to what we supposed – namely, that a critical economic situation would be reflected in more hard news reporting. One explanation might be that higher advertising revenues help fund high-cost, high-quality investigative reporting. In contrast, a news organization is less likely to produce hard news when hard news costs in the country are higher ($B = −.742, p < .05$) or when significant time has elapsed since the last general election ($B = −.016, p < .05$). In a nutshell, the macro-level indicators are good predictors of the amount of hard or soft news produced by news organizations and should thus be further considered in comparative communication research (see Model 3 in Table 9.3).

Discussion and conclusions

While the dichotomous concept of hard and soft news has been widely used in investigations of news, internationally comparative analyses have been scarce. The purpose of this chapter has been to explore the character of political news with respect to two dimensions of Reinemann and colleagues' (2012) multidimensional model – namely, the topic dimension and the style dimension. In order to do so, we created a hard/soft news index for each individual news item and average index values for media organizations, types of media, and countries. We then explored the relationships between the index and the event environment, various characteristics of media organizations (meso-level), and the political and media systems in the various countries (macro-level). The results can be summarized as follows.

First, the prevalence of harder or softer news items in political coverage strongly differs in the democracies we investigated. The differences between the countries at the top and at the bottom of the hard news ranking are notable. Second, the bivariate analyses show significant relationships between the average degree of hard news in the different news outlets and their organizational characteristics as well as the respective countries' contexts. Third, the multivariate analyses, in which all factors were mutually controlled, reveal that medium type explains the extent to which more hard news or less hard news is published. As one might have expected, public service television and broadsheet newspapers generally provide their audiences with a harder news diet than tabloid papers and commercial television. These findings confirm a series of prior studies on hard and soft news (e.g., Reinemann et al. 2012). No general difference was found between broadsheets and public service newscasts or between online and offline services. This result is in line with findings from more recent studies (e.g., Oschatz et al. 2014) indicating that more general differences in audiences and the quality profiles of different media seem to be more important for explaining the character of news than whether it is published online or offline. Fourth, the same analysis reveals that a country's political and economic situation as well as the situation in the media market have a strong impact on the amount of hard news items – far stronger than the impact of organizational-level factors. Surprisingly, the greater the adspend as a percentage of GDP in a country, the greater the likelihood of hard news. This result is contrary to what we expected and seems to be a counterintuitive finding at first sight. Our hypotheses – that there would be across-the-board ecological effects of media market structure (strength of public service television, production costs of hard news) and event-driven effects of the political and economic situation – were supported.

In sum, based on the multivariate analysis, we do not find support for H1 because online media do not carry more soft news than offline media. We neither find support for H6 since there was no evidence that the number of paid-for daily newspapers explained the share of hard news in the countries under investigation. With regard to H10, political competition did not predict hard and soft news well (although the regression coefficient points in the hypothesized direction), thus we cannot support this hypothesis either. In contrast, we found support for H2 to H5, H7, and H9. Finally, H8 points to an important association between adspend as a percentage of GDP and hard/soft news. The relationship was significant but went in the opposite direction from what we expected. Possible explanations are multifaceted and illustrate the complexity of integrating macro-level indicators in such models. The explanations include the following: first, in small media markets, the (small) size of the advertising market may result in floor effects of adspend as a percentage of GDP. Second, the ownership structure of the media outlets may influence the general acceptance of either more or less advertising as a country-specific tradition. Third, political polarization may lead to polarized advertising, which fosters disparities of adspend. Fourth, advertising agency commissions are not equally transparent in the analyzed countries and thus may blur the amount of adspend on which the statistical analyses are based. Fifth, newspapers rely country-specifically on both advertising and the selling price, which may impact the total adspend in a country. Sixth, the severity of the financial crisis may have engendered country-specific, time-lagged effects on the advertising market. Further analyses will therefore have to take a closer look at the specific relationships in the countries investigated.

Taking a broader perspective, our results, on the one hand, confirm findings of other studies that focused on a single country or on a few countries (see earlier). On the other hand, the comparative perspective, the inclusion of different kinds of television channels and newspapers as well as online news, and the investigation of the effects of several meso- and macro-level characteristics mark a step forward in research on the character of political news coverage in Western democracies. Our results show that the differences between different types of media organizations remain significant even in the light of extraordinary events like the European financial crisis and the varying economic and political situations. Our findings support approaches like the two-component model of news selection or the concept of event-driven news, which suggest including both stable structural and situational factors to explain news coverage (see Kepplinger and Ehmig 2006). Besides the effects of the political and economic situation, the *ecological effects* of strong public service television are an especially important finding because they tap into the ongoing discussion about the necessity of PSB. Obviously, public service television contributes to a general climate in which media are more likely to report about politics in more substantial ways. The PSB market share (media market shares being indicators that represent the size of audiences that are used to and prefer certain ways of political reporting) also seems to affect the standards to which other media adhere when reporting politics.

Despite its merits, the present analysis also has its limitations. First, our analysis focused on political coverage and did not include other topics that can be supposed to be especially important in tabloid newspapers and commercial television. This focus, however, makes the differences between the types of media organizations even more remarkable because they are still apparent in the core of political coverage and do not stem only from a different preferences for hard and soft topics. Second, the fact that we did not find systematic differences between online and offline media deserves further scrutiny because we cannot be sure that on- and offline news items referred to the same topics or events. Third, due to inter-country reliability problems, we were not able to include one of the three dimensions of hard/soft news as proposed by Reinemann and colleagues (2012). Our index thus only represents the political substance and the emotionality of a news item but not the way the news is framed with respect to its individual or societal focus. These limitations, however, do not undermine the analyses that are presented but instead should be taken as incentive for further and more detailed analyses of what drives and constitutes the way political news is presented in media across the globe.

Note

1 The regression models described here were also run with the individual news items as the unit of analysis (N = 7,794). These analyses yielded almost identical results with respect to the predictors being influential and the sizes of effects. The major difference between the analysis on the media organizational level and the level of individual news items is the amount of variance being explained by the models. Whereas the most comprehensive model (Model 3) explains only 12 percent of the variance of the hard news index in individual news items, it explains 48 percent of the variance of the average hard news index calculated for the 160 news organizations.

Chapter 10

Cross-conceptual architecture of news

Carsten Reinemann, Sebastian Scherr, and James Stanyer with Toril Aalberg, Peter Van Aelst, Rosa Berganza, Frank Esser, David Nicolas Hopmann, Nicolas Hubé, Guido Legnante, Jörg Matthes, Stylianos Papathanassopoulos, Susana Salgado, Tamir Sheafer, Jesper Strömbäck, and Claes de Vreese

Introduction

While the other chapters in this volume have treated each of the six key concepts in depth, it is important to consider the relationships between them and the extent to which they are interconnected. Indeed, some scholars have made connections, at least theoretically, between a number of different developments (e.g., Patterson 1993). Several advantages flow from such a cross-conceptual approach. Specific concepts can be related to each other, which gives readers some idea of how they may interact. For example, the degree of personalization and negativity in the news may be related but may also operate independently. Understanding these cross-concept relationships further can improve our insights into journalists' processes of news construction. It is highly likely that decisions about the selection and construction of news are based on a combination of content features rather than on individual features of events or topics. This line of reasoning was already a key idea in the early studies on news factors, which hypothesized that different content features would add up to the specific news value of an event (e.g., Galtung and Ruge 1965).

In addition, cross-conceptual analyses may also inspire future analysis of news *effects* on audiences. Indeed, it can be argued that news reception and effects may best be explained when individual content features are seen in combination. Scholars often include multiple content features such as visibility and the candidate evaluation in the news (Hopmann, Vliegenthart, de Vreese, and Albæk 2010). In our case, for example, the effects of game and strategy framing might well depend on whether the context of an article is positive or negative in tone, whether the news is hard or soft, and whether a story is balanced or one sided. Along these lines, cross-conceptual analyses may help establish more representative methods and more complex messages for experimental research, strengthening their ecological validity. In doing so, we get a step closer to understanding the contingencies of media effects.

Indeed, in recent years, some scholars have begun examining more closely how different content features interact, both on the level of individual news items and in the coverage of different news outlets, to better understand the complexity in journalists' work to which media audiences are exposed. Very few of these studies have been internationally comparative or included different kinds of media outlets (but see Esser and Umbricht 2013). In this cross-conceptual chapter, we show that political communication research and journalism studies can benefit from comparisons and cross-conceptual analyses of key concepts. In the end, this approach will improve our understanding of journalistic and political communication cultures across countries (see Hanitzsch and Mellado 2011; Pfetsch and Esser 2014). As we know little about how the key concepts investigated here interconnect in the news media of our 16 countries, we will take a look at how they occur in individual news items. Before that, we theorize about the possible connections between concepts, leading us to formulate several hypotheses. We then sketch out the methodological aspects of our analysis, present our results, conclude with a short discussion, and add suggestions for future research.

Interconnections between key concepts: theory and research question

The notion that, rather than the single characteristics of news reports, the specific *combination* of content features best serve to explain their selection by journalists and their effects on audiences is not new. For example, early theorizing on news factors explicitly postulated that the newsworthiness of events would be a result of the cumulation of news factors and that they could also complement each other (e.g., Galtung and Ruge 1965). More recent research has looked at the way various news factors are combined in individual news items to get a sense of their structure. Methodologically, this research has been based on, among other methods, factor analysis (e.g., Sommer et al. 2013). Moreover, the effects of the combination of news factors on news decisions have been investigated using both survey data (e.g., Kleinnijenhuis, van Hoof, Oegema, and de Ridder 2007) and experiments (e.g., Kepplinger and Ehmig 2006). Also, framing research has explicitly focused on the combination of content features. For example, researchers have investigated the structure of political coverage by measuring a number of frame elements and then clustering them to arrive at empirically constructed frames (e.g., Semetko and Valkenburg 2000; for an overview, see Matthes and Kohring 2008). However, the cross-concept approach has not generally been a common feature of the literature on the concepts that we are interested in here.

Several studies do provide some insight into a number of possible interconnections. For example, when discussing the attractiveness of game and strategy frames, Aalberg (2014) argues that those frames reflect journalism's focus on drama, conflict, negativity, elite individuals or political groups, and the tendency towards personalization. This reasoning would imply that negativity, game framing, and personalization might go together in news reports. Similarly, Brants and van Praag (2006, p. 31) argue that an interpretive style in journalism should be characterized by a more critical outlook and less substance. This reasoning would mean that negativity should also go together with interpretation and soft news.

One of the few studies explicitly linking various concepts in a longitudinal and cross-national perceptive has been conducted by Esser and Umbricht (Esser and Umbricht 2013, 2014; Umbricht and Esser 2013). They look at the combination of content features as indicators of specific national news cultures. In their study of political affairs coverage in British, French, German, Italian, Swiss, and US newspapers, they used objectivity, opinion orientation, negativity, scandalization, sensationalization, and emotionalization to characterize different styles of reporting – for example, a Swiss-Germanic, an Italian, and an American style. Interestingly, they found that those styles of reporting could not be easily integrated into existing media system typologies, which means that system differences do not seem to directly translate into differences of news content. Methodologically, in addition to analyzing the co-occurrence of news characteristics on the basis of overall percentages in the countries, they also applied correspondence analyses and identified two dimensions on which news coverage differed across countries. This chapter's logic is similar to Esser and Umbricht's approach. Our analysis broadens the scope in terms of countries, looks at individual items – both offline and online – and focuses, in part, on different concepts.

A key question arising from the cross-conceptual approach is why some characteristics of news should go together and others not? Certainly, some news report features have the same causes. For example, economic pressures and commercialization are argued to drive a softening of news and an increase in negativity and personalization since they are seen as strategies that attract audiences (e.g., Patterson 2000). Moreover, the rise of interpretive journalism, strategy framing, and negativity can be traced back to more proactive and professionalized political public relations activities, which are countered by political journalists who want to defend their autonomy (Aalberg 2014; Patterson 2000).

Assessing the relationship between the different concepts gives us a unique handle on news performance, not only in a cross-nationally comparative perspective, but in a theoretically novel and broader perspective. The underlying question (RQ1) for this chapter is how strategy/game framing, interpretive journalism, negativity, balance, personalization, and the hard/soft character of news interconnect in political coverage. We parcel out this inquiry by looking at how types of media (RQ2) and countries (RQ3) differ in the interconnections between strategy/game framing, interpretive journalism, negativity, balance, personalization, and the hard/soft character of news.

Method

To investigate to what extent the key concepts presented in this book show up and interact in the same news articles, media outlets, and countries we use a standardized version of the concepts analyzed in the preceding chapters. This approach not only allows us to calculate comparable descriptive statistics reflecting the presence of each concept in the various types of media and nations but also to identify common structures and concept clusters for political media coverage across our 16 Western democracies. By standardizing the key concepts and by applying a comprehensive perspective, we are able to carve out the extent to which similar concept combinations are actively shaping political news across media outlets and countries. In addition, it will become obvious whether similar concept clusters are present in countries regarded as having similar types of media systems or journalistic cultures (Pfetsch and Esser 2014).

To address the earlier research questions, we rely on indicators that best represent each concept's basic idea. Once these indicators were identified, the six concepts were standardized. Values for each concept were recoded to values ranging from 0 ("concept is not present") to 1 ("concept is very much present"), so that descriptive comparisons and interactions across media types and countries, and between key concepts, can be made based upon individual news items ($N =$ 7,797). We use simple correlations, factor analyses, and cluster analyses across all countries and for different types of media (commercial television and websites, public service television and websites, mass-market newspapers and websites, upmarket newspapers and websites) and single countries. For the sake of comparative analyses, we investigated similar correlation matrices and factor structures across countries. To our knowledge, this study is the first time that such an approach has been applied systematically in a cross-national study spanning several key concepts.

Game-strategy index

The measure for game/strategy framing is a mean index ranging from 0 ("no strategic game frame") to 1 ("strategic game frame"). The index is based upon five indicators of news stories that frame politics as a game, as a personality contest, as strategy, and as personal relationships between political actors not related to issue positions.

Interpretive journalism

The measure for interpretive journalism is a sum index of three indicators that show whether given political news items contain journalistic interpretations, explanations, or overt commentaries on political issues. It was crucial here that journalists themselves explicitly convey what they think.

Negativity

The measure for negativity is a mean index based upon four indicators of news stories that present politics in a negative tone. For the coding, the overall impression a news item conveyed was decisive (see also Chapter 6 on negativity).

Balance (neutrality)

Our measure of balance (neutrality) is based on the favorability coding for the first five actors appearing in a news story, reflecting the degree to which actors were depicted in either neutral or judgmental terms (for a discussion of balance and neutrality as dimensions of media impartiality, see Jandura and Friedrich 2014; see also Chapter 7 on balance).[1]

Personalization

Personalization was measured as the ratio of human actors versus institutions mentioned in a news item.

Hard and soft news

The hard versus soft character of news items was measured as an additive index variable containing the political substance and the emotionality of reporting.

Results

Standardized key concepts in comparison

Looking at the standardized values for the key concepts across countries, two basic findings stand out (see Table 10.1). First, the variance across countries differs considerably between concepts. It is smallest for negativity (with most values around 0); medium for personalization and game/strategy framing; and largest for interpretive journalism, balance, and hard/soft news.[2] This finding means that media coverage in our 16 Western democracies tends to be rather similar with respect to the way political actors and processes are evaluated but rather different with respect to the amount of political substance presented and the way it is emotionalized, interpreted, and evaluated. Second, most countries deviate from the overall means for not more than two concepts. Taking one standard deviation as the cutoff criterion, this conclusion is true for 13 of the 16 countries, with Norway and Switzerland being closest to the overall concept averages. Three countries stand out by being different from the others on three or more concepts. This conclusion is true for France, which deviates three times, and Portugal and Spain, deviating in four of the six concepts. France ranks above average when it comes to interpretive journalism and game/strategy framing but has a below-average value for hard news. Portugal stands out with an above-average rating in negativity and an above-average amount of hard news, while interpretive journalism and a balanced presentation of actors is much less common than in the other countries. This result might in part be due to the impact of the economic crisis. And finally, the Spanish media had less game/strategy coverage, less interpretation, and less personalization but a rather high amount of hard news. As the examples of these most deviating countries show, each country's media seem to be characterized by a specific pattern of

Table 10.1 Standardized key concepts in comparison – deviations from overall means

	Strategy/game ΔM	Interpretation ΔM	Negativity ΔM	Balance (neutrality) ΔM	Personalization ΔM	Hard news ΔM	Above-average means n	Below-average means n
Austria	**+.11**	+.04	**+.06**	+.02	−.05	+.06	2	–
Belgium	−.07	**−.13**	−.02	+.04	+.01	+.06	–	1
Denmark	**−.14**	+.01	−.01	+.02	−.04	+.05	–	1
France	**+.13**	**+.15**	+.02	+.03	+.06	**−.11**	2	1
Germany	+.05	+.02	**−.04**	−.02	−.06	−.04	–	1
Greece	**+.11**	+.05	+.01	−.03	+.05	**−.13**	1	1
Israel	−.04	+.07	+.00	−.07	+.03	**−.15**	–	1
Italy	−.07	−.08	−.01	+.02	**+.12**	**−.14**	1	1
Netherlands	−.03	−.03	−.04	**+.13**	−.02	−.01	1	–
Norway	−.05	−.09	+.00	+.03	+.03	+.09	–	–
Portugal	+.02	**−.15**	**+.05**	**−.36**	−.07	**+.14**	2	2
Spain	**−.11**	**−.19**	−.01	+.08	**−.13**	**+.21**	1	3
Sweden	−.01	**+.18**	**+.06**	+.02	+.00	−.07	2	–
Switzerland	+.03	+.05	−.03	−.10	−.07	+.08	–	–
UK	+.00	−.04	+.02	**+.17**	**+.09**	+.06	2	–
US	+.04	**+.19**	−.05	+.06	+.05	−.10	1	–
M	.27	.36	.60	.71	.53	.63	–	–
SD	.27	.48	.20	.33	.22	.28	–	–

M, mean; *SD*, standard deviation.

a Based on individual news items ($N = 7,797$).
b Table entries are differences to overall concept mean values across countries.
c Values printed bold indicate positive or negative differences larger than one standard deviation (based on country values).

156 Carsten Reinemann et al.

Table 10.2 Standardized key concepts in comparison per media outlet type[a,b,c]

Variables	Commercial television (television/web)		Public service television (television/web)		Mass-market newspaper (print/web)		Upmarket newspaper (print/web)	
	M (SD)		M (SD)		M (SD)		M (SD)	
Strategy/game frame	.25	(.27)[x]	.24	(.26)[x]	.25	(.26)[x]	.30	(.28)[y]
Interpretation	.33	(.47)[y]	.23	(.42)[x]	.38	(.49)[z]	.41	(.49)[z]
Negativity	.60	(.19)[y]	.58	(.20)[x]	.60	(.20)[y]	.61	(.20)[y]
Balance (neutrality)	.73	(.31)[x]	.75	(.31)[x]	.68	(.35)[y]	.70	(.33)[y]
Personalization	.55	(.22)[y]	.55	(.20)[y]	.55	(.20)[y]	.51	(.23)[x]
Hard news	.62	(.28)[y]	.67	(.25)[z]	.58	(.29)[x]	.64	(.29)[y]

M, mean; SD, standard deviation.

a Table entries are means of standardized concept values (with standard deviations in parentheses).
b Means with different superscripts (x, y, z) differ significantly ($p < .05$).
c Post-hoc test according to Duncan.

political coverage. Whether these findings also mean that the connections between concepts are different will be investigated in the following section (Table 10.2).

To get an idea of the differences between the various types of media, we compared the prevalence of our concepts in commercial and public service television newscasts and mass-market and upmarket newspapers (each including their respective websites). Clearly, public service television stands out as carrying a relatively low amount of interpretive journalism and negativity (although the latter difference to the other media is very small) while at the same time being more focused on hard news than the other media and more balanced than the newspapers. The upmarket newspapers, however, are characterized by an above-average level of strategy/game framing and interpretation, while being low on personalization. The mass-market newspapers carry an especially low amount of hard news, combined with a rather high degree of interpretation. And finally, commercial television's most noticeable characteristics are that it has less interpretation than newspapers but more than public service broadcasting (PSB) television and that its coverage is as balanced as PSB television's, which also means that commercial television is more balanced than political newspapers (Table 10.2).

Correlations between key concepts across countries and media

Calculating correlations between our six concepts gives a first impression of their relationships. Generally, we find a substantial number of highly significant positive and negative coefficients representing small to moderate correlations. Which

Table 10.3 Correlations between standardized key concepts across countries and media[a,b]

Variables	Strategy/ game	Interpretation	Negativity	Balance (neutrality)	Personalization	Hard news
Strategy/game	–					
Interpretation	.27**	–				
Negativity	.23**	.15**	–			
Balance (neutrality)	–.14**	–.14**	–.12**	–		
Personalization	.05**	.01	–.02*	.00	–	
Hard news	–.10**	–.15**	–.04**	.13**	–.27**	–
M	.27	.36	.60	.71	.53	.63
SD	.27	.48	.20	.33	.22	.28

M, mean; SD, standard deviation.

a Intercorrelations for key concepts of political communication in a comparative sample of 16 countries are presented.
b N = 7,746 to 7,796 articles; the number of articles varies due to the coding procedure.
* $p < .05$, ** $p < .01$ (one-tailed).

concepts go together, and which ones do not? Leaving aside very small correlations (< .10), game and strategy–framed news items tend to be more interpretive and negative, rather unbalanced and softer (i.e., less substantial and more emotionalized). Similarly, interpretive items tend to be more negative and strategically framed, be less balanced, and carry less hard political information. In addition, negativity and balance are negatively correlated, which makes sense because we would expect a clear and unambiguous negative portrayal of actors to also be reflected in the overall negative tone of a story. And finally, personalization is negatively correlated to hard news, although one indicator of hard news is the presence of political actors. This finding means that personalized news items tend to have less political substance, whereas news items with more political substance tend to involve more institutional actors (Table 10.3).

These results show that the six key concepts investigated here are not independent from each other. In fact, their correlations are such that they do not represent distinct concepts. However, this finding does not supersede the analysis of their underlying structure. Therefore, we calculated a factor analysis (oblique rotation) of the concepts, which reveals two factors. The first factor represents the evaluative and interpretive character of news. It comprises of interpretive elements, game and strategy framing, negativity, and balance, with the latter concept being negatively related to this factor. This finding suggests that this first factor represents the extent to which journalists themselves come to the forefront of political coverage and present their own view of events. Moreover, it suggests that, if journalists are acting that way, they do so mostly in the context of rather negative and unbalanced stories. The second factor seems to represent the dichotomy of person versus substance. We find a high factor loading for personalization and for the

Table 10.4 Factor analysis of standardized key concepts across countries and media[a,b,c]

Scale	Factor loadings		Communalities
	I	II	
Strategy/game frame	**.70**	−.09	.49
Interpretation	**.65**	−.15	.43
Negativity	**.61**	.13	.41
Balance (neutrality)	**−.49**	.11	.24
Personalization	−.04	**−.80**	.65
Hard news	−.24	**.78**	.63
Eigenvalues	1.63	1.22	
Percentage of variance	27%	20%	

a Factor loadings higher than .40 are in boldface.
b N = 7,746 to 7,797 articles; the number of articles varies due to the coding procedure.
c Oblique rotation.

hard/soft character of the news items (Table 10.4). Analyzing the factor structures separately for PSB newscasts, commercial television, and upmarket and mass-market newspapers yields almost identical results.

All in all, across all countries and media, the six key concepts that we focus on in this analysis seem to represent two underlying dimensions that shape the way political news is presented in the media of Western democracies. One dimension represents the degree of evaluation and interpretation, and the other, the amount of political substance. These dimensions are obviously important in guiding journalists' construction of the political world and can therefore be assumed to also affect the way that audiences perceive political processes and the functioning of democracy. In the next step of our analysis, we will take a look at whether this structure is common to all the countries.

Interconnections of key concepts in country comparison

The relationships between the key concepts in individual news items represent the typical way in which political information is conveyed in news reporting. As stated earlier, these structures both represent common patterns of news construction by journalists and the typical mixture of content features that confront media audiences. Analyzing the factor structures in each country separately, however, also reveals some differences. First of all, there are only two countries in which, not two, but three factors were found: Israel and the United States. In the other 14 countries, the analyses resulted in two factors. However, correlations between concepts were not the same in all countries. Only six countries mirrored the pattern found in the overall cross-country analysis with strategy/game, interpretation, negativity, and balance loading on the first factor and personalization and hard/soft characteristics loading on the second factor. This finding was true for Austria, Belgium, Germany, the Netherlands, Spain, and Sweden. Here, more strategy and game framing, more interpretation, and more negativity went together with less balance. In addition, substantial news indicators were negatively related to personalization. The pattern in France was similar. The only difference was that the hard/soft news indicators had a stronger link to the interpretive/evaluative factor than to the personality factor.

The second largest group of countries showing the same factor structure consists of Norway, Portugal, Switzerland, and the United Kingdom. Here, strategy/game, interpretation, and negativity made up for the first factor, with which they positively correlated. In contrast, balance, personalization, and hard news characteristics loaded on the second. In those countries, more political substance and more balance went together with less personalization, and vice versa. Denmark and Italy are the two remaining countries that are similar, with a two-factor concept structure. In both countries, strategy/game and personalization go together. However, the direction of the relationship is completely different. In Denmark, strategy/game correlates positively with the factor and negatively with personalization. This finding suggests that strategy and game frames coverage combines with a focus on institutions – mainly political parties. In contrast, in the Italian media, strategy and game framing goes together with a more personalized focus, probably indicating that individual actors play a stronger role in coverage here. The last two-factor country, Greece, shows a unique structure with strategy and game framing, negativity, and hard news indicators loading on the first factor, and interpretation, balance, and personalization loading on the second factor. Here, news items with game and strategy framing tend to be more negative and less substantial. In addition, more balanced news items appear to be more personalized and less interpretive. This pattern was not to be seen in any other included country (Table 10.5).

Finally, Israel and the United States are the only countries with a three-factor structure. In Israel, strategy and game framing, interpretation, and negativity relate to the first factor, and personalization and hard news characteristics, to the second factor. Balance established a factor of its own, again indicating a slightly different pattern of presenting political news. What about the benchmark nation of political communication research – the United States? Here, more interpretation and game and strategy framing were related to less balance. In addition, more political substance was connected to less personalization. And finally, negativity made up for another third factor. This pattern of results makes the United States the only country where negative reporting was not connected to any other key concepts or the respective factors (Table 10.5).

Clusters of news items

Up to this point, we have looked at the correlations between our key concepts. In this section, we use the factors found in the earlier analysis to answer the question, how many news items share a specific profile of those key concepts? We therefore

Table 10.5 Factor structures of standardized key concepts in country comparison[a,b,c]

	Strategy/game	Interpretation	Negativity	Balance (neutrality)	Personalization	Hard news	Explained variance (%)
2 Factors							
Austria	■	■	■	■			52
					O	O	
Belgium	■	■	■	■			47
					O	O	
Germany	■	■	■[d]	■			50
					O	O	
Netherlands	■	■	■	■			45
					O	O	
Spain	■	■	■	■			48
					O	O	
Sweden	■	■	■[e]	■			52
					O	O	
Norway	■	■	■				43
				O	O[f]	O	
Portugal	■	■	■				48
				O	O	O	
Switzerland	■	■	■				50
				O	O	O	
UK	■	■	■				51
				O	O[g]	O	
Denmark	■				■		53
		O	O[h]	O		O	
	■						53

France	■	■	■	■		■i	54
					O		
Greece	■		■			■	44
		O		O	O		
3 Factors							
Israel	■	■	■				63
			O				
					♦	♦	
US	■	■		■			63
		O					
					♦	♦	

a Factor analysis based on individual news items (N = 465–477 articles per country; oblique rotation).

b Identical symbols represent key concepts that commonly go together in news articles in Western democracies (based on oblique factor analysis).

c Equal symbols and shades of grey (■,O,♦) symbolize the same factors. For example, in Austria, two types of news items (depicted by two shades of grey and the two symbols ■,O) explain 52% of the existing variance; these news items either contain strategy/game, interpretation, negativity, and balance (neutrality) elements or combine personalization and hard news. In the United States, on the contrary, we find three types of news items that explain 63% of the variance: the first type of news item (■) combines elements of strategy/game, interpretation, and balance; the second type of news item (O) contains mainly negativity; and the third type of news item (♦) combines personalization and hard news.

d In Germany, the factor loading for balance was rather small (−.365).

e In Sweden, negativity loaded quite high on the substance factor it was not assigned to (−.518).

f In Norway, personalization loaded quite high on the evaluative/interpretive factor it was not assigned to (−.462).

g In the UK, the personalization index also loaded quite high on the strategy/interpretation factor (.324).

h In Denmark, the negativity load was almost equally high on both factors (with a loading of .501 for the strategy/personalization factor it was not assigned to).[7] In the US, game/strategy (.432) and personalization (.514) also loaded quite high on the third negativity factor it was not assigned to.

i In France, the hard news index also loaded quite high on the substance factor to which it was not assigned (.516).

performed a series of cluster analyses based on the factor loadings derived from the overall cross-country factor analysis. The number of clusters is determined on visual inspection (so-called elbow criterion). This procedure aims at selecting a cluster solution that is not too heterogeneous after another fusion of clusters. Based on the elbow criterion, it turned out that a four-cluster solution is most convincing. The individual clusters can be characterized by the prevalence of the key concepts, the types of news stories represented, the media in which the items were published, and the topics covered.

Cluster 1 comes to about one-third of all news items (30 percent of all items; $n = 3,337$). The stories in this cluster are more hard news–oriented and more balanced than the average news item but have less strategic framing, less interpretation, and less negativity. Almost nine out of ten of these news items are regular, fact-oriented news stories covering a wide range of issues, with an above-average share of 'hard topics,' such as macroeconomics (21 percent), social affairs (10 percent), and labor (7 percent). Reports on party politics and elections, the functioning of democracy (makes about 7 percent), and miscellaneous topics are underrepresented in this group of news reports. This cluster of news stories can therefore be labeled *issue-focused hard news coverage.*

The news items in cluster 2 (31 percent of all items; $n = 2,363$) have a profile very similar to Cluster 1 with respect to strategic framing, interpretation, negativity, and balance. Moreover, the overwhelming majority of these items consist of regular, fact-oriented news stories. In contrast to the first group of reports, however, Cluster 2 stories are much more personalized and include fewer indicators of political substance. Cluster 2 stories, although well represented in all types of media, are a bit more frequent on television and in the mass-market newspapers, and they tend to cover party politics, justice, and miscellaneous topics more often than the items of the issue-focused cluster. This cluster of news stories can therefore be labeled *actor-focused news coverage.*

The third cluster of news items accounts for 22 percent of all items ($n = 1,707$). In contrast to the first two clusters, Cluster 3 is characterized by an above-average amount of strategy framing, interpretation, and negativity. At the same time, the reports contain a lot of political substance (i.e., hard news indicators). Although the majority of these reports are regular news stories, a considerable portion consists of reportages and background stories (12 percent) and editorials or commentaries (19 percent). An above-average share of items in this cluster deals with the functioning of democracy, but the dominant topics are hard policy issues like macroeconomics (21 percent), social affairs (7 percent), and labor (7 percent). More than half of these stories were run in upmarket newspapers. This cluster can therefore be called *issue-focused interpretive coverage.*

Finally, the news reports included in the fourth cluster (17 percent; $n = 1,338$) are negative, interpretive, and personalized and show the most strategic framing. Regarding their journalistic genre, only half of these items are regular news stories, whereas 27 percent can be identified as editorials or commentaries and 20 percent as reportages and background reports. Almost half of them appeared in upmarket newspapers, but they are also frequent in mass-market newspapers. With respect to the topics covered, we find the highest shares taken by party politics and elections (39 percent) and stories dealing with the functioning of democracy (13 percent). The items in this cluster seem to represent the kind of stories that scholars have in mind when they write about subjective, interpretive, and negative coverage with a potential negative effect on citizens' views of politics. We therefore label this group of news items *strategy-focused interpretive coverage* (Table 10.6).

Table 10.6 Characteristics of news item clusters based on key concept factor structure[a]

	Issue-focused hard news coverage Cluster 1 (N = 2,337)	Actor-focused news coverage Cluster 2 (N = 2,363)	Issue-focused interpretive coverage Cluster 3 (N = 1,707)	Strategy-focused interpretive coverage Cluster 4 (N = 1,338)
Key concept values (ΔM)				
Strategy/game	.13	.15	**.43**	**.51**
Interpretation	.11	.18	**.60**	**.79**
Negativity	.54	.50	**.74**	**.71**
Balance	**.84**	**.78**	.57	.52
Personalization	.41	**.67**	.40	**.69**
Hard news	**.85**	.49	**.75**	.35
Media organization (%)[b]				
Public broadcasting television	**21**	**22**	16	11
Commercial television	17	19	15	16
Upmarket newspaper	45	36	**52**	**49**
Mass-market newspaper	17	23	18	24
Type of news story (%)[c]				
News story	**89**	**83**	64	47
Reportage/background	5	7	**12**	**20**
Editorial/column/commentary	2	4	**19**	**27**
Other	4	6	5	7
Topic (top 8 issues)[d]				
Macroeconomics/taxes	**20**	12	**21**	9
Party politics/elections	4	**16**	11	**39**
Functioning of democracy	6	8	11	**13**
Justice	7	9	6	6
Social affairs	**10**	6	**7**	3
Other (disasters, sports, royals)	2	**12**	2	**8**
Foreign affairs	5	**8**	6	4
Labour	**7**	3	**7**	2

a Based on individual news items (N = 7,797).
b χ^2 = 180.26, p < .001, Cramer's V = .088.
c χ^2 = 1197.21, p < .001, Cramer's V = .227.
d χ^2 = 1636.98, p < .001, Cramer's V = .265.

As the final step of our analysis, we compare the importance of the 4 clusters in our 16 countries. This analysis should give us a clear idea of how politics is typically presented in the different nations and thus of journalistic cultures regarding content production. Taking *issue-focused news coverage* first, journalists in France, Greece, Israel, Italy, Sweden, and the United States seem to include very little of this type of coverage in their media outlets. At the opposite end of the spectrum is Spain, with a hard news share way above the average. As we have seen, the economic situation of the Eurozone crisis may have contributed to this exceptional result. Belgium, Denmark, the Netherlands, Norway, Switzerland, and the United Kingdom use this kind of coverage in more than one-third of all news items.

In several countries, a low preference for issue-focused hard news coverage occurs with an above-average preference for *actor-focused news coverage*. This pattern is found, for example, in France, Greece, Israel, Sweden, the United States, and – most notably – Italy. It is the predominant type of reporting in these countries, with more than half of all the news items falling into this category. But it is especially uncommon in Portugal, Spain, and Switzerland. *Issue-focused interpretive coverage* is most common in Austria and Portugal (more than 40 percent of news items) and in Switzerland (more than one-third of stories). And finally, *strategy-focused interpretive coverage* is most common in France, Greece, the United States, Israel, and Italy, where between one-fourth and one-third of the news items belong to this category (Figure 10.1).

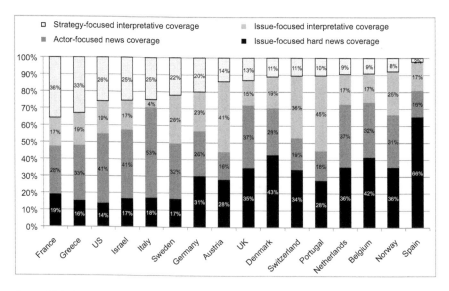

Figure 10.1 Size of news item clusters according to key concepts in country comparison. Clusters based on individual news items (N = 7,746).

Conclusion

Despite some attempts to explore how different key concepts of political communication interconnect in news coverage, the vast majority of existing studies tend to concentrate on single concepts, and in those cases where several are examined, concepts tend to be treated as if they were separate from one another. Existing cross-conceptual studies have been largely theoretical and certainly not internationally comparative, involving different media (for exceptions, see the work by Esser and Umbricht). By adopting a cross-conceptual approach, this chapter enriched our understanding of how different content features interact on the level of individual news items across 16 countries. The chapter showed that the six key concepts investigated in the book are not independent from each other. The underlying structure of their interrelationships is shown with a factor analysis revealing two factors. The first factor comprises interpretive and evaluative elements; the second largely represents the dichotomy of person versus substance. As we noted, these two factors can be regarded as important, deep structures that seem to guide journalists' construction of the political world. Based on this pattern of findings, we were able to run cluster analyses to determine how many news items share a specific profile of those key concepts, identifying four key cross concept clusters. The study found that 30 percent of all news items were dominated by *issue-focused hard news*, 31 percent by *actor-focused news*, 22 percent by *issue-focused interpretive coverage*, and 17 percent by *strategy-focused interpretive coverage*. We can see that issue-oriented coverage still makes up for the majority of political news coverage in Western democracies and that strategy-focused reports only represent a rather small part of overall political coverage. However, comparing the cluster patterns in the various countries also shows huge differences in the importance of the different types of coverage (see Figure 10.1).

One of the most remarkable findings is that Israel and the United States are unique in their composition of news clusters, with low shares of issue-oriented coverage and a huge amount of actor- and strategy-focused reports. Political coverage in most European countries differs from this news composition, especially with respect to issue-focused hard news, which plays a much bigger role. This outcome speaks against uncritically transferring results and the focus of research from the United States to Europe. Instead, future research on European media should put a stronger focus on the specific patterns important in the European and national contexts. Nonetheless, some European countries seem to have rather similar coverage to Israel and United States. Obviously, the picture is more complex than a simple Europe versus United States dichotomy. Future research will have to dig even deeper into the various reasons responsible for the differences and similarities between European countries.

Another important aspect that we want to point out is the context dependency of the global news media climate of 2012 that interacts with the theoretical concepts presented in this book. Contrary to Hallin and Mancini's (2004) pivotal research on comparative political communication, our study showed that issues in the news are treated differently in different countries. At this time, we can only speculate about what influences journalistic coverage on politically relevant issues and what factors have been omitted so far in comparative research. A plausible explanation, for instance, would be changes in public opinion towards certain issues that influence journalists' news coverage. The salience of an issue may differ highly in different countries, depending on their political communication cultures, the state of public discussion, and the time that has elapsed since the issue was raised. For example, the economic crisis and the role of international institutions like the European Union, the World Bank, and the International Monetary Fund might have led to more (institutional) hard news coverage in some countries but at the same time – with an increasingly hostile public opinion – increased the amount of negativity in the news.

This chapter has provided an important first step to clarify the relationships between key concepts and to present empirical evidence of their prevalence in the political news coverage of 16 Western democracies. In the concluding chapter, we relate these findings to the book's overall endeavor – the quest for good news.

Notes

1 The measure of balance applied in this chapter does not refer to balanced reporting about one specific actor. Instead, a news item is judged as balanced when some actors are judged very favorable and others very unfavorable (see also the chapter on balance, Chapter 7, which applies a different measure of balance).

2 The distribution of the balance (neutrality) indicator shows one extreme outlier, which is Portugal. While the average cross-country measure is .71, Portugal only arrives at .34, indicating a comparatively high share of actors that were not presented in a neutral or ambivalent tone but in an evaluative tone. Leaving out Portugal reduces the standard deviation to .07, which would put Israel and Spain among the countries deviating considerably from the cross-country balance indicator.

Appendix

Game-strategy index. It was coded whether the story makes a reference to public opinion at least once (1) or not (0), whether the story makes a reference to politicians, parties, or other actors 'winning' or 'losing' (elections, debates, public opinion or in general) (1) or not (0), whether the story uses language of sports or war at least once (1) or not (0), whether the story makes references to politicians or parties strategies or tactics for legislative debates, governing negotiations, favorable news coverage, or elections for achieving other forms of political success (1) or not (0), and whether the story makes reference to how a political actor (a party, a politician, a candidate, a government, coalition, campaign) is performing, working, or doing its job (1) or not (0) (see also the chapter on game/strategy framing).

Interpretive journalism. The interpretive journalism index was recoded so that it only indicates whether (1) or not (0) these elements are present. More specifically, it was coded whether the news story includes journalistic explanations or interpretations of the reasons behind events or actions (1) or not (0), whether the story includes journalistic speculations about future consequences of events (1) or not (0), and whether the journalist includes overt commentary when covering events and actions (1) or not (0) (see also the chapter on interpretive journalism).

Negativity. It was coded whether a news story as a whole conveys a primarily conflictual impression of politics, political records, conditions, and views (1) or not (0), whether a given news story as a whole primarily convey indications of incapability in politics (1) or not (0), and whether the overall tone of the story was negative (1) or not (0). Moreover, it was coded for the first five actors appearing in a news story, whether the report primarily conveys a negative impression of politics, political records, conditions or views (1) or not (0).

Balance (neutrality). It was coded whether a news story conveys a favorable, unfavorable, or neutral/ambivalent impression of an actor. To construct the balance measure, the favorability codings were condensed into a mean index that included the favorability of the first five actors for each news item coded so that it ranges from 0 "(positively or negatively) polarized news" to 1 "neutral or ambivalent news." Higher values are then indicative of balanced (neutral) news.

Personalization. For the first five actors appearing in a news story, it was coded whether they were a specific person (1) or an institutional or organizational actor (0). To build a measure of personalization, first, a sum index for the number of specific persons as well as for the institutional or organizational actors was calculated for each news item. Second, both indices were transformed so that values near 0 are indicative of 'no personalization' and values near 1 are indicative of 'personalization' (see also the chapter on personalization).

Hard and soft news. It was coded whether political actors, decision-making-authorities, policy-plans, and groups affected were mentioned (1) in a given news item or not (0), whether an article was predominantly unemotional (1) or emotional (0). All indicators of a hard or soft news story were transformed into an additive index that was transformed so that it ranges from 0 "story contains no hard news indicators" to 1 "story contains all hard news indicators" (see also the chapter on hard/soft news).

Chapter 11

Conclusion

Assessing news performance

*Claes de Vreese, Carsten Reinemann,
Frank Esser, and David Nicolas Hopmann
with Toril Aalberg, Peter Van Aelst, Rosa Berganza,
Nicolas Hubé, Guido Legnante, Jörg Matthes,
Stylianos Papathanassopoulos, Susana Salgado,
Tamir Sheafer, James Stanyer, and Jesper Strömbäck*

Introduction

At the outset, we asked if there is any good news about the news and, if so, where the good news is. In academic research and public discussions about news and democracy, one finds different interpretations of the state of current news provision. A tendency towards pessimism about current news performance is commonplace. Although there is an overall proliferation of both traditional and newer forms of online news availability and supply (Esser, de Vreese et al. 2012), many suggest that the *performance* of news providers is getting worse. In more or less explicit terms, the decreasing quality of news is seen as having a negative impact on the quality of political life and democracy. Set against the pessimism and caution in the public debate and literature on news quality and the performance of political journalism, we were not optimistic that we would find good-quality news or that we would be able to offer some good news as a positive antidote, so to speak, to the pervasive pessimism in the literature.

Using six key concepts – strategy and game framing, interpretive journalism, negativity, political balance, personalization, and hard versus soft news – as indicators of news performance, we systematically assessed news in 16 Western democracies. The starting point for our work was that 'news performance' implies that media have different functions (see Chapter 1). At a basic level, most agree that the news media should provide information, context and analysis, a platform for public debate, and scrutiny of power holders (McQuail 1992). News performance refers to the reality of news practices and how they manifest themselves in media outcomes across types of media systems, news organizations, and journalistic communities. Thus, we measure the quality of news performance by the use of strategy and game framing, interpretive journalism, negativity, political balance, personalization, and hard and soft news.

What did we find? We first summarize our key findings per concept, then look across the different concepts, and propose the conditions under which we are most likely to find good news. In terms of covering politics as a *strategic game*, we find that most political news in most countries during regular time periods is largely *not* framed as a strategic game. Some issues, typically related to party politics, are more often framed as a strategic game, but the use of strategy and game frames are not necessarily, as previously assumed, higher in tabloid newspapers and commercial broadcasters compared to elite newspapers and public broadcasters. Looking at *interpretive journalism*, we find that it is common across countries, although it differs significantly with respect to its prevalence, its various forms, and the type of media where it is most often found.

Looking at *negativity*, we find large country differences. Country-specific events were better able to explain overall negativity than differences in political systems, journalistic cultures, or political communication cultures. Negativity is highest in media systems with high levels of commercialism and competition and in media organizations that are geared towards commercial goals (as opposed to public service obligations). The tendency to cover politics in negative terms is stronger in the offline than online editions of media outlets and is strongest in stories that deal with negatively connoted issues, such as scandals, crises, or conflicts. Moving on to *political balance,* we find that the visibility of political actors across countries is fairly balanced. The analysis shows that by far most appearances of politicians are either neutral or balanced, rarely colored in a positive or negative light.

In terms of *personalization,* we looked at whether individual politicians or political institutions are the main actors in news stories and whether the media focus on a broad range of politicians or only on a limited number of leaders. We find that individual politicians are more prominent in the news compared to political institutions. The degree of personalized political coverage, however, varies strongly across countries. The greater the number of television channels (which represents the competitiveness of the media market) and the greater the degree of federalism (which represents the concentration of power within the political system), the more personalization in the news. Looking at *hard and soft news,* we find that the prevalence of harder and softer news strongly differs between countries. Multivariate analyses show that the medium type, a country's political and economic situation, and the state of the media market significantly predict the hard or soft character of individual news items.

Finally, analyzing across the different concepts (in Chapter 10), we find that game- or strategy-framed news tends to be more interpretive and negative, rather unbalanced, and softer. In the same vein, interpretive news tends to be more negative and strategically framed, be less balanced, and carry less hard political information. Negativity and balance are negatively correlated; we would expect a clear, unambiguous, negative portrayal of actors to be reflected in a story's overall negative tone. And finally, personalization is negatively correlated to hard news, such that personalized news tends to have less political substance, whereas news items with more political substance tend to have more institutional actors. Looking cross-nationally, we observed that Spain, Denmark, Belgium, the Netherlands, Norway, and the United Kingdom have the most issue-focused coverage, whereas Austria, Portugal, Greece, and Sweden have the least. News in France, Greece, the United States, Israel, and Italy is the most focused on framing politics as a strategic game. We will return to these dimensions, the ranking of countries, and the antecedents of news performance. But it is important to note that using the six key concepts as indicators of news performance, we do *not* find a pervasive and uniform pattern of 'bad news' with little political substance. In several instances, we even find indications of quality news.

Key dimensions of political news

Often when analyzing news, the focus is on one or two key features, such as the amount of strategy coverage versus substantive news coverage or how intensely the news is actor focused versus issue focused. Scholars rarely take the opportunity to explore news across several dimensions, even though such an approach makes sense, not only because the conceptual demarcation between different elements of interest is less clear than is often assumed, but also because (and in part as a function of this blurring of borders between the concepts) different elements co-occur, of which research has found clear traces.

We propose four clusters of news coverage based on our empirical findings (see Chapter 10). Cluster 1 is dubbed *issue-focused hard news coverage*. News stories in this cluster are more hard news–oriented and more balanced than the average news item but have less strategic framing, less interpretation, and less negativity. News items are regular, fact-oriented news stories covering a wide range of issues with an above-average share of hard topics such as macroeconomics. As shown in Figure 11.1, this type of news is largely found in Spain, Denmark, Belgium, and the Netherlands. But Israel, Sweden, Greece, and the United States have the least of this type of news.

Cluster 2 is labeled *actor-focused news coverage*. It is similar to Cluster 1 with respect to strategic framing, interpretation, negativity, and balance. It, too, features regular, fact-oriented news stories, but they are much more personalized and include fewer indicators of political substance. As shown in Figure 11.2, this type

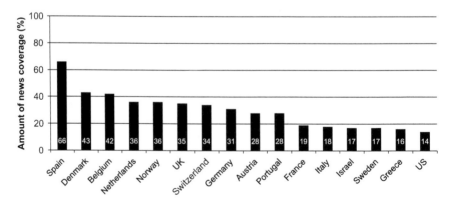

Figure 11.1 Amount of issue-focused hard news coverage per country (percentages).

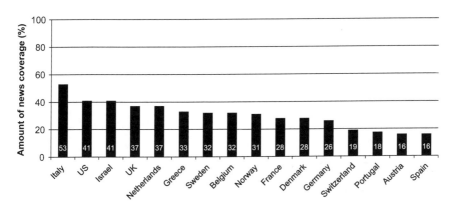

Figure 11.2 Amount of actor-focused news coverage (percentages).

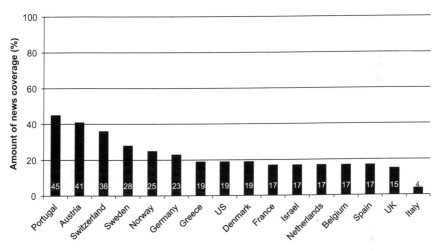

Figure 11.3 Amount of issue-focused interpretive coverage (percentages).

of news is mostly found in Italy, the United States, Israel, and the United Kingdom and less so in Switzerland, Portugal, Austria, and Spain.

Cluster 3 is called *issue-focused interpretive coverage*. It is characterized by an above-average amount of strategy framing, interpretation, and negativity. At the same time, these news reports contain a good deal of political substance (i.e., hard news indicators). As shown in Figure 11.3, issue-focused interpretive news is found most in Portugal, Austria, Switzerland, and Sweden and least in Belgium, Spain, the United Kingdom, and Italy.

Finally, Cluster 4 is named *strategy-focused interpretive coverage*. Here, we find negative, interpretive, personalized news, and the most strategic framing. This category includes not only news but also editorials and commentaries, reportage and background reports. This type of news has the highest share of

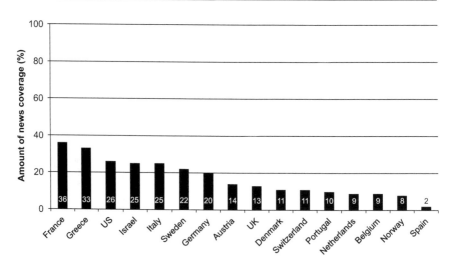

Figure 11.4 Amount of strategy-focused interpretive coverage (percentages).

party politics, elections, and stories dealing with the functioning of democracy. As shown in Figure 11.4, this type of news is especially prevalent in France, Greece, the United States, Israel, and Italy and is least prevalent in the Netherlands, Belgium, Norway, and Spain.

Figure 11.5 illustrates the different dimensions as a radar chart. It becomes clear that news in France, Greece, the United States, and Israel (and in part Italy) stands out as scoring relatively *high* on the actor-focused and strategy-focused interpretive news coverage dimensions and relatively *low* on the issue-focused hard news, with a more mixed picture regarding issue-focused interpretive news. Conversely, news in Denmark, Belgium, the Netherlands, and Norway – ceteris paribus – score higher on issue-focused hard news and lower on strategy-focused interpretive news.

As an illustration of the relationship between the different dimensions, on the one hand, and the differences in between countries, on the other hand, we briefly zoom in on the news in the United States (Figure 11.6), Germany (Figure 11.7), and Norway (Figure 11.8). News in the United States (Figure 11.6) is characterized by a (relatively speaking) high share of strategy coverage, high share of actor-based news, moderate share of issue-focused interpretive news, and low share of issue-focused hard news. News in Germany (Figure 11.7) is characterized by a somewhat moderate score on all four dimensions. News in Norway (Figure 11.8) scores very low on the strategy-interpretive dimension, relatively high on the issue hard news, and moderate on the remaining two dimensions.

In sum, the cross-national comparisons suggest that, in particular, news in France, Greece, the United States, Israel, and, in part, Italy stands out for being more strategic, interpretive, and actor based than news elsewhere. Danish, Belgian, Dutch, and Norwegian news scores higher on the hard issue dimension and

Conclusion: assessing news performance 173

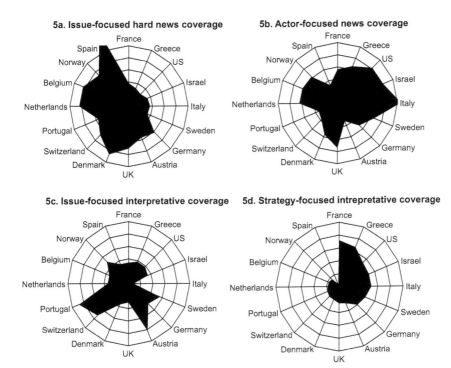

Figure 11.5 Dimensions of news. Each of the four fields represents a percentage of coverage per country by either issue-focused hard news (5a), actor-focused news (5b), issue-focused interpretive news (5c), or strategy-focused interpretive news (5d). Each ring represents an additional 10%, which results in a maximum of 50% for the outer ring. Spain, with a 66% share in issue-focused hard news coverage out of its total coverage, therefore extends beyond the outer ring.

lower on the strategy dimension. The empirical findings do not provide a clear-cut picture that translates into a one-dimensional categorization of 'good' versus 'bad' news provision or 'excellent' versus 'appalling' news performance. However, we find traces of a north–south divide; southern Europe, Israel, and the United States share patterns in news provision in contrast to northwestern Europe, represented by parts of Scandinavia, Germany, and the Belgium–Netherlands nexus. Overall, however – confirming our research group's earlier findings (Esser, Strömbäck, and de Vreese 2012) – more deeply rooted dimensions are relevant for understanding and classifying news patterns in contemporary media systems. One dimension that stands out is political economy; both in our previous study and in the study at hand, explanatory factors such as strong competition, private broadcast ownership, and heavy dependence on commercial logics turned out to be disadvantageous for news performance quality. Another aspect that stands out is the United States case, which may no longer be as exceptional as it was long made out to be in the literature (e.g., Patterson 2000).

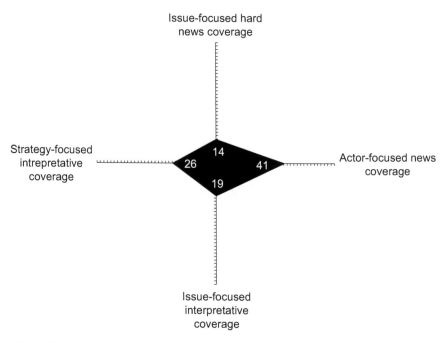

Figure 11.6 Dimensions of news coverage per dimension in the United States (percentages).

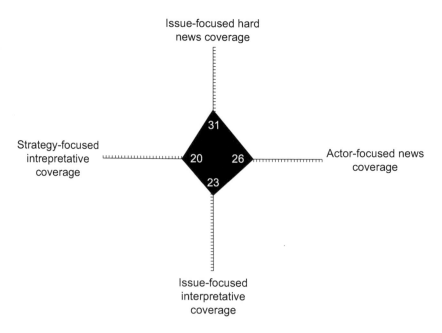

Figure 11.7 Dimensions of news coverage per dimension in Germany (percentages).

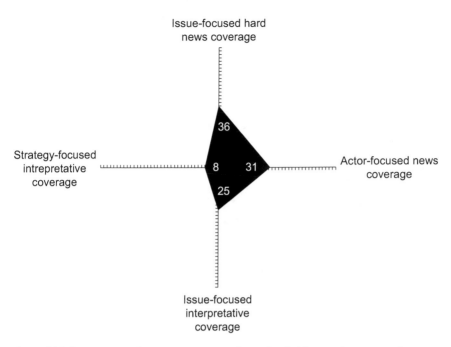

Figure 11.8 Dimensions of news coverage per dimension in Norway (percentages).

Everyday democracy

Our analysis focuses, deliberately, on routine news. We do not include election periods or news focused around large and important events. Obviously, in so doing, we do not argue that political news during elections is unimportant. On the contrary, these few weeks of heightened political interest and activity are the cornerstone of democracy and the epitome of aligning citizens' preferences and elected representatives. However, elections are not the only time at which representative democracy is at play. The provision of news about politics in the interim period – that is, the 95 percent of the time when an election is not taking place – is crucial for the linkage between citizens and politics. This notion is also gaining momentum in the political science literature, and the term 'between-election democracy' eloquently captures the idea that representative democracy necessitates responsive political representatives also in the long periods between elections (Esaiasson and Narud 2013). The bulk of political communication research focuses on election periods, and many of the observations about the quality of news and the performance of news media pertain to elections. Patterson's (1993) *Out of Order* made a clear argument why the news content during elections is suboptimal and damaging to democracy. He is especially critical of the growing attention that is paid to polls and horse race news. His analysis focuses on election periods in particular, and his conclusion is that the news media are charged with a task that they are not equipped to fulfill; they therefore fall short of our expectations. The system is dysfunctional, out of order. We ask in this book if the same kind of conclusion pertains to nonelection news. It goes without saying that an assessment of news performance should also consider the bigger part of the electoral cycle, when elections are absent. Again, based on our analysis, we do *not* find support for a sweeping conclusion about 'system failure.' Although one can be critical of contemporary news for many reasons, the picture that emerges is one where the overall supply of political news is rich in both amount and content.

Antecedents of good news?

We have identified different clusters of news reporting and scored the countries on each cluster as well as across the cluster dimensions. We now turn to the antecedents of different news performance. In Chapter 3, we outlined our conceptual approach and made a distinction between factors shaping political news at the (1) event level, (2) media organization level, (3) media system level, and (4) political system level. In each chapter, we discussed the different explanations. In general, there are certain news styles that have a higher degree of event dependency. For example, strategy game news is inherent to elections, though not absent outside elections, and negative news prevails mostly in relation to certain topics. At the level of media organizations, the distinction between public and commercial broadcasters is clearly still relevant to understanding news content and performance differences. Commercial broadcasters provide more interpretive, more negative, more personalized, and more soft news than their public service counterparts. For mass-market versus upmarket newspapers, the picture is more diverse, with upmarket newspapers, for example, scoring higher on hard news but also on strategy game coverage and negativity – perhaps, in part, as a function of longer pieces and more attention to the behind-the-scenes aspects of politics. At the level of media systems, we find that the degree of competition in a media system is a positive predictor of, for example, personalization and negativity. At the political systems level, the degree of federalism has a strong negative impact on personalization, whereas the number of parties in government has a positive impact on the degree of game strategy news framing. Our study also included both online and offline news. Here, we found very little that was substantively meaningful and minimal systematic variation when controlling for other factors, suggesting a rather high degree of resemblance between the online and offline news supply and that the same kind of 'media logic' is prevalent in both offline and online news (Strömbäck and Esser 2014). Looking across the different explanatory levels, we find that the *media organizational level* – in particular, the distinctions commercial/public service and mass market/upmarket – is highly relevant for understanding variation in news content. Table 11.1 summarizes a selection of our hypothesized effects and the empirical findings.

Conclusion: assessing news performance   177

Table 11.1 Multilevel framework of factors that shape political news

Levels of influence	Hypothesized effects on news performance (selected examples)	Empirical relationships found
Event level		
Bad economic situation	More hard news	Not supported
Proximity to elections	More game/strategy news	Supported
Issue context:		
e.g., crime and corruption	More negative news	Supported
e.g., intra party conflict	More game/strategy news	Supported
Media organizational level		
Mass-market oriented editorial mission (e.g., in commercial TV or popular press)	More personalized news	Partly supported
	More soft news	Supported
	More strategic news	Partly supported
	More interpretive news	Supported
Public service mission	More balanced news	Partly supported
Online channel	More negative news	Not supported
Media system level		
High market competition	More personalized news	Partly supported
	More negative news	Partly supported
	More interpretive news	Partly supported
High market commercialization	More negative news	Not supported
	More interpretive news	Not supported
	More soft news	Supported
Low competition and commercialization	More hard news	Partly supported
High journalistic professionalism and independence (i.e., distance to politics)	More negative news	Not supported
	More strategic news	Not supported
	More interpretive news	Not supported
Political system level		
Small number of competing parties	More strategic news	Supported
	More negative news	Not supported
High number of parties (i.e., need for negotiations and coalitions)	More hard news	Not supported
Majoritarian electoral system	More personalized news	Not supported
Low federalism, high power concentration	More personalized news	Supported
	More negative news	Not supported
Stronger party standing in preceding election or current poll standing	More visibility	Supported

News performance and democratic quality

Answering the question of where the *best* news performance is to be found is obviously a task with normative implications. The answer will depend on the standards that are applied to the media and on the perceived role that they play in a democracy. As summarized by Strömbäck (2005), when the procedural and competitive models of democracy are combined, the demands for political journalism are to (1) provide reliable information that can be acted upon, if necessary, (2) provide an overview of political events, (3) monitor and watch political elites and power holders, and (4) offer alternatives in political discussions. How do we interpret our findings in that light?

First, we contend that *none* of the included countries have news that is void of substance or focused solely on strategy. Neither is it heavily negative or grossly biased. So the first observation must necessarily be that things are not pervasively bad.

Second, some differences are striking. We see a pattern emerge where news in countries like France, Greece, Israel, the United States, and Italy is less focused on substance and more on strategy; it is more negative, more actor biased, and more interpretive. The opposite is the case in Scandinavian countries and the central west of the European continent (Belgium, Germany, the Netherlands). Here, the news is more varied and overall more substantive and hard-news focused.

Third, media organizations matter. Public service broadcasting is good for news performance, provided that the public broadcaster has the necessary financial and political autonomy from power holders.

In all cases, however, news provides an overview of current events, balanced information, and a diverse range of topics and approaches. Perhaps the real question is therefore by what bar should one judge political news performance? Other scholars have suggested that the bar for the average citizen and 'average' news medium should not be placed too high. John Zaller (2003) has argued that most citizens are only marginally interested in politics and that the news media should – as a minimum – function as a 'burglar alarm,' such that even the inattentive and politically uninterested citizen will be exposed to major political issues. Zaller (2003) posits that this minimum is perhaps both sufficient and rational since diving into deep and contextualized knowledge about politics does little for citizens' political empowerment or decision-making impact.

We find Zaller's model too minimalistic and believe that we should demand more – both of citizens and of the political news media. According to Bennett (2009), problems occur if the alarm rings too frequently or if it does not ring at all. Our findings suggest that the news media deliver more than just burglar alarm coverage. In line with Albæk, van Dalen, Jebril, and de Vreese (2014), we suggest that "political journalism should not be treated complacently." Although we find no reason to 'ring the alarm bell' or activate the burglar alarm on the part of the media, our findings clearly show that strong public service organizations and journalists that are not tightly bound by commercial or political pressures are where the news performance is best.

Approach and shortcomings

In this book, we took an explicit comparative approach to our study of political news. The study is part of a larger endeavor in which we hope to promote not only comparative research but also a *systematic* approach, which calls for standardized ways of operationalizing key concepts and for particular attention to theory-driven, systematically tested explanations (Esser et al. 2012). As we have expressed elsewhere (e.g., Esser, de Vreese et al. 2012), we share earlier observations about the virtue of comparative research (e.g., Blumler, McLeod, and Rosengren 1992; Esser and Pfetsch 2004; Hallin and Mancini 2004), but we also acknowledge that political communication scholars still have a long way to go to further develop the conceptual consistency and the infrastructure for comparative research. In pursuing this, we believe that a combination of large-scale comparative studies and small-scale, in-depth case studies should complement each other.

Our own study is obviously not without limitations. First of all, we would like to highlight that the project was completed without the backing of a large-scale grant. Systematic comparative research is cumbersome and requires resources. However, with this project, we have shown that pooling modest resources and agreeing to an approach, a design, and a measurement can yield insightful comparative research. This lesson is an important one.

When resources are pooled, comparative research can be carried out on a shoestring. That said, in the long run, comparative research needs to develop infrastructure, which requires larger endeavors and greater resources.

Looking at the project in more detail, we believe that our research could be improved by expanding the scope of the design. We have focused, purposely, on an 'in-between' period of democracy. Obviously, a design that would allow a comparison between our routine period and election times would yield very interesting observations and offer comparative conclusions about these different aspects of democratic processes (see also Van Aelst and de Swert 2009; Binderkrantz and Green-Pedersen 2009; Falasca 2014). Second, the scope of the media sample could be expanded. We include television, newspapers, and online news, but in terms of both the sampling period and media outlets, it would be beneficial to span out more to assess temporal and outlet differences and similarities in greater detail. In particular, the sampling of online news is limited by looking only at the online counterparts of offline news providers. Even so, we believe that our choice made sense for reasons of comparability between online and offline news and of the sites' popularity and wide use.

Third, our analysis neglects the role of visuals. The importance of visuals in news provision has been reiterated time and again (Graber 2003; Grabe and Bucy 2009; Nagel, Maurer, and Reinemann 2012), but too often, as in our case, they have been neglected and have not been integrated into the actual coding scheme. We echo the long list of scholars pleading to pay more attention to the role of visuals, also in comparative political communication research. Finally, we are aware that any attempt to standardize comes at the cost of losing details. Already, when developing the conceptual framework for this study (Esser, de Vreese et al. 2012), we acknowledged that the measures proposed for each of the six key concepts were not exhaustive. The empirical application of these measures led to further confinement and simplification, and thereby a de facto loss of detail and information. At the same time, the challenge of cross-national comparative content analysis also yielded inter-coder reliability scores for some of the new items that merit further conceptual attention and that need to be improved in future research.

In addition to these explicit shortcomings, our comparative endeavor yielded interesting discussions about the levels and units of analysis in comparative research. Descriptions and analyses can be conducted at the individual news story level, the aggregated media outlet level, or the country level. In many descriptive analyses, we refer to the sum of individual news stories, whereas most explanatory analyses are conducted at the media outlet level. A second issue is one of comparability. As noted earlier, media type is an important explanation, but a mass newspaper in one country is not exactly the same in another. Undoubtedly, those who know both *The Sun* (United Kingdom) and *De Telegraaf* (Netherlands) would agree that these are not identical newspapers, just like a 15-minute public service news broadcast in Germany is not identical to a 60-minute public broadcasting news show in Spain. These examples point to a broader issue of comparability and functional equivalence of the units being compared. Our study has not solved these challenges but merely adds to the cautionary warnings that should be issued when making conclusions about types of units.

A final reflection concerns explanations that failed to fall into their expected place. In recent years, much work has been done at the level of systems (see also Chapter 3). In our analyses of variation in news content, this level did not yield strong explanations, and our empirical findings did not reproduce the systematic pattern that could be expected based on, for example, Hallin and Mancini's (2004) typology of countries. We take this outcome not so much as a disqualification of existing work at the systems level but rather as an indicator that explanations of news content features require other crucial factors to be included (see also Boomgaarden et al. 2013). System-level classifications have perhaps greater value as heuristics for systems differences and similarities than as specific explanatory factors.

The future of news: sobering appraisals of new challenges

Our book focuses on political news as it is understood in a relatively conventional and contemporary sense – that is, on news that is provided by key national news organizations via television, newspapers, and online. It is a truism that the news landscape is rapidly changing. News is no longer accessible merely in prescheduled television shows or in papers printed at night. New digital and networked technologies have emerged while many traditional political journalism outlets with clear-cut schedules have declined (Kuhn and Kleis-Nielsen 2014). The news business is now a 24/7 affair, and in recent years, new players have entered the field offering niche news, specialized news, citizen-based news, and the widespread sharing and liking of news on social media. This change poses the question of how our own study relates to these new realities of news supply and use. Scholarship has long clung to a "mass public model of political communication research," which is now changing towards a "more fragmented model of political communication" (Tewksbury and Rittenberg 2012), dubbed by others a "hybrid communication system" (Chadwick 2013). We are fully aware of this shift, but the question remains what conclusions should be drawn from it.

The old mass public model understands political communication basically as a top-down process where elites in the media and political sphere control information. The public occupies a much weaker position, unable to do other than receive or ignore these elite-centered messages. In the new evolving system, however, traditional media are losing influence, whereas the audience is gaining importance. New possibilities are opening up for people to become more selective and active, and these shifts in consumption patterns and in mass self-communication have implications. Although the changes appear to be evolutionary rather than revolutionary, people increasingly have the option of becoming involved in the creation and distribution of political information, observable in multiple forms of citizen journalism and user-generated content. Greater involvement leads to a potentially greater dispersion of providers, platforms, practices, and subpublics and thereby to a "more fragmented model" of political communication (see Tewksbury and Rittenberg 2012). Some commentators are already declaring the death of traditional journalism (Charles 2014; McChesney and Pickard 2011), while others are celebrating the rise of digital networks and crowd-sourced intelligence (Bennett 2015). Future scholarship will show to what extent these predictions are right.

We readily concede that our study is more concerned with the realities of today. But although our study focuses mainly on established news providers, we found them in the middle of a transitional process, making changes to adapt to new demands and requirements. Many of these organizations are trying to turn themselves into more agile operators as they embrace new processes and approaches to news. One manifestation of this development is that they are all employing different platforms to engage with the public, and for that reason, we decided to study both their offline and online news supply. And we focused specifically on those news organizations that still hold the largest audiences and the greatest agenda-setting power in their respective countries. We do realize that many functions of journalism will no longer be provided solely by the closed ecosystem of 'traditional' media organizations but by a more open, fluid, hybrid system that accommodates a wider range of sources, including blogs and social media. It is very likely, however, that a fair number of large general news providers – today's print, broadcast, and digital leaders – will also dominate the provision of political information in the future (Picard 2014). We have taken great efforts to identify those leaders and include them in our sample. After all, most people continue to use well-established sources such as the BBC, *The Guardian*, *The New York Times*, or CNN when consuming online news (Newman and Levy 2014; Shehata and Strömbäck 2014). Moreover, many of the news items that people share on social media platforms tend to originate from these well-established sources or relate to traditional media formats (Curran, Fenton, and Freedman 2012).

The six features of news performance that we have studied (strategy and game framing, interpretive journalism, negativity, political balance, personalization, and hard and soft news) are part of a 'news logic' that has developed over a long period in the transorganizational field of legacy media. This incremental process was based on common professional beliefs, norms, relationships, and routines and was a typical course to follow for news media to emerge "as institutions" (Esser 2013; Strömbäck and Esser 2014). Whether these institutionalized elements of news logic and news performance will stay the same or change under the influence of an increasing 'social media logic' remains to be seen. Our expectation is that certain forms of journalism – whether practiced inside or outside the brick walls of news organizations – will stay the same.

The greatest differences between mass media logic and network media logic concern the production, distribution, and consumption of messages, as Klinger and Svensson (2014) have pointed out.[1] But they also emphasize that the elements of news logic and news performance that we have studied remain significant because "the majority of relevant information still comes from journalistic content production, is distributed via established mass media and is used by individuals with routinized media menus" (Klinger and Svensson 2014, p. 11). New players such as Buzzfeed, Facebook, Google News, or Twitter are good examples since they remain reliant on external sources and repackage information derived from traditional news providers. Further, their output is limited in democratic value due to self-imposed reductions (such as maximum message length on Twitter or the conversion of everything to headline-grabbing lists at Buzzfeed).

Nevertheless, we fully agree that the "political information cycle" (Chadwick 2011) in Western democracies will be increasingly shaped by the *combined* forces of conventional and network media, which act in tandem to shape the news agenda. And we also agree with Cushion (2015), who argues that "amidst much of the hype and excitement about the latest technologies reshaping the new media landscape, it is important not to lose sight of old media which continue to exert their influence on most political information environments" (p. 162). The "political information environments" that Cushion refers to were defined by us in an earlier publication as mediated public spaces through which political information flows via different channels (Esser, de Vreese et al. 2012). The idea of 'environment' emphasizes, in particular, the supply and performance of news to which citizens are exposed.

Changes in the supply side of the news environment lead to the final question: what will and what should be the future added value of political journalism. Thomas Patterson (2014), in his recent book, argues that the news media need to provide a new kind of added value, which he dubs "knowledge-based journalism," which he characterizes as

Conclusion: assessing news performance 183

a conceptual reorientation of the way media members frame issues and conduct the information-gathering process. . . . This is not a call for dry policy stories, but a shift in the way the press should contextualize partisan claims and ground anecdotes in wider intellectual frameworks and research findings.

In the light of our news classification, Patterson's recommendations might be a call for political journalism to be not only issue based but also interpretive. However, even if political journalism adjusts continuously to cater for citizens as critical consumers in media markets, an audience is not guaranteed. Current research is divided on what proliferation in choice does for news consumption (see Prior 2013 for an overview): are some citizens increasingly tuning in while others tune out? Or do they become selective (along the lines of political preferences)? Or do citizens still get 'trapped' by the news as inadvertent audience members in a high-choice era? Only future, systematic, comparative research can answer such questions. For now, we can only conclude that, as regards the supply side, good news is out there. As we continue to discuss and study the changing role of political journalism in a global world, this conclusion is an important one to add to the literature and to the public and political debate about news performance.

Note

1 Klinger and Svensson (2014) argue that the 'production' of messages in *mass media logic* refers to content that is generated and selected extensively by professional journalists according to news values, whereas in *network media logic* this is done by (lay) users according to their individual preferences and anticipated attention gain. 'Distribution' of messages in *mass media logic* means content selected by expert/professional gatekeepers – based on established news values – and distributed to a fixed audience of subscribers, whereas in *network media logic*, it means that users distribute popular content as intermediaries – almost like chain letters – through networks of like-minded others. Media 'consumption' in *mass media logic* refers to a location-bound mass audience that uses professionally preselected messages rather passively, whereas in *network media logic* the process occurs within like-minded peer networks, based on selective exposure driven by own interests and oriented towards interaction through practices of constant updating.

References

Aalberg, T. (2014). Issues, events and frames in political media coverage. In C. Reinemann (Ed.), *Political communication: Handbooks of communication science*, Vol. 18 (pp. 375–388). Berlin: De Gruyter Mouton.

Aalberg, T., and Curran, J. (2012). *How media inform democracy: A comparative approach.* London: Routledge.

Aalberg, T., Strömbäck, J., and de Vreese, C. H. (2012). The framing of politics as strategy and game: A review of concepts, operationalizations and key findings. *Journalism* 13(2): 162–178.

Aalberg, T., Van Aelst, P., and Curran, J. (2010). Media systems and the political information environment: A cross-national comparison. *The International Journal of Press/ Politics* 15(3): 255–271.

Aarts, K., Blais, A., and Schmitt, H. (Eds.). (2011). *Political leaders and democratic elections.* Oxford: Oxford University Press.

Adam, S., and Maier, M. (2010). Personalization of politics: A critical review and agenda for research. In C. Salmon (Ed.), *Communication yearbook 34* (pp. 213–257). New York: Routledge.

Albæk, E., Van Dalen, A., Jebril, N., and de Vreese, C. H. (2014). *Political journalism in comparative perspective.* New York: Cambridge University Press.

Asp, K. (2003). *Medieval 2002 — Partiskheten och valutgången.* Göteborg: JMG Arbetsrapport nr. 13, Göteborgs Universitet.

Asp, K. (2007). Fairness, informativeness and scrutiny. *Nordicom Review, Jubilee Issue* 31–49: 28.

Assembleia da República. (April 11, 2011). Law no. 8/2011, of 11 April. Available at www. anacom.pt/render.jsp?contentId=1105532.

Balmas, M., Rahat, G., Sheafer, T., and Shenhav, S. R. (2014). Two routes to personalized politics: Centralized and decentralized personalization. *Party Politics* 20(1): 37–51.

Balmas, M., and Sheafer, T. (2013). Leaders first, countries after: Mediated political personalization in the international arena. *Journal of Communication* 63(3): 454–475.

Barnhurst, K. (2003). The makers of meaning: National public radio and the new long journalism, 1980–2000. *Political Communication* 20(1): 1–22.

Barnhurst, K. G., and Mutz, D. (1997). American journalism and the decline in event-centered reporting. *Journal of Communication* 47(4): 27–53.

Baum, M. A. (2003). Soft news and political knowledge: Evidence of absence or absence of evidence? *Political Communication* 20(2): 173–190.

Bennett, W. L. (1996). *News: The politics of illusion.* New York: Longman.

References 185

Bennett, W. L. (2009). *News: The politics of illusion.* 8th ed. New York: Longman.

Bennett, W. L. (2015). Changing societies, changing media systems: Challenges for communication theory, research and education. In S. Coleman, G. Moss, and K. Parry (Eds.), *Can the media serve democracy? Essays in honour of Jay G. Blumler* (pp. 151–163). Basingstoke: Palgrave Macmillan.

Benson, R. (2008). Normative theories of journalism. In W. Donsbach (Ed.), *The international encyclopedia of communication* (pp. 2561–2597). Oxford: Wiley-Blackwell.

Benson, R., Blach-Ørsten, M., Powers, M., Willig, I., and Zambrano, S. V. (2012). Media systems online and off: Comparing the form of news in the United States, Denmark, and France. *Journal of Communication* 62(1): 21–38.

Benson, R., and Hallin, D. (2007). How states, markets and globalization shape the news: The French and U.S. national press, 1965–97. *European Journal of Communication* 22(1): 27–48.

Binderkrantz, A. S., and Green-Pedersen, C. (2009). Policy or processes in focus? *International Journal of Press/Politics* 14(2): 166–185.

Bittner, A. (2011). *Platform or personality? The role of party leaders in elections.* Oxford: Oxford University Press.

Blumler, J. G., and Gurevitch, M. (1995). *The crisis of public communication.* London: Routledge.

Blumler, J. G., and Gurevitch, M. (2001). "Americanization" reconsidered: U.K.-U.S. campaign communication across time. In W. L. Bennett and R. M. Entman (Eds.), *Mediated politics: Communication and the future of democracy* (pp. 380–403). New York: Cambridge University Press.

Blumler, J. G., and Kavanagh, D. (1999). The third age of political communication: Influences and features. *Political Communication* 16(3): 209–230.

Blumler, J. G., McLeod, J. M., and Rosengren, K. E. (1992). An introduction to comparative communication research. In J. G. Blumler, J. M. McLeod, and K. E. Rosengren (Eds.), *Comparatively speaking: Communication and culture across space and time* (pp. 3–18). Newbury Park: Sage.

Boomgaarden, H. G., de Vreese, C. H., Schuck, A.R.T., Azrout, R., Elenbaas, M., van Spanje, J.H.P., and Vliegenthart, R. (2013). Across time and space: Explaining variation in news coverage of the European Union. *European Journal of Political Research* 52(5): 608–629.

Boumans, J. W., Boomgaarden, H. G., and Vliegenthart, R. (2013). Media personalisation in context: A cross-national comparison between the UK and the Netherlands, 1992–2007. *Political Studies* 61(1): 198–216.

Bourdieu, P. (1998). *On television.* New York: The New Press.

Brandenburg, H. (2005). Political bias in the Irish media: A quantitative study of campaign coverage during the 2002 general election. *Irish Political Studies* 20(3): 297–322.

Brants, K., and van Praag, P. (2006). Signs of media logic: Half a century of political communication in the Netherlands. *Javnost* 13(1): 25–40.

Brekken, T., Thorbjørnsrud, K., and Aalberg, T. (2012). News substance: The relative importance of soft and de-contextualized news. In T. Aalberg and J. Curran (Eds.), *How media inform the democracy: A comparative approach* (pp. 64–78). New York: Taylor & Francis.

Brettschneider, F. (1997). The press and the polls in Germany, 1980–1994: Poll coverage as an essential part of election campaign reporting. *International Journal of Public Opinion Research* 9(3): 248–265.

186 References

Cappella, J. A., and Jamieson, K. H. (1997). *Spiral of cynicism*. New York: Oxford University Press.

Caspari, M., Schönbach, K., and Lauf, E. (1999). Bewertung politischer Akteure in Fernsehnachrichten. *Media Perspektiven* 1999(5): 270–274.

Chadwick, A. (2011). Britain's first live televised party leaders' debate: From the news cycle to the political information cycle. *Parliamentary Affairs* 64(1): 24–44.

Chadwick, A. (2013). *The hybrid media system*. Oxford: Oxford University Press.

Charles, A. (Ed.). (2014). *The end of journalism: Industry, technology and politics*. Oxford: Peter Lang.

Cohen, J. (2008). *The presidency in the era of 24 hour news*. Princeton, NJ: Princeton University Press.

Coleman, J. S. (1990). *Foundations of social theory*. Cambridge: Harvard University.

Conseil supérieur de l'audiovisuel. (2009). *Délibération du 21 juillet 2009 relative au principe de pluralisme politique dans les services de radio et de télévision*. Paris: CSA.

Conseil supérieur de l'audiovisuel. (2011). *Recommandation n° 2011–3 du 30 novembre 2011 à l'ensemble des services de radio et de télévision concernant l'élection du Président de la République*. Paris: CSA.

Cook, T. E. (1998). *Governing with the news*. Chicago: University of Chicago Press.

Croteau, D., and Hoynes, W. (2006). *The business of media: Corporate media and the public interest*. Thousand Oaks, CA: Pine Forge.

Curran, J., Coen, S., Aalberg, T., and Iyengar, S. (2012). News content, media consumption and current affairs knowledge. In T. Aalberg and J. Curran (Eds.), *How media inform the democracy: A comparative approach* (pp. 81–97). New York: Taylor & Francis.

Curran, J., Fenton, N., and Freedman, D. (2012). *Misunderstanding the Internet*. London: Routledge.

Curran, J., Iyengar, S., Lund, A. B., and Salovaara-Moring, I. (2009). Media system, public knowledge and democracy: A comparative study. *European Journal of Communication* 24(1): 5–26.

Curran, J., Salovaara-Moring, I., Coen, S., and Iyengar, S. (2010). Crime, foreigners and hard news: A cross-national comparison of reporting and public perception. *Journalism* 11(1): 3–19.

Cushion, S. (2012). *The democratic value of news: Why public service media matter*. Basingstoke: Palgrave Macmillan.

Cushion, S. (2015). *News and politics: The rise of live and interpretive journalism*. London: Routledge.

Dalton, R. J., McAllister, I., and Wattenberg, M. P. (2000). The consequences of partisan dealignment. In R. J. Dalton and M. P. Wattenberg (Eds.), *Parties without partisans: Political change in advanced industrial democracies* (pp. 37–63). Oxford: Oxford University Press.

Darras, E. (2005). Media consecration of the political order. In R. N. Benson and E. Neveu (Eds.), *Bourdieu and the journalistic field* (pp. 156–173). Cambridge: Polity.

De Swert, K., Belo, A., Kamhawi, R., Lo, V., Mujica, C., and Porath, W. (2013). Topics in foreign and domestic television news. In A. Cohen (Ed.), *Foreign news on television: Where in the world is the global village?* (pp. 41–62). New York: Peter Lang.

Deuze, M. (2002). National news cultures: A comparison of Dutch, German, British, Australian, and U.S. journalists. *Journalism & Mass Communication Quarterly* 79(1): 134–149.

de Vreese, C. H. (2003). Television reporting of second-order elections. *Journalism Studies* 4(2): 183–198.

de Vreese, C. H. (2008). News coverage of politics. In L. L. Kaid and C. Holtz-Bacha (Eds.), *Encyclopedia of political communication*, Vol. 2 (pp. 496–501). Los Angeles: Sage.

de Vreese, C. H. (2009). Journalistic news frames. In P. D'Angelo and J. Kuypers (Eds.), *Doing framing analysis* (pp. 187–214). New York: Routledge.

de Vreese, C. H., Banducci, S. A., Semetko, H., and Boomgaarden, H. G. (2006). The news coverage of the 2004 European parliamentary election campaign in 25 countries. *European Union Politics* 7(4): 477–504.

de Vreese, C. H., and Elenbaas, M. (2010). Political publicity and spin. In K. Brants and K. Voltmer (Eds.), *Political communication in postmodern democracy* (pp. 75–91). Basingstoke: Palgrave.

de Vreese, C. H., Lauf, E., and Peter, J. (2007). The media and European parliament elections: Second-rate coverage of a second-order event? In W. van der Brug and C. van der Eijk (Eds.), *European elections and domestic politics: Lessons from the past and scenarios for the future* (pp. 116–130). Notre Dame, IN: University of Notre Dame Press.

de Vreese, C. H., and Semetko, H. A. (2002). Cynical and engaged: Strategic campaign coverage, public opinion and mobilization in a referendum. *Communication Research* 29(6): 615–641.

de Vreese, C. H., and Tobiasen, M. (2007). Conflict and identity: Explaining turnout and anti-integrationist voting in the Danish 2004 elections for the European parliament. *Scandinavian Political Studies* 30: 87–111.

de Vreese, C. H. and Vliegenthart, R. (2012). Europe: a laboratory for comparative communication research. In I. Volkmer (Ed.), *Handbook of global media research* (pp. 470–486). Oxford: Wiley-Blackwell.

D'Haenens, L., Jankowski, N., and Heuvelmann, A. (2004). News in online and print newspapers: Differences in reader consumption and recall. *New Media & Society* 6: 363–381.

Djerf-Pierre, M., and Weibull, L. (2008). From public educator to interpreting ombudsman: Regimes of political journalism in Swedish public service broadcasting 1925–2005. In J. Strömbäck, M. Ørsten, and T. Aalberg (Eds.), *Communicating politics: Political communication in the Nordic countries* (pp. 195–214). Gothenburg: Nordicom.

Donsbach, W. (2010). The global journalist: Are professional structures being flattened? In B. Dobek-Ostrowska, M. Glowacki, K. Jakubowicz, and M. Sükösd (Eds.), *Comparative media systems: European and global perspectives* (pp. 153–170). Budapest, Hungary: CEU Press.

Dunaway, J. (2013). Media ownership and story tone in campaign news. *American Politics Research* 41(1): 24–53.

Elmelund-Præstekær, C., and Hopmann, D. N. (2012). Does television personalise voting behaviour? Studying the effects of media exposure on voting for candidates or parties. *Scandinavian Political Studies* 35(2): 117–140.

Engesser, S., and Franzetti, A. (2011). Media systems and political systems: Dimensions of comparison. *International Communication Gazette* 73(4): 273–301.

Esaiasson, P., and Narud, H. M. (2013). *Between-election democracy*. Essex: ECPR Press.

Esser, F. (2008). Dimensions of political news cultures: Sound bite and image bite news in France, Germany, Great Britain and the United States. *International Journal of Press/Politics* 13(4): 401–428.

Esser, F. (2013). Mediatization as challenge: Media logic versus political logic. In H. Kriesi, S. Lavenex, F. Esser, J. Matthes, M. Bühlmann, and D. Bochsler (Eds.), *Democracy in the age of globalization and mediatization* (pp. 155–176). Basingstoke: Palgrave Macmillan.

188 References

Esser, F., de Vreese, C., Strömbäck, J., Van Aelst, P., Aalberg, T., Stanyer, J., . . . Reinemann, C. (2012). Political information opportunities in Europe: A longitudinal and comparative study of 13 television systems. *International Journal of Press/Politics* 17(3): 247–274.

Esser, F., and Hanitzsch, T. (2012). On the why and how of comparative inquiry in communication studies. In F. Esser and T. Hanitzsch (Eds.), *Handbook of comparative communication research* (pp. 3–22). London: Routledge.

Esser, F., and Pfetsch, B. (Eds.). (2004). *Comparing political communication: Theories, cases, and challenges.* New York: Cambridge University Press.

Esser, F., and Strömbäck, J. (2012a). Comparing election campaign communication. In F. Esser and T. Hanitzsch (Eds.), *The handbook of comparative communication research* (pp. 289–307). New York: Routledge.

Esser, F., and Strömbäck, J. (2012b). Comparing news on national elections. In F. Esser and T. Hanitzsch (Eds.), *The handbook of comparative communication research* (pp. 308–326). London: Routledge.

Esser, F., and Strömbäck, J. (Eds.). (2014). *Mediatization of politics: Understanding the transformation of Western democracies.* Basingstoke: Palgrave Macmillan.

Esser, F., Strömbäck, J., and de Vreese, C. H. (2012). Reviewing key concepts in research on political news journalism: Conceptualizations, operationalizations, and propositions for future research. *Journalism* 13(2): 139–143.

Esser, F., and Umbricht, A. (2013). Competing models of journalism? Political affairs coverage in U.S., British, German, Swiss, French and Italian newspapers. *Journalism* 14: 989–1007.

Esser, F., and Umbricht, A. (2014). The evolution of objective and interpretative journalism in the Western press: Comparing six news systems since the 1960s. *Journalism & Mass Communication Quarterly* 91(2): 229–249.

European Audiovisual Observatory. (2011). *Yearbook television, cinema, video and on-demand audiovisual services in Europe*, Vols. 1 and 2. Strasbourg: EAO.

Falasca, K. (2014). Political news journalism: Mediatization across three news reporting contexts. *European Journal of Communication* 29(5): 583–597.

Fallows, J. (1996). *Breaking the news: How the media undermine American democracy.* New York: Vintage.

Fallows, J. (1997). *Breaking the news.* New York: Vintage.

Farnsworth, S. J., and Lichter, R. S. (2011). *The nightly news nightmare: Television's coverage of US presidential elections, 1988–2008.* 3rd ed. Lanham, MD: Rowman & Littlefield.

Farrell, D. (2001). *Electoral systems. A comparative introduction.* Hampshire: Palgrave.

Fournier, P., Nadeau, R., Blais, A., Gidengil, E., and Nevitte, N. (2004). Time-of-voting decision and susceptibility to campaign effects. *Electoral Studies* 23(4): 661–681.

Freedman, P., and Goldstein, K. (1999). Measuring media exposure and the effects of negative campaign ads. *American Journal of Political Science* 43(4): 1189–1208.

Fretwurst, B. (2015a). Reliabilität und Validität von Inhaltsanalysen: Mit Erläuterungen zur Berechnung des Reliabilitätskoeffizienten 'Lotus' mit SPSS. In W. Wirth, K. Sommer, M. Wettstein, and J. Matthes (Eds.), *Qualitätskriterien in der Inhaltsanalyse* (pp. 176–203). Köln: Halem.

Fretwurst, B. (2015b). Lotus manual. Available at www.iakom.ch/lotusEnglish.html.

Galtung, J., and Ruge, M. H. (1965). The structure of foreign news: The presentation of the Congo, Cuba and Cyprus crises in four Norwegian newspapers. *Journal of Peace Research* 2(1): 64–91.

References 189

Gans, H. (1979). *Deciding what's news: A study of CBS evening news, NBC Nightly News, Newsweek and Time.* New York: Pantheon.

Gerstlé, J., Davis, D., and Duhamel, O. (1991). Television news and the construction of political reality in France and the United States. In L. Kaid, J. Gerstlé, and K. Sanders (Eds.), *Mediated politics in two cultures: Presidential campaigning in the United States and France* (pp. 119–143). New York: Praeger.

Giddens, A. (1984). *The constitution of society: Outline of the theory of structuration.* Cambridge: Polity.

Grabe, M. E., and Bucy, E. P. (2009). *Image bite politics: News and the visual framing of elections.* New York: Oxford University Press.

Graber, D. A. (2003). The media and democracy: Beyond myths and stereotypes. *Annual Review of Political Science* 6(1): 139–160.

Green-Pedersen, C., Mortensen, P. B., and Thesen, G. (2015). The incumbency bonus revisited: Causes and consequences of media dominance. *British Journal of Political Science* FirstView. doi: http://dx.doi.org/10.1017/S0007123415000022

Groeling, T. (2013). Media bias by the numbers: Challenges and opportunities in the empirical study of partisan news. *Annual Review of Political Science* 16(1): 129–151.

Gurevitch, M., and Blumler, J. G. (1990). Political communication systems and democratic values. In J. Lichtenberg (Ed.), *Democracy and the mass media* (pp. 269–289). Cambridge: Cambridge University Press.

Gurevitch, M., and Blumler, J. G. (2004). State of the art of comparative political communication research: Poised for maturity? In F. Esser and B. Pfetsch (Eds.), *Comparing political communication: Theories, cases, and challenges* (pp. 325–343). New York: Cambridge University Press.

Hallin, D. C., and Mancini, P. (2004). *Comparing media systems: Three models of media and politics.* Cambridge: Cambridge University Press.

Hallin, D. C., and Mancini, P. (2012). TK. Comparing media systems: A response to critics. In F. Esser and T. Hanitzsch (Eds.), *Handbook of Comparative Communication Research* (pp. 207-220). New York: Routledge.

Hamilton, J. T. (2004). *All the news that's fit to sell: How the market transforms information into news.* Princeton, NJ: Princeton University Press.

Hanitzsch, T. (2011). Populist disseminators, detached watchdogs, critical change agents and opportunist facilitators: Professional milieus, the journalistic field and autonomy in 18 countries. *International Communication Gazette* 73(6): 477–494.

Hanitzsch, T., and Berganza, R. (2012). Explaining journalists' trust in public institutions across 20 countries: Media freedom, corruption and ownership matter most. *Journal of Communication* 62(5): 794–814.

Hanitzsch, T., and Donsbach, W. (2012). Comparing journalism cultures. In F. Esser and T. Hanitzsch (Eds.), *The handbook of comparative communication research* (pp. 262–275). New York: Routledge.

Hanitzsch, T., Hanusch, F., Mellado, C., Anikina, M., Berganza, R., Cangoz, I., . . . Kee Wang Yuen, E. (2011). Mapping journalism cultures across nations: A comparative study of 18 countries. *Journalism Studies* 12(3): 273–293.

Hanitzsch, T., and Mellado, C. (2011). What shapes the news around the world? How journalists in eighteen countries perceive influences on their work. *International Journal of Press/Politics* 16: 404–426.

Harcup, T., and O'Neill, D. (2001). What is news? Galtung and Ruge revisited. *Journalism Studies* 2(2): 261–280.

190 References

Hart, R. (1992). *Seducing America: How television charms the modern voter*. London: Sage.

Hofstetter, C. R. (1976). *Bias in the news – Network television coverage of the 1972 election campaign*. Columbus: Ohio State University Press.

Holtz-Bacha, C., and Strömbäck, J. (Eds.). (2012). *Opinion polls and the media: Reflecting and shaping public opinion*. Basingstoke: Palgrave Macmillan.

Hopmann, D. N. (2014). Politicians, parties and political candidates in the news media. In C. Reinemann (Ed.), *Handbook of communication sciences: Volume political communication* (pp. 389–407). Berlin: De Gruyter Mouton.

Hopmann, D. N., Elmelund-Præstekær, C., Vliegenthart, R., de Vreese, C. H., and Albæk, E. (2012). Party media agenda-setting: How parties influence election news coverage. *Party Politics* 18(2): 173–191.

Hopmann, D. N., and Skovsgaard, M. (2014). *Forskningsmetoder i journalistik og politisk kommunikation*. Copenhagen: Hans Reitzels Forlag.

Hopmann, D. N., Van Aelst, P., and Legnante, G. (2012). Political balance in the news: A review of concepts, operationalizations and key findings. *Journalism* 13(2): 240–257.

Hopmann, D. N., Vliegenthart, R., de Vreese, C. H., and Albæk, E. (2010). Effects of election news coverage: How visibility and tone influence party choice. *Political Communication* 27(4): 389–405.

Hox, J. (2002). *Multilevel analysis: Techniques and applications*. Mahwah, NJ: Lawrence Erlbaum.

Iyengar, S. (2011). *Media politics: A citizens' guide*. 2nd ed. New York: WW Norton.

Iyengar, S., Norpoth, H., and Hahn, K. S. (2004). Consumer demand for election news: The horserace sells. *Journal of Politics* 66(1): 157–175.

Jackson, D. (2011). Strategic media, cynical public? Examining the contingent effects of strategic news frames on political cynicism in the United Kingdom. *International Journal of Press/Politics* 16(1): 75–101.

Jandura, O., and Friedrich, K. (2014). The quality of political media coverage. In C. Reinemann (Ed.), *Political communication: Handbooks of communication science*, Vol. 18 (pp. 351–373). Berlin: De Gruyter Mouton.

Kaid, L. L., and Strömbäck, J. (2008). Election news coverage around the world: A comparative perspective. In J. Strömbäck and L. L. Kaid (Eds.), *Handbook of election news coverage around the world* (pp. 421–431). New York: Routledge.

Karvonen, L. (2010). *The personalization of politics: A study of parliamentary democracies*. Colchester: ECPR.

Kepplinger, H. M., and Ehmig, S. (2006). Predicting news decisions: An empirical test of the two-component theory of news selection. *Communications* 31(1): 25–43.

Kleinnijenhuis, J. (2008). Negativity. In W. Donsbach (Ed.), *The international encyclopedia of communication* (pp. 3188–3192). Malden, MA: Blackwell.

Kleinnijenhuis, J., van Hoof, A.M.J., Oegema, D., and de Ridder, J. A. (2007). A test of rivaling approaches to explain news effects: News on issue positions of parties, real-world developments, support and criticism, and success and failure. *Journal of Communication* 57(2): 366–384.

Klinger, U., and Svensson, J. (2014). The emergence of network media logic in political communication: A theoretical approach. *New Media and Society* 17, 1241–1257. Online first. doi:10.1177/1461444814522952

Kreft, I., and de Leeuw, J. (1998). *Introducing multilevel modeling*. London: Sage.

Kriesi, H. P. (2012). Personalization of national election campaigns. *Party Politics* 18(6): 825–844.

References 191

Krippendorff, K. (2004). *Content analysis – An introduction to its methodology*. London: Sage.

Kuhn, R. (2013a). The box trumps the net? Mediatising the 2012 presidential campaign. *Parliamentary Affairs* 66(1): 142–159.

Kuhn, R. (2013b). The media and the 2012 presidential election. *Modern & Contemporary France* 21(1): 1–16.

Kuhn, R., and Nielsen, R. K. (2014). *Political journalism in transition: Western Europe in a comparative perspective*. London: I.B. Tauris.

Lavrakas, P. J., and Traugott, M. W. (2000). Why election polls are important to a democracy: An American perspective. In P. J. Lavrakas and M. W. Traugott (Eds.), *Election polls, the news media, and democracy* (pp. 3–19). New York: Seven Bridges.

Lawrence, R. G. (2000a). Game-framing the issues: Tracking the strategy frame in public policy news. *Political Communication* 17(2): 93–114.

Lawrence, R. G. (2000b). *The politics of force: The media and the construction of police brutality*. Berkeley, CA: University of California Press.

Leckner, S., and Facht, U. (2010). *A sampler of international media and communication statistics 2010*. Gothenburg: Nordicom.

Lengauer, G., Esser, F., and Berganza, R. (2012). Negativity in political news: A review of concepts, operationalizations and key findings. *Journalism* 13(2): 179–202.

Lijphart, A. (1999). *Patterns of democracy: Government forms and performance in thirty-six countries*. New Haven: Yale University Press.

Lijphart, A. (2012). *Patterns of democracy: Government forms and performance in thirty-six countries*. 2nd ed. New Haven: Yale University Press.

Luhmann, N. (2000). *The reality of the mass media*. Stanford: Stanford University Press.

Mancini, P., and Hallin, D. C. (2012). Some caveats about comparative research in media studies. In H. A. Semetko and M. Scammell (Eds.), *Sage handbook of political communication* (pp. 509–517). Thousand Oaks, CA: Sage.

Matthes, J., and Kohring, M. (2008). The content analysis of media frames: Toward improving reliability and validity. *Journal of Communication* 58: 258–279.

McAllister, I. (2007). The personalization of politics. In R. J. Dalton and H. D. Klingemann (Eds.), *The Oxford handbooks of political science: The Oxford handbook of political behaviour* (pp. 571–588). Oxford: Oxford University Press.

McChesney, R., and Pickard, V. (2011). *Will the last reporter please turn out the lights: The collapse of journalism and what can be done to fix it*. New York: The New Press.

McCombs, M., and Reynolds, A. (2002). News influence on our pictures of the world. In J. Bryant and D. Zillmann (Eds.), *Media effects: Advances in theory and research* (pp. 1–18). Mahwah, NJ: Lawrence Erlbaum.

McManus, J. H. (1994). *Market driven journalism: Let the citizen beware?* London: Sage.

McManus, J. H. (2009). The commercialization of news. In K. Wahl-Jorgensen and T. Hanitzsch (Eds.), *The handbook of journalism studies* (pp. 218–233). London: Routledge.

McNair, B. (2000). *Journalism and democracy: An evaluation of the political public sphere*. London: Routledge.

McQuail, D. (1992). *Media performance*. London: Sage.

Meyrowitz, J. (1985). *No sense of place: The impact of electronic media on social behaviour*. New York: Oxford University Press.

Moy, P., and Pfau, M. (2000). *With malice toward all? The media and public confidence in democratic institutions*. Westport: Praeger.

References

Mullainathan, S., and Shleifer, A. (2006). The market for news. *American Economic Review* 95(4): 1031–1053.

Mutz, D. C., and Young, L. (2011). Communication and public opinion. *Public Opinion Quarterly* 75(5): 1018–1044.

Nagel, F., Maurer, M., and Reinemann, C. (2012). Is there a visual dominance in political communication? How verbal, visual, and vocal communication shape viewers' impressions of political candidates. *Journal of Communication* 62(5): 833–850.

Negrine, R., Holtz-Bacha, C., Mancini, P., and Papathanassopolous, S. (2007). *The professionalisation of political communication*. Bristol: Intellect.

Neuendorf, K. A. (2002). *The content analysis guidebook*. London: Sage.

Neveu, E. (2002). Four generations of political journalism. In R. Kuhn and E. Neveu (Eds.), *Political journalism: New challenges, new practices* (pp. 22–43). London: Routledge.

Newman, N., and Levy, D. (Eds.). (2014). *Reuters institute digital news report 2014*. Oxford: Reuters Institute. Available at https://reutersinstitute.politics.ox.ac.uk.

Nir, L. (2012). Cross-national differences in political discussion: Can political systems narrow deliberation gaps? *Journal of Communication* 62(3): 553–570.

Norris, P. (2000). *A virtuous circle: Political communications in postindustrial societies*. Cambridge: Cambridge University Press.

Norris, P. (2009). Comparative political communications: Common frameworks or Babelian confusion? *Government & Opposition* 44(3): 321–340.

Oegema, D., and Kleinnijenhuis, J. (2000). Personalization in political television news: A 13-wave survey study to assess effects of text and footage. *Communications* 25: 43–60.

Ofcom. (2014). *Review of Ofcom list of major political parties for elections taking place on 22 May 2014*. London: Ofcom. Available at http://stakeholders.ofcom.org.uk/consultations/major-political-parties-2014/statement.

O'Neill, D., and Harcup, T. (2009). News values and selectivity. In K. Wahl-Jorgensen and T. Hanitzsch (Eds.), *The handbook of journalism studies* (pp. 161–174). New York: Routledge.

Oschatz, C., Maurer, M., and Haßler, J. (2014). (R)Evolution der Politikberichterstattung im Medienwandel. *Medien & Kommunikationswissenschaft* 62: 25–41.

Pan, Z., and McLeod, J. (1991). Multilevel analysis is mass communication research. *Communication Research* 18(2): 14–173.

Patterson, T. E. (1993). *Out of order*. New York: Vintage.

Patterson, T. E. (2000). *Doing well and doing good: How soft news and critical journalism are shrinking the news audience and weakening democracy-and what news outlets can do about it*. Cambridge, MA: Harvard University, John F. Kennedy School of Government, Joan Shorenstein Center on the Press, Politics and Public Policy.

Patterson, T. E. (2000). The United States: News in a free-market society. In R. Gunther and A. Mughan (Eds.), *Democracy and the media: A comparative perspective* (pp. 241–265). New York: Cambridge University Press.

Patterson, T. E. (2003). *The vanishing voter*. New York: Vintage.

Patterson, T. E. (2014). *Informing the news: The need for knowledge based journalism*. New York: Vintage.

Peter, J. (2003). Country characteristics as contingent conditions of agenda setting: The moderating influence of polarized elite opinion. *Communication Research* 30(6): 683–712.

Peter, J., and Lauf, E. (2002). Reliability in cross-national content analysis. *Journalism and Mass Communication Quarterly* 79(4): 815–832.

References 193

Pfetsch, B., and Esser, F. (2014). Political communication in comparative perspective: Key concepts and new insights. In C. Reinemann (Ed.), *Political communication: Handbooks of communication science,* Vol. 18 (pp. 87–105). Berlin: De Gruyter Mouton.

Picard, R. G. (2004). Commercialism and newspaper quality. *Newspaper Research Journal* 25(1): 54–65.

Picard, R. G. (2014). The future of the political economy of press freedom. *Communication Law and Policy* 19(1): 97–107.

Plasser, F. (2005). From hard to soft news standards? How political journalists in different media systems evaluate the shifting quality of news. *International Journal of Press/ Politics* 10(2): 47–68.

Plasser, F., and Lengauer, G. (2009). Wie "Amerikanisch" sind Europäische Fernsehwahlkämpfe? In S. H. Kaspar, S. Schumann, and J. R. Winkler (Eds.), *Politik–Wissenschaft–Medien. Festschrift für Jurgen W. Falter zum 65. Geburtstag* (pp. 323–346). Wiesbaden: VS Verlag.

Plasser, F., Pallaver, G., and Lengauer, G. (2009). Die (trans-)nationale Nachrichtenlogik in Mediendemokratien. Politischer TV-Journalismus im Wahlkampf zwischen transatlantischer Konvergenz und nationaler Divergenz [The (trans)national news logic in media democracies. Political TV journalism in election campaigns between transatlantic convergence and national divergence]. In F. Marcinkowski and B. Pfetsch (Eds.), *Politik in der Mediendemokratie* [Politics in mediated democracy] (pp. 174–202). Wiesbaden, Germany: VS Verlag.

Popescu, M. (2011). *European media systems survey: Results and documentation.* Colchester, UK: Department of Government, University of Essex. Available at http://media systemsineurope.org.

Popescu, M., Gosselin, T., and Pereira, J. S. (2010). *European media systems survey 2010 data set.* Colchester, UK: Department of Government, University of Essex. Available at www.mediasystemsineurope.org.

Popper, K. R. (1963/1994). Models, instruments and truth: The status of the rationality principle in the social sciences. In K. R. Popper (Ed.), *The myth of the framework* (pp. 154–184). New York: Routledge.

Preston, P. (2009). *Making the news: Journalism and news cultures in Europe.* London: Routledge.

Prior, M. (2013). Media and political polarization. *Annual Review of Political Science* 16(1): 101–127.

Quandt, T. (2008). (No) News on the world wide web? A comparative analysis of online news in Europe and the United States. *Journalism Studies* 9(5): 717–738.

Rahat, G., and Sheafer, T. (2007). The personalization(s) of politics: Israel, 1949–2003. *Political Communication* 41(1): 65–80.

Reese, S. D. (2007). Journalism research and the hierarchy of influences model: A global perspective. *Brazilian Journalism Research* 3(2): 29–42.

Reid, S. A. (2012). A self-categorization explanation for the hostile media effect. *Journal of Communication* 62(3): 381–399.

Reinemann, C. (2004). Routine reliance revisited: Exploring media importance for German political journalists. *Journalism & Mass Communication Quarterly* 81(4): 857–876.

Reinemann, C., and Baugut, P. (2014). Political journalists as communicators. In C. Reinemann (Ed.), *Political communication* (pp. 325–350). Berlin: De Gruyter Mouton.

Reinemann, C., Stanyer, J., Scherr, S., and Legnante, G. (2012). Hard and soft news: A review of concepts, operationalizations and key findings. *Journalism* 13(2): 221–239.

194 References

Reinemann, C., and Wilke, J. (2007). It's the debates, stupid! How the introduction of televised debates changed the portrayal of chancellor candidates in the German press, 1949–2005. *The Harvard International Journal of Press/Politics* 12(4): 92–111.

Ridout, T., and Franz, M. (2008). Evaluating measures of campaign tone. *Political Communication* 15(2): 158–179.

Riffe, D., Lacy, S., and Fico, F. G. (2005). *Analyzing media messages – using quantitative content analysis in research*. London: Lawrence Erlbaum.

Rogers, W. (1994). Regression standard errors in clustered samples. *Stata Technical Bulletin* 3(13). Available at http://econpapers.repec.org/article/tsjstbull/y_3a1994_3av_3a3_3ai_3a13_3asg17.htm.

Rössler, P. (2012). Comparative content analysis. In F. Esser and T. Hanitzsch (Eds.), *The comparative handbook of communication research* (pp. 459–468). London: Routledge.

Rozell, M. J. (1996). *The press and the Bush presidency*. Westport: Praeger.

Sabato, L. J. (1991). *Feeding frenzy*. New York: Free.

Salgado, S., and Strömbäck, J. (2012). Interpretive journalism: A review of concepts, operationalizations and key findings. *Journalism* 13(2): 144–161.

Schiffer, A. (2006). Assessing partisan bias in political news: The case of local senate election coverage. *Political Communication* 23(1): 23–39.

Schmitt, K. M., Gunther, A. C., and Liebhart, J. L. (2004). Why partisans see mass media as biased. *Communication Research* 31(6): 623–641.

Schneider, M., Schönbach, K., and Semetko, H. (1999). Kanzlerkandidaten in den Fernsehnachrichten und in der Wählermeinung – Befunde zum Bundestagswahlkampf 1998 und früheren Wahlkämpfen. *Media Perspektiven* 1999(5): 262–269.

Schönbach, K., De Ridder, J., and Lauf, E. (2001). Politicians on TV news: Getting attention in Dutch and German election campaigns. *European Journal of Political Research* 39(4): 519–531.

Schuck, A.R.T., Boomgaarden, H. G., and de Vreese, C. H. (2013). Cynics all around? The impact of election news on political cynicism in comparative perspective. *Journal of Communication* 63(2): 287–311.

Schuck, A.R.T., Vliegenthart, R., Boomgaarden, H. G., Elenbaas, M., Azrout, R., van Spanje, J., and de Vreese, C. H. (2013). Explaining campaign news coverage: How medium, time and context explain variation in the media framing of the 2009 European parliamentary elections. *Journal of Political Marketing* 12(1): 8–28.

Schuck, A.R.T, Vliegenthart, R., and de Vreese, C. H. (2016). Who's afraid of conflict? The mobilizing effect of conflict framing in campaign news. *British Journal of Political Science* 46(1), 177–194.

Schudson, M. (1978). *Discovering the news: A social history of American newspapers*. New York: Basic.

Schudson, M. (1999). Social origins of press cynicism in portraying politics. *American Behavioral Scientist* 42(6): 998–1008.

Semetko, H. (2003). Political bias in the media. In D. Johnston (Ed.), *Encyclopedia of international media and communications 3* (pp. 517–525). Amsterdam: Academic.

Semetko, H. A., Blumler, J. G., Gurevitch, M., and Weaver, D. H. (1991). *The formation of campaign agendas: A comparative analysis of party and media roles in recent American and British elections*. Hillsdale, NJ: Lawrence Erlbaum.

Semetko, H. A., and Valkenburg, P. M. (2000). Framing European politics: A content analysis of press and television news. *Journal of Communication* 50(2): 93–109.

Seymour-Ure, C. (1974). *The political impact of mass media*. London: Constable.

Shehata, A. (2007). Facing the Muhammad cartoons: Official dominance and event-driven news in the Swedish and American elite press. *International Journal of Press/Politics* 12(4): 131–153.

Shehata, A. (2014). Game frames, issue frames, and mobilization: Disentangling the effects of frame exposure and motivated news attention on political cynicism and engagement. *International Journal of Public Opinion Research* 26(2): 157–177.

Shehata, A., and Strömbäck, J. (2011). A matter of context: A comparative study of media environments and news consumption gaps in Europe. *Political Communication* 28(1): 110–134.

Shehata, A., and Strömbäck, J. (2014). Mediation of political realities: Media as crucial source of information. In F. Esser and J. Strömbäck (Eds.), *Mediatization of politics: Understanding the transformation of Western democracies* (pp. 93–113). Basingstoke: Palgrave Macmillan.

Shenhav, S. R., and Sheafer, T. (2008). From inter-party debate to inter-personal polemic: Media coverage of internal and external party disputes in Israel, 1949–2003. *Party Politics* 14(6): 706–725.

Shoemaker, P., and Reese, S. D. (1991). *Mediating the message:. Theories of influences on mass media content.* New York: Longman.

Shoemaker, P., and Reese, S. D. (2014). *Mediating the message in the 21st century: A media sociology perspective.* New York: Routledge.

Shoemaker, P. J., and Cohen, A. A. (2006). *News around the world: Content, practitioners, and the public.* New York: Routledge.

Shoemaker, P. J., Eichholz, M., Kim, E., and Wrigley, B. (2001). Individual and routine forces in gatekeeping. *Journalism & Mass Communication Quarterly* 78(2): 233–246.

Shoemaker, P. J., and Reese, S. D. (1996). *Mediating the message: Theories of influence on mass media content.* White Plains, NY: Longman.

Shoemaker, P. J., and Vos, T. P. (2009). *Gatekeeping theory.* New York: Routledge.

Skewes, E. A. (2007). *Message control: How news is made on the presidential campaign trail.* Lanham, MD: Rowman and Littlefield.

Soloski, J. (1989). News reporting and professionalism: Some constraints on the reporting of news. *Media, Culture and Society* 11: 207–228.

Sommer, D., Fretwurst, B., Sommer, K., and Gehrau, V. (2013). Nachrichtenwert und Gespräche über Medienthemen. *Publizistik* 57(4): 381–401.

Sonck, N., and Loosveldt, R. (2008). Making news based on public opinion polls: The Flemish case. *European Journal of Communication* 23(4): 490–500.

Soroka, S. (2014). *Negativity in democratic politics: Causes and consequences.* New York: Cambridge University Press.

Stanyer, J. (2013). *Intimate politics: Politicians and declining privacy in the media age.* Cambridge: Polity.

Starkey, G. (2007). *Balance and bias in journalism: Representation, regulation and democracy.* Hampshire: Palgrave Macmillan.

Steele, C. A., and Barnhurst, K. G. (1996). The journalism of opinion: Network coverage in U.S. presidential campaigns, 1968–1988. *Critical Studies in Mass Communication* 13(3): 187–209.

Strömbäck, J. (2005). In search of a standard: Four models of democracy and their normative implications for journalism. *Journalism Studies* 6(3): 331–345.

Strömbäck, J. (2008). Swedish election news coverage: Towards increasing mediatization. In J. Strömbäck and L. L. Kaid (Eds.), *The handbook of election news coverage around the world* (pp. 160–174). New York: Routledge.

196 References

Strömbäck, J. (2012). The media and their use of opinion polls: Reflecting and shaping public opinion. In C. Holtz-Bacha and J. Strömbäck (Eds.), *Opinion polls and the media: Reflecting and shaping public opinion* (pp. 1–22). Basingstoke: Palgrave Macmillan.

Strömbäck, J. (2013). Den medialiserade valrörelsejournalistiken. In J. Strömbäck and L. Nord (Eds.), *Kampen om opinionen. Politisk kommunikation under svenska valrörelser* (pp. 119–149). Stockholm: SNS Förlag.

Strömbäck, J., and Aalberg, T. (2008). Election news coverage in democratic corporatist countries: A comparative study of Sweden and Norway. *Scandinavian Political Studies* 31(1): 91–106.

Strömbäck, J., and Dimitrova, D. V. (2006). Political and media systems matter a comparison of election news coverage in Sweden and the United States. *Harvard International Journal of Press/Politics* 11(4): 131–147.

Strömbäck, J., and Dimitrova, D. V. (2011). Mediatization and media interventionism: A comparative analysis of Sweden and the United States. *International Journal of Press/Politics* 16(1): 30–49.

Strömbäck, J., and Esser, F. (2014). Mediatization of politics: Towards a theoretical framework. In F. Esser and J. Strömbäck (Eds.), *Mediatization of politics: Understanding the transformation of Western democracies* (pp. 3–28). Basingstoke: Palgrave Macmillan.

Strömbäck, J., and Kaid, L. L. (2008a). A framework for comparing election news coverage around the world. In J. Strömbäck and L. L. Kaid (Eds.), *The handbook of election news coverage around the world* (pp. 1–18). New York: Routledge.

Strömbäck, J., and Kaid, L. L. (Eds.). (2008b). *The handbook of election news coverage around the world*. New York: Routledge.

Strömbäck, J., and Luengo, Ó. G. (2008). Polarized pluralist and democratic corporatist models: A comparison of election news coverage in Spain and Sweden. *International Communication Gazette* 70(6): 547–562.

Strömbäck, J., and Shehata, A. (2007) Structural biases in British and Swedish election news coverage. *Journalism Studies* 8(5): 798–812.

Strömbäck, J., and Van Aelst, P. (2010). Exploring some antecedents of the media's framing of election news: A comparison of Swedish and Belgian election news. *International Journal of Press/Politics* 15(1): 41–59.

Sullivan, M. (2012). He said, she said, and the truth. *New York Times*, September 16, p. SR12.

Swanson, D. L., and Mancini, P. (1996). *Politics, media and modern democracy: An international study of innovations in electoral campaigning and their consequences*. Westport, CN: Praeger.

Takens, J., van Atteveldt, W., van Hoof, A., and Kleinnijenhuis, J. (2013). Media logic in election campaign coverage. *European Journal of Communication* 28: 277–293.

Tewksbury, D., and Rittenberg, J. (2012). *News on the Internet: Information and citizenship in the 21st century*. New York: Oxford University Press.

Tresch, A. (2009). Politicians in the media: Determinants of legislators' presence and prominence in Swiss newspapers. *International Journal of Press/Politics* 14(1): 67–90.

Tsfati, Y. (2007). Hostile media perceptions, presumed media influence, and minority alienation: The case of Arabs in Israel. *Journal of Communication* 57(4): 632–651.

Tuchman, G. (1973). Making news by doing work: Routinizing the unexpected. *American Journal of Sociology* 79(1): 110–131.

Umbricht, A., and Esser, F. (2013). Changing political news? Long-term trends in American, British, French, Italian, German and Swiss press reporting. In K. Raymond and

K. N. Rasmus (Eds.), *Political journalism in transition: Western Europe in a comparative perspective* (pp. 195–217). London: I.B. Tauris.

Umbricht, A., and Esser, F. (2014). Changing political news? Long-term trends in American, British, French, Italian, German and Swiss press reporting. In R. Kuhn and R. Kleis Nielsen (Eds.), *Political journalism in transition: Western Europe in a comparative perspective* (pp. 195–218). London: I.B. Tauris.

Umbricht, A., and Esser, F. (2015). The push to popularize politics: Understanding the audience-friendly packaging of political news in six media systems since the 1960s. *Journalism Studies* 17(1): 100–121.

Valentino, N., Beckmann, M. N., and Buhr, T. A. (2001). A spiral of cynicism for some: The contingent effects of campaign news frames on participation and confidence in government. *Political Communication* 18(4): 347–367.

Vallone, R., Ross, L., and Lepper, M. R. (1985). The hostile media phenomenon: Biased perception and perceptions of media bias in coverage of the Beirut massacre. *Journal of Personality and Social Psychology* 49(3): 577–585.

Van Aelst, P., Brants, K., Van Praag, P. H., de Vreese, C. H., Nuytemans, M., and Van Dalen, A. (2008). The fourth estate as superpower? An empirical study on perceptions of media power in Belgium and the Netherlands. *Journalism Studies* 9(4): 494–511.

Van Aelst, P., and de Swert, K. (2009). Politics in the news: Do campaigns matter? A comparison of political news during election periods and routine periods in Flanders (Belgium). *Communications* 34(2): 149–168.

Van Aelst, P., Sheafer, T., and Stanyer, J. (2012). The personalization of mediated political communication: A review of concepts, operationalizations and key findings. *Journalism* 13(2): 203–220.

Van Biezen, I., Mair, P., and Poguntke, T. (2012). Going, going, . . . gone? The decline of party membership in contemporary Europe. *European Journal of Political Research* 51(1): 24–56.

Van Dalen, A., Albæk, E., and de Vreese, C. H. (2011). Suspicious minds: Explaining political cynicism among political journalists in Europe. *European Journal of Communication* 26(2): 147–162.

Van Dalen, A., de Vreese, C. H., and Albæk, E. (2012). Different roles, different content? A four-country comparison of the role conceptions and reporting style of political journalists. *Journalism* 13(7): 903–922.

Walgrave, S., and Van Aelst, P. (2006). The contingency of the mass media's political agenda setting power: Toward a preliminary theory. *Journal of Communication* 56(1): 88–109.

Weaver, D., and Loeffelholz, M. (2008). Questioning national, cultural and disciplinary boundaries: A call for global journalism research. In M. Loeffelholz and D. Weaver (Eds.), *Global journalism research: Theories, methods, findings, future* (pp. 3–12). London: Blackwell.

Weaver, D. H., and Willnat, L. (2012). *The global journalist in the 21st century*. New York: Routledge.

Weintraub, A. E., and Pinkleton, B. E. (1995). Positive and negative effects of political disaffection on the less experienced voter. *Journal of Broadcasting & Electronic Media* 39(2): 215–235.

Wilke, J., and Reinemann, C. (2001). Do the candidates matter? Long-term trends of campaign coverage – A study of the German press since 1949. *European Journal of Communication* 16(3): 291–314.

198 References

Wolfsfeld, G. (2011). *Making sense of media & politics: Five principles of political communication*. New York: Routledge.

Zaller, J. (2003). A new standard of news quality: Burglar alarms for the monitorial citizen. *Political Communication* 20(2): 109–130.

Zaller, J. R. (1999). *A theory of media politics: How the interests of politicians, journalists, and citizens shape the news*. Unpublished manuscript. Available at www.sscnet.ucla.edu/polisci/faculty/zaller/media%20politics%20book%20.pdf.

Zaller, J. R. (2001). The rule of product substitution in presidential campaign news. In E. Katz and Y. Warshel (Eds.), *Election studies: What's their use?* (pp. 247–270). Boulder, CO: Westview.

Zeh, R., and Hopmann, D. N. (2013). Indicating mediatization? Two decades of election campaign television coverage. *European Journal of Communication* 28(3): 225–240.

Zeldes, G. A., Fico, F. G., Carpenter, S., and Diddi, A. (2008). Partisan balance and bias in network coverage of the 2000 and 2004 presidential elections. *Journal of Broadcasting & Electronic Media* 52(4): 563–580.

Zittel, T., and Gschwend, T. (2008). Individualised constituency campaigns in mixed-member electoral systems: Candidates in the 2005 German elections. *West European Politics* 31(5): 978–1003.

Index

actor-focused news coverage 162–5, 170–5
adversarialism 71, 75

balance, political 3–6, 8, 20, 28, 31, 92–4, 96–7, 99–102, 110, 168–9, 182

campaigns: election 27, 32, 35, 39, 43, 48–9, 72, 80, 92, 94–5, 109, 113, 128; political 47
commercial broadcasting 7, 14, 35, 42, 63, 68, 78, 82, 89, 97, 99–101, 135, 137, 140, 169, 176
commercialization, commerciality 1, 5, 27, 29, 54, 56, 62, 75–6, 78–9, 80, 84–6, 88, 90, 115, 124–5, 131, 133, 152, 177
comparative research 1, 6–7, 9–10, 14–17, 20, 22, 24, 26–8, 31–3, 37, 43, 49, 50, 52, 54–5, 57, 68, 70, 72–3, 90–1, 98, 108–10, 113–16, 122, 128, 131–3, 135–6, 146–8, 151–3, 157, 165–6, 179–80, 183
competition 5, 8, 24, 27, 29, 31, 36–7, 45–6, 48, 51, 55, 63–9, 72, 75, 78, 84, 88, 90, 92, 99–102, 115, 117, 128–9, 133, 134–5, 140, 147, 169, 173, 176–8
conflict 4, 8, 18, 25, 27, 29, 31–2, 34, 52, 72–3, 75–7, 79–83, 89–90, 109, 151, 167, 169, 177
cross-national research 1, 3–4, 7–10, 20, 22–3, 32, 36, 39–40, 42–4, 72, 78–9, 82, 98, 106, 152–3, 158, 162, 166, 169, 172, 180
cynicism 1, 34, 48, 71, 82

democracy 1, 4–5, 11, 20, 30–1, 33, 35, 42, 47, 59, 71, 80–1, 89, 92–5, 105, 113, 115–16, 121–2, 131, 135, 137, 139, 144, 147–8, 153–4, 158, 161–3, 165–6, 168, 172, 175, 178–9, 182

diversity 6, 23, 78, 71, 74, 78, 84, 90, 176, 178

economic conditions 8, 26–7, 75, 78, 80–1, 118, 134–5, 141–2, 145–8, 152, 154, 164, 166, 169, 177
election results 15, 104–5, 111
electoral systems 27, 30–2, 114, 116–17, 124–8, 130, 177
entertainment 35, 44
event-driven news 73, 132, 147–8

federalism 8, 27, 31, 75, 78, 84–5, 87, 90, 105, 109, 116, 117, 122, 124–8, 130, 169, 176–7
framing: conflict 32; effects 34–5, 150; game 5, 7, 16, 24, 28, 32–49, 52, 151, 152–3, 156, 158–9, 166, 168–9, 182; issue 17–18, 38, 42; strategy 3, 5–6, 7, 9, 17–18, 28, 33–49, 150–4, 156–9, 162, 166, 168–9, 171, 182

ideology 4–5, 13, 24
incumbency status, bonus 94, 96–7, 110
inter-coder reliability 7, 10, 17–21, 180
interconnections of key concepts 150–3, 156–9, 165–6
issue-focused hard news coverage 162–5, 170, 172–5
issue-focused interpretive coverage 162–5, 171–3

journalism: critical 65, 69, 74–5, 79–80, 95–6, 107, 152; descriptive 33, 52–3, 58, 89; fact-focused 53; interpretive 1, 3–7, 16–18, 28–30, 32, 50–70, 152–4, 156, 166–9, 182; source-driven 53
journalistic culture 24, 36, 43, 52, 55–6, 67–8, 76, 115, 153, 64, 169

200 Index

journalistic independence 30, 54, 57, 65, 67, 101–2

journalistic professionalism 5, 11, 27, 29, 38, 43–4, 46, 53, 56–7, 65, 67, 78, 84, 87, 90, 96, 100–2, 177

journalist(s), role of 52, 81, 183

media: audiences 42, 151, 158; effects 150; influence 31; interventionism 51; logic 34, 176, 182–3; ownership 4, 24, 28, 78, 82, 89, 124, 148, 173; system 5–6, 8, 11, 14, 20–1, 23–4, 27, 29–31, 36–7, 44, 54–5, 64–5, 67–70, 72, 76, 84–5, 88–91, 103, 111, 113, 115, 117, 123, 125, 128–9, 131, 133–6, 141–2, 144–7, 152–3, 168–9, 173, 176–7

mediatization 34, 51, 128

mobilization 4, 48, 71

negative news coverage 2–6, 8–9, 16, 18, 23–4, 27–31, 34, 52, 54, 71–91, 96, 98, 102, 107, 150–63, 166–71, 176–8

news 2–6, 8–9, 23, 26–8, 30, 32, 131–7, 139–49, 152, 154, 159, 167–9, 176–7, 182; hard news 1–4, 6, 9, 26–7, 29–31, 76, 78, 84–7, 90, 131–42, 145–7, 149, 154–5, 167, 169–78; online 13–14, 27–8, 43, 46, 51, 56, 61–2, 64–5, 67–70, 72–3, 78, 81–2, 87–90, 97, 99–102, 116–17, 124–6, 132–7, 139–40, 145–9, 152, 168–9, 176–7, 179–82; performance 1, 3–6, 9, 22–3, 27, 32, 152, 168–70, 173, 176–8, 182–3; values 25, 28, 30, 34, 92, 96, 100, 103, 115, 132, 150, 183

news factors 25, 132, 150–1

news management 54, 75

newspapers: broadsheet 11, 25, 28, 35, 48, 124, 132, 137, 140–1, 145, 147; mass-market 7, 13–15, 27, 35, 42–3, 46, 47, 51, 56, 63, 65, 67, 69–70, 97, 99–101, 115, 124–6, 132, 135, 140, 145–6, 153, 146, 158, 162–3; popular 13, 74, 82, 89; quality 73–4, 89, 135; tabloid 14, 25, 28, 35, 42, 74, 132, 135, 137, 140–1, 145, 147–8, 169; upmarket 7, 11–14, 28, 35, 42–3, 46–7, 51, 56, 62–5, 67, 69–70, 73–4, 78, 82–3, 87–9, 97, 99–103, 115,

117, 124–6, 132, 135–6, 140, 146, 153, 156, 162–3, 167

newsworthiness 24–5, 34, 75, 96, 102, 109, 151

opinion polls 31, 34, 38–9, 96, 104, 108, 111

partisan bias 93, 96–7, 110

personalization 3–6, 8–9, 20, 23–4, 27–9, 31–2, 81, 99, 112–17, 119–20, 122–4, 126, 128–30, 132, 150–2, 154–63, 167–71, 176–7, 182

political balance *see* balance, political

political institutions 8, 15, 71, 74, 89, 112–16, 119–20, 122, 124, 128, 169

political parties 7–8, 15, 37–8, 44, 47–8, 74, 84, 94–7, 99, 103–9, 111, 113, 119, 121, 129, 159

political system 5–6, 8, 11, 23–4, 27, 30–1, 34, 36, 38, 43, 45–6, 70, 74, 75, 84–5, 89–90, 105, 109, 111–12, 114–17, 123–4, 129, 136, 142, 144–5, 169, 176–7

politicization, polarization 4–5, 11, 57, 74–5, 78–80, 89, 148, 167

professionalism, professional norms 5, 11, 27, 29–30, 36, 38, 43–4, 46, 54, 56–7, 65, 67, 75, 78, 84–5, 87, 90, 100–2, 177

public opinion 3–4, 18, 37–9, 45, 48, 96, 107–8, 166

public relations 24, 54, 152

public service mission/broadcasting 11, 14, 17, 36, 44, 48, 56, 62

sampling: period 15–16, 135, 179; unit 11

scandal(s) 8, 71–2, 74, 80–1, 90, 152, 169

selective exposure 183

skepticism 30, 54, 71, 73, 75

social media 181–2

spin 36, 43

strategy-focused interpretive coverage 163–5, 171–2

tabloidization *see* newspapers, mass-market

tone, tonality 8–9, 18, 72, 74, 76–7, 79–80, 82–3, 89, 93–4, 97, 99, 106, 110–11, 150, 153, 157, 166–7, 169, 175

watchdog 4, 23, 56, 73, 79, 81, 109